D1348180

BLACK'S NEW TESTAMENT COMMENTARIES

GENERAL EDITOR: HENRY CHADWICK, D.D.

COMPANION VOLUME I

# THE BIRTH OF
# THE NEW TESTAMENT

# THE BIRTH OF
# THE NEW TESTAMENT

**C. F. D. MOULE**
FELLOW OF CLARE COLLEGE
UNIVERSITY OF CAMBRIDGE

**ADAM & CHARLES BLACK**
LONDON

FIRST PUBLISHED 1962
SECOND EDITION, WITH MINOR REVISIONS, 1966
REPRINTED 1971, 1973, 1976 AND 1978
A. AND C. BLACK LIMITED
35 BEDFORD ROW, LONDON WCI
© 1962, 1966 CHARLES FRANCIS DIGBY MOULE
ISBN 0 7136 0995 8

PRINTED IN GREAT BRITAIN BY
BILLING & SONS LIMITED, GUILDFORD, LONDON AND WORCESTER

*To*
*THE SENATUS ACADEMICUS*
*OF THE*
*UNIVERSITY OF ST ANDREWS*
*as a token of gratitude for*
*their greatly honouring me*
*with the degree of*
*Doctor of Divinity*

# ACKNOWLEDGMENTS

OF all to whom I am consciously indebted (and this is a very large number) I must specially express my gratitude to Dr Henry Chadwick, who first suggested that I should write a book to go in his series, and whose frequent readings of drafts and patient help have rescued me from many mistakes and considerably enriched the material. All the errors that still remain, both of commission and omission, are in spite of his labours. Gratitude is due, further, to Mr G. M. Styler for kindly contributing an excursus. I must also thank very warmly the two typists who did the bulk of the transcription (often from very difficult manuscripts), Mrs A. N. Thompson and Mrs A. de Q. Robin, Mrs Milne, who brought order and clarity to several heavily corrected and altered sheets of notes, and the publisher and printer who have shown much courtesy and skill.

Apart from many relevant publications which I have no doubt overlooked, a good deal of important material has come to hand too late for even a reference. I must ask the authors of all such works for their indulgence if they have not been consulted.

Biblical quotations, with a few exceptions, are for the Old Testament from the *Revised Standard Version of the Bible*, copyrighted 1946 and 1952 by the Division of Christian Education of the National Council of the Churches of Christ in the U.S.A., and for the New Testament from *The New English Bible* by permission of the copyright owners and publishers, the Oxford and Cambridge University Presses.

C. F. D. M.

# CONTENTS

# ABBREVIATIONS

| | |
|---|---|
| *Ang. Theol. Rev.* | *Anglican Theological Review* (Evanston, Ill.). |
| *B.J.R.L.* | *Bulletin of the John Rylands Library* (Manchester). |
| *Bibl. Zeitschr.* | *Biblische Zeitschrift* (Paderborn). |
| CD | 'Damascus' Document or 'Zadokite Fragments' (from the Cairo Geniza; ed. C. Rabin, *The Zadokite Documents*, ²1958). |
| *Canad. Journ. of Theol.* | *Canadian Journal of Theology* (Toronto). |
| *Cath. Bib. Quarterly* | *Catholic Biblical Quarterly* (Washington). |
| *E.T.* | *Expository Times* (Edinburgh). |
| *H.T.R.* | *Harvard Theological Review* (Cambridge, Mass.). |
| *I.C.C.* | *International Critical Commentary.* |
| *I.L.N.T.* | J. Moffatt, *Introduction to the Literature of the New Testament* (³1918). |
| *J.B.L.* | *Journal of Biblical Literature* (Philadelphia). |
| *J.N.T.S.* | Journal called *New Testament Studies* (Cambridge). |
| *J.R.S.* | *Journal of Roman Studies* (London). |
| *J.T.S.* | *Journal of Theological Studies* (Oxford). |
| *M.T.* | Massoretic Text. |
| *N.E.B.* | *The New English Bible* (1961). |
| *Nov.T.* | *Novum Testamentum* (Leiden). |
| *par., pars.* | parallel(s). |
| *Proc. Brit. Acad.* | *Proceedings of the British Academy* (Oxford). |
| 1QS | (i.e. *Serek hayyaḥad*, the Rule of the Community from cave 1 at Qumran) *Manual of Discipline* (Eng. trans. and notes, W. H. Brownlee, 1951). |
| *R.B.* | *Revue Biblique* (Jerusalem). |
| *R.G.G.* | *Die Religion in Geschichte und Gegenwart* (²1927–1932; ³1957–). |
| *Rev. d'Hist. et de Philos.* | *Revue d'Histoire et de Philosophie religieuses* (Paris). |
| *Rev. Qum.* | *Revue de Qumran* (Paris). |
| S.-B. | H. L. Strack and P. Billerbeck, *Kommentar zum Neuen Testament aus Talmud und Midrasch* (1922–28). |
| *S.N.T.S.* | *Studiorum Novi Testamenti Societas* (Bulletins i-iii, 1950–52, Oxford; preceding *J.N.T.S.*). |

| | |
|---|---|
| Stevenson | J. Stevenson, *A New Eusebius : Documents illustrative of the History of the Church to* A.D. *337* (1957). |
| *T.B.* | *The Babylonian Talmud* (Eng. trans. by I. Epstein, incomplete, Soncino Press, 1935). |
| *T.J.* | *The Jerusalem Talmud* (ed. Krotoschin, 1866). |
| *T. und U.* | *Texte und Untersuchungen zur Geschichte der altchristlichen Literatur* (1882 ff.). |
| *T.W.N.T.* | *Theologisches Wörterbuch zum Neuen Testament* (ed. †G. Kittel and G. Friedrich, 1933–). |
| *Test.* | *Testaments of the Twelve Partriarchs* (ed. R. H. Charles, 1908) ; *Benj.* = *Benjamin*, etc. |
| *Th. Zeitschr.* | *Theologische Zeitschrift* (Basel). |
| *Theol. Literaturz.* | *Theologische Literaturzeitung* (Leipzig). |
| W.-H. | B. F. Westcott and F. J. A. Hort, *The New Testament in the Original Greek* (editio maior, 2 vols., text and introduction, 1881 ; editio minor, text only, 1896). |
| *Z.N.T.W.* | *Zeitschrift für die neutestamentliche Wissenschaft* (Berlin). |
| *Z.Th.K.* | *Zeitschrift für Theologie und Kirche* (Tübingen). |

## CHAPTER I

# INTRODUCTORY

THE character and purpose of this book need explanation. It does not set out to be an introduction to the New Testament in the ordinarily accepted sense of the word, for it attempts no systematic investigation of the authorship, date, and composition of each writing. Already there are sufficient works on these lines. Yet neither is it primarily a theology of the New Testament, although in fact a number of theological issues will come up for discussion. What it tries to do is to investigate the circumstances which led to the making of the New Testament. It is concerned with the birth of Christian scripture—or, still more, with its antenatal period.

The steady pressure of biblical research has fortunately brought about an atmosphere in which it is much easier than it used to be to remember the living community, and there is less danger now of imagining a study-table procedure[1] and mere 'scissors-and-paste' methods behind those vivid and practical documents. Indeed, there are already many books dealing with

---

[1] To speak of 'study-tables' literally in the New Testament period, and indeed, until as late as perhaps the eighth century, would, incidentally, be an anachronism even in connexion with scholarly study. B. M. Metzger has recently enquired further into the curious fact (already noted by others before him) that writing at a table seems to have been a comparatively late development. The scribes of antiquity either stood (for relatively brief notes), or sat on a stool or bench, or even on the ground, and rested their material on their knees. See B. M. Metzger, 'The Furniture of the Scriptorium at Qumran', *Rev. Qum.* i. 4 (1959), 509-515; and 'When did Scribes begin to use Writing Desks?', *Akten des XI. internationalen Byzantinisten-Kongresses, 1958* (Munich, 1960), 355 ff.; and, cited there, such earlier authorities as Theodor Birt, *Die Buchrolle in der Kunst* (1907); W. Sanday (ed.), *Studies in the Synoptic Problem by Members of the University of Oxford* (1911), 16 ff.; A. Dain, *Les Manuscrits* (1949), 22; Jaroslav Černý, *Paper and Books in Ancient Egypt* (1952), 14; T. C. Skeat, 'The Use of Dictation in Ancient Book-Production', *Proc. Brit. Acad.* 42 (1956), 138.

the life and worship of the early Christian communities in which the New Testament took shape.[1] But there still remains, it seems, a place for an attempt, within the compass of a single book of reasonable size,[2] to bring together, in a composite picture, the main features of the complex circumstances from which, under the guidance of God, there emerged, first a number of separate units of material, and then eventually the process which collected some of it into Christian scriptures, while much else was left aside or even repudiated.

This book looks at the New Testament in the light thrown on the earliest days of the Christian Church by such techniques as that of 'form criticism'[3] (although by no means all the standard findings of form criticism are here accepted); and it attempts to place in their setting in life and thought the processes which led up to the writing of early Christian books and the beginnings of the process of the selection from among them of what we call the scriptures of the New Testament. This will take us into many fields of language, history, and theology where many mistakes are sure to be made, many factors overlooked, many false guesses offered. But it will have been worth while if it leads readers back again to the New Testament with an imagination more alive to the questions that need to be asked—and especially

[1] In addition to the literature on 'form criticism', n. 3 below, the books on worship in New Testament times are relevant; see p. 11, n. 1, below.

[2] M. Albertz, *Die Botschaft des Neuen Testaments* (4 vols., 1947–57) is magnificent but bulky.

[3] This is the term generally used in English for the German *die formgeschichtliche Methode*, the method (of critical investigation) which proceeds by reconstructing the history of the forms assumed by each unit of tradition as it passes from mouth to mouth and place to place. Among introductions to the method and discussion of its scope and limitations see B. S. Easton, *The Gospel before the Gospels* (about 1928); V. Taylor, *The Formation of the Gospel Tradition* (1933; [2]1953); R. H. Lightfoot, *History and Interpretation in the Gospels* (Bampton Lectures, 1935); *The Gospel Message of St Mark* (1950), 98 ff.; M. Dibelius, *From Tradition to Gospel* (Eng. trans., 1934, of *Die Formgeschichte des Evangeliums*, 1919); *A Fresh Approach to the New Testament and Early Christian Literature* (Eng. version, 1936); R. Bultmann, *Die Geschichte der synoptischen Tradition* ([2]1931); H. Riesenfeld, *The Gospel Tradition and its Beginnings* (1957, also in the report of the Oxford 'Four Gospels' Congress, *Studia Evangelica* (*T. und U.* 73), 1959, and in *The Gospels Reconsidered*, Blackwell, 1960); C. F. D. Moule in *Lond. Quarterly and Holborn Review* (April 1958), 87 ff.; O. Cullmann, 'Unzeitgemässe Bemerkungen zum "historischen Jesus" der Bultmannschule', from the Evangelische Verlagsanstalt, Berlin, 1960; B. Gerhardsson, *Memory and Manuscript* (1961).

the questions that actually were asked in those early days and from which the New Testament took its genesis.

Two or three things at least may surprise the reader. One is that, while the general approach is that represented by 'form criticism', the conclusions are often more conservative than is typical of that approach. The Acts, in particular, is treated with more credence (some would say credulity) than by many scholars. This is not (consciously, at least) in the interests of any conservatism as such. It is because the Acts, taken at its face value, seems to me in the main coherent and in keeping with the rest of the evidence.

It may be surprising, secondly, that in the course of this enquiry, so little is said about evangelism. But although evangelism is absolutely inseparable from the life of the Church (when it is alive), it did not directly generate very much early Christian literature. In those days, before books could be very readily reproduced in quantity, literature was less prominent as a medium of propaganda than it is today. The initial *kerygma* or proclamation was spoken: when it came to be expanded into a written Gospel, it seems to have become explanatory rather than (primarily) evangelistic. If there are exceptions, these are perhaps the Gospels of Luke and John, which were possibly meant for non-Christian readers.

Once again, the paucity of allusions to the whole world of Hellenic thought and religion will seem to some readers to be a grave distortion of the picture. But I find myself among those who detect the minimum of such influence in the New Testament, as far as basic themes are concerned; and, where it leaves its mark, it seems to me to be more often by way of recoil from it than acceptance of it. This is not to deny that there are numerous borrowings of words and phrases and even ideas from the Hellenic world, but these are on a level shallower than that of the basic themes. The substance is usually Hebraic, even when the terms are Hellenic—except when (as is often the case) something quite original to Christianity is presented, which can be traced neither to Jew nor Greek, as such, but simply to Christ.[1]

[1] But, in any case, J. Barr's *The Semantics of Biblical Language* (1961) constitutes a very important warning against sweeping classifications of concepts as 'Greek' or 'Hebrew'.

One further remark must be made at this point, by way of anticipating surprise. Much of the ground covered or implied in this book has been deeply studied already and there are many monographs on certain aspects of it. It seemed, therefore, a waste of time to attempt to retell the whole story in equal detail. Some aspects, on the other hand, have hitherto been comparatively neglected; and there are certain suggestions and guesses (some of them perhaps new) which seemed worth putting forward tentatively. As a result, the proportions are uneven, less space being devoted to the well studied and well documented aspects than to the less familiar.

This introductory chapter offers one or two examples of the kind of question that must be asked. The last chapter will sum up the findings and also some of the questions that remain unanswered. In between the two, come sections portraying the Church from various angles: at worship, explaining itself, defending itself, building itself up, manifesting its different local characteristics, searching for authority. Each angle of view helps us towards an understanding of the genesis of various component parts of the New Testament or of the whole of the collection: for none of it was an academic exercise—it was simply the response of the Spirit of God within the Church to the challenges of its environment and history.

Take, now, by way of illustrating the problems confronting us, a couple of typical phenomena—two new genres of literature offered by the New Testament. First, the 'Gospel'. Imagine (if possible) that an otherwise educated person of our own day, with absolutely no knowledge of Christianity or its literature, were suddenly presented with St Mark's Gospel. What would he make of it? He would quickly recognize that it was quite unlike any other genre of writing known to him. It is concerned with Jesus of Nazareth, yet there is no description of his personal appearance, practically no attempt to date the action, only the barest indications of its place. It starts with no family history or background, it presents little ordered sequence of events. It springs straight into what it describes as good news, εὐαγγέλιον, and points to the coming of John as the fulfilment of a certain passage in the Old Testament. From this jumping-off point it goes on, through a series of brief, loosely linked paragraphs

4

describing the activity, or (more rarely) the sayings, of Jesus, to a proportionately very long account of his arrest, trial, and execution; and at the point where the tomb is found empty it seems to end abruptly—for the few verses which follow are patently from a later hand and constitute a summary of the traditions about the sequel.

This is certainly not biography, real or fictional. Yet neither is it an ethical or moralistic writing. It has no real parallels before it. It is the first extant specimen of a new genre: it is what we have learnt to call 'a Gospel', although the term εὐαγγέλιον is used by Mark himself not for his book but for its contents.[1] How did it ever come to be written, and why? Part of the answer is becoming clearer than it used to be. In the first place, what may be called the Gospel 'form' or 'shape' can be traced back behind this Gospel book, and evidently arose out of an effort to put into a few words an explanation of what Christians had heard and seen and what had brought them to their present convictions.

The reason why they belonged together as a distinct community was that they had been through certain events, about the significance of which they shared a common conviction, and that they believed themselves charged to bear witness to them. And this is how their witness ran:

A certain Jew named Jesus had, during his lifetime, been marked out as God's special representative by supreme goodness, and by exceptional deeds of power, such as the healing and the rescue of those who were in the grip of evil, and by his exceptionally powerful words. He had been cruelly put to death by Gentiles at the instigation of his fellow-Jews. But God had brought him back to life. All this was in fact in line with God's plan for his People as it may be traced in the Jewish Scriptures. Thus it is clear that Jesus is God's supreme Agent for the rescue of his People from evil and for the fulfilment of his purpose in the world. And this constitutes a challenge to you who hear to trust him

[1] For the significance of the word, see W. Schneemelcher's ed. of E. Hennecke, *Neutestamentliche Apokryphen* (³1959), and A. D. Nock's criticisms in *J.T.S.*, n.s., xi. (1960), 64 f., where he doubts whether the noun εὐαγγέλιον can rightly be called a distinctively sacral term, or whether its use by Christians is in *rivalry* to the (very different) εὐαγγέλια of the Caesar-cult. See also the interesting note in *Überlieferung und Auslegung im Matthäus-Evangelium*, G. Bornkamm, G. Barth, and H. J. Held (1960), 47 n. 2.

and give him your allegiance, and be baptized into membership in him.

This is at once less and much more than mere narrative: it is a declaration of conviction about the significance of a few events. And St Mark's Gospel is a filling out of this brief framework of declaration (short of the last two clauses) with some circumstantial detail: it is the story of God fulfilling and bringing to a climax in Jesus the age-long destiny of his People. Thus a hitherto unknown genre of writing seems to have sprung from the explanatory elaboration and expansion of a very early, very spontaneous, spoken proclamation. Substantially, it is neither biography nor moral exhortation, it is neither history nor ethics. It springs straight from Christian witness: it is the elaboration of a herald's announcement. So beautiful an early Christian writing as the *Epistle to Diognetus* (to be found among 'The Apostolic Fathers') serves, by way of contrast, to throw into relief this strangely different type of book. The *Epistle to Diognetus* is a gracious little statement about God's generous love to man and about Christian qualities. It is not a Gospel.

But although so new and unprecedented, the Christian proclamation is nothing if not rooted in the antecedent life of Judaism. Although it constituted a direct indictment of the Jews for sentencing their King to death, it was, in the same breath, paradoxically good news for them. For the crime of Judaism—so it declared—had unwittingly led to the placing of the coping-stone on the structure of God's salvation-plan for Israel. The stone rejected by the expert masons turned out to have come into its own, through that very process of rejection, as the most vital member of the building. And Israel's salvation lay in admitting the crime, and entering, through repentance and baptism, into union with this Jesus, who was the divinely anointed King of Israel, the Lord of Glory. However, St Mark's Gospel stops short of that last step. It represents an elaboration only of the Christian proclamation—the statement of fact and conviction which precedes and leads up to that final appeal to repent and be baptized.

There is no evidence that any complete Gospel existed before St Mark's; but before he set to work there were probably sheets of papyrus already circulating on which were written, in Aramaic (and possibly Hebrew) or in Greek, anecdotes or sayings such as eventually went into his composition. Several phenomena point in this direction. There are traces in Mark of the use of various sources—perhaps one which called the apostles 'the Twelve',[1] perhaps another identical with a sayings-collection or group of collections drawn upon also by Matthew and Luke;[2] there are traces, even earlier, in some of the epistles, of traditions (whether written or oral) of the sayings of Jesus and possibly of some incidents from his life;[3] and the arguments already framed in Rom. ix-xi can be paralleled from the subsequently written Gospels.[4] At all events traditions containing what we know as evangelic material can be certainly discerned in the background, before ever our extant Gospels took shape. But not an entire Gospel: Mark's seems to be the first example of that. After Mark, however, a large number of others came to be written, as well as collections of sayings of Jesus. Many of these other writings have been lost, and we know of them, if at all, only by name or through brief quotations in other writers. Of others, besides the other canonical Gospels, we have fragments or even almost complete copies. Only recently a Coptic sayings-collection has been retrieved.

But the only ones besides Mark which were ultimately retained by the general consensus of Christians throughout the world were Matthew, Luke, and John. For some years the traditions of Jesus seem to have flowed in many more or less parallel channels; but in the end these four Gospels emerged above the welter—or possibly were in fact the only complete Gospels ever to take shape. Their mutual relations, as is well known, are the subject of close study and controversy. It is remarkable that only two of the four bear apostolic names, while the other two bear the names of individuals who were not apostles. In these latter cases one might have expected at least the authority of communities rather than of non-apostolic individuals; but there it is. And in any case, all these attributions are

---

[1] E. Meyer, *Ursprung und Anfänge des Christentums*, i (1924), 133 ff.

[2] For 'Q' in Mark, see (e.g.) B. H. Streeter in *Studies in the Synoptic Problem by Members of the University of Oxford* (ed. W. Sanday, 1911), 165 ff.; B. W. Bacon, *The Gospel of Mark* (1925), 11, n. 7.

[3] See pp. 144 ff. below.

[4] J. Munck, *Christus und Israel: eine Auslegung von Röm. 9-11* (1956), 22.

7

traditional: none of the Gospels explicitly carries an author's name within it (though Jn xxi. 24, a note indicating the author, is now part of the Gospel).

Meanwhile (and this brings us to our other new genre, the New Testament epistle), before even Mark was written, and at the stage when the Good News was being proclaimed almost exclusively by word of mouth, leading evangelists like Paul of Tarsus found occasion to write letters of advice and exhortation to the communities they had founded. No Christian letter has so far been conclusively dated earlier than the earliest datable Pauline letter; and it is possible that it was Paul who brought this other new genre of Christian literature into existence—for a new genre it is. The literary letter, such as Cicero's, and the incidental papyrus letter of antiquity (at least in the forms it assumed in Egypt) are well known; but never before had the world seen anything quite like these very long letters almost wholly concerned not with personal details but with matters of Christian doctrine and conduct, introduced by and ending with new and distinctively Christian formulae of greeting and fare-well. Even the few letters contained within Old Testament scripture are not comparable with these.

The Pauline letters, whether or not absolutely the pioneers of their type, were certainly followed by others, and even by homilies artificially cast in epistolary form. Some of Paul's, and some by other writers, were evidently treasured by the recipient communities, and eventually came to be collected—how, is an obscure and fascinating question (see below, pp. 199 ff.)—and ranked alongside the Gospels as recognized Christian literature: 'the Gospel' and 'the Apostle' stood side by side, somewhat as 'the Law' and 'the Prophets' of the Hebrew scriptures. The New Testament letters reflect an enormously interesting variety of situations, in face of which, once again, one is compelled to ask Why?—Why did this problem or that present itself, and why did St Paul and the communities he represented give this answer and not that? Why did the early Church break out from the conservatism of Jewish ritual requirements? What controlled the decisions reached regarding the relations of Christians with pagans?

In addition to the Gospels and Epistles, there are the Acts and the Apocalypse; and behind much of the New Testament there lie, no doubt, earlier and more fragmentary documents—component pieces, absorbed and transformed so as to be usually beyond assured reconstruction. The circumstances in which such a medley of writings of a new type was created and then sifted and established in authority alongside, even above, the scriptures of the Old Testament—this is our story. One of the morals of it is that the only hope of reconstructing and understanding the genesis of the Christian scriptures is in asking Why? at every turn: Why this and not that? Why such and such an omission? Why this decision and not that? This book sets out chiefly to ask 'Why?' and only by this route, if at all, to arrive at any answers to the question 'How?'

Another of its morals, however, is the remarkable degree of unity that was achieved through all the differences and varieties. If it is asked why this happened, the only answer is that the common factor holding all together is devotion to the person of Jesus Christ—the historical Jesus acknowledged as Messiah and Lord. In the chapter on variety and uniformity in the early Church (Chapter IX), an attempt is made to do justice to the very wide range of diversity in emphasis as between different individuals and different traditions. But the rainbow spectrum thus presented is undeniably thrown by one luminary alone. Common to every writing of the New Testament, without even the exception of the Epistle of James, is devotion to Jesus Christ. Whether he is viewed as the Davidic Messiah or as the pre-existent Word of God, it is to Jesus that each writer acknowledges allegiance. All except Matthew, Mark, Titus, and the Johannine Epistles style Jesus 'Lord'; and the excepted writings all use comparable, if not even more significant terms—'Son of God', or 'Saviour'.

If there is anything equally conspicuous that the New Testament documents possess in common besides this distinctively Christian allegiance—this common confession of the incarnate Lord—it might be that, with few exceptions, they are Jewish writings, or, without any exception, monotheistic. This only makes it the more remarkable that, strictly maintaining their monotheism and without the slightest concession in this respect to pagan thought, they all adopt this attitude of reverence for Jesus.

Some discussion will be devoted in Chapter X to the process of selection which ultimately segregated the books of the New Testament from other Christian writings, and it will be seen that an important factor was this 'Christ-centredness'—this test of devotion to Jesus as Christ and Lord. Any Christology that attempted to resolve this tension—for tension there is in any confession of the incarnation—tended to be ejected, however reverent might be its form, and even if an apostolic name were attached to it.

In a word, the apostolic proclamation about Jesus was the unifying factor; or, more deeply defined, it is to the Spirit of God himself, through Jesus Christ our Lord, that the unity-in-diversity of the New Testament is to be traced.

## CHAPTER II

# THE CHURCH AT WORSHIP[1]

NOBODY reading the New Testament with a grain of imaginative insight could fail to recognize that considerable blocks of its material glow with the fervour of worship. But in comparatively recent years the glow has (seemingly, at least) been blown into a flame by reason of a special concern with worship which has pervaded all departments of Christian practice and research. In England the liturgical revival and the practical experiments associated with the 'Parish and People' movement[2] have gone hand in hand with a new appraisal of the setting of much biblical literature, especially the Psalms, along lines already pioneered in Scandinavia by such scholars as Sigmund Mowinckel, and elsewhere on the Continent by others.[3] As a result, the tendency today is to assume a liturgical context wherever it is in the faintest degree possible, rather than to start from other assumptions.

This has brought a great deal of fresh understanding, and thrown a vivid awareness of corporate life and movement and poetry into passages which had been treated far too statically and individualistically and prosaically; the words have begun to sing themselves, the mind's eye to see the rhythm of processions and the swing of censers. If anything, this fashion has overreached

[1] For this subject generally, see: P. G. S. Hopwood, *The Religious Experience of the Primitive Church prior to the Influence of Paul* (1936); J. Jeremias, *The Eucharistic Words of Jesus* (Eng. trans., 1955, of 2nd German ed., 1949); Bo I. Reicke, *Diakonie, Festfreude und Zelos, in Verbindung mit der altchristlichen Agapenfeier* (1951); O. Cullmann, *Early Christian Worship* (Eng. version, 1953; cf. *Les Sacrements dans l'Évangile johannique,* 1951); Bo I. Reicke, *Glaube und Leben der Urgemeinde; Bemerkungen zu Apg. 1-7* (1957); E. Schweizer, *Church Order in the New Testament* (Eng. trans., 1961, of *Gemeinde und Gemeindeordnung im neuen Testament,* 1959); C. F. D. Moule, *Worship in the New Testament* (1961).

[2] See the journal *Parish and People* as a mirror of this movement.

[3] As an example of S. Mowinckel's work, see his *Psalmenstudien II. Das Thronbesteigungsfest Jahwäs und der Ursprung der Eschatologie* (1922); another famous figure in this connexion is H. Gunkel (e.g. *Die Psalmen: Reden und Aufsätze* (1913)).

itself a trifle, and our professors are in danger of crying worship, worship where there is no worship. The liturgical clue is a useful guide but it can become a snare; and a distinguished Dutch scholar has rightly complained of a certain 'panliturgism' invading New Testament scholarship.[1]

But all this is only a caveat against abuse of the new insight: it remains perfectly true that many of the component parts of the New Testament were forged in the flame of devotion and that worship has left its stamp on its whole vocabulary; and it is to the Christians at worship that we now turn, as an important part of our study of the birth and growth of the New Testament. Or rather, we must start with the Jewish Church at worship.

Christian worship,[2] like Christian literature, was continuous with, and yet in marked contrast to, Jewish worship. Like the Christian scriptures, it grew out of words borrowed, out of traditions remembered, and out of inspired utterances; and, as with the scriptures, so in worship, the Jesus who was remembered was found to be the same Jesus who was experienced and who was present wherever two or three were assembled in his name. Christian worship was continuous with Jewish worship and yet, even from the first, distinctive.

As is well known, the Temple at Jerusalem continued, until its destruction in A.D. 70, if indeed it was completely destroyed even then,[3] to be the focus of Jewish worship. The Jewish synagogue (an institution of obscure origin, but perhaps dating virtually from the time of the exile) was in essence simply a 'gathering together' (which is what the Greek, *synagoge*, means) of a local group to hear the scriptures read aloud, to praise God and pray to him together, and to be instructed. In theory at any rate, the synagogue system was not an alternative to the Temple cultus. Religion on the level of its national consciousness and in its official form still found expression in the sacrificial cultus at the single Temple, the one centre of world Judaism.[4]

---

[1] W. C. van Unnik, 'Dominus Vobiscum', in *New Testament Essays in mem. T. W. Manson*, ed. A. J. B. Higgins (1959), 272.
[2] The next 7 pages are borrowed (by kind permission of the Lutterworth Press) from my book *Worship in the New Testament* (1961).
[3] See p. 121, n. 3 and p. 123, n. 4 below.
[4] For certain parallels between Temple and synagogue, and for the derivative nature of the synagogue's status, see *T.W.N.T.*, s.v. συναγωγή.

Indeed, even when a worshipper was not himself offering a sacrifice, his prayers seem often to have been offered actually in the Temple, or at least linked with the hours at which sacrifice was offered. In Lk. i. 10 the whole congregation pray in the court while Zecharias offers the incense in the Holy Place (cf. Rev. viii. 3 f.); in Acts iii. 1 Peter and John go up to the Temple at the hour of prayer which was also the hour of the evening sacrifice (see Exod. xxix. 39, etc.); and in Acts x. 30 a God-fearing Gentile prays at the same evening hour. So in the Old Testament, in 1 Kings xviii. 36 Elijah's prayer and offering on Mount Carmel are at the time of the offering of the oblation (cf. Ezra ix. 5); and in Dan. vi. 10 Daniel prays towards Jerusalem three times a day (cf. Ps. lv. 17). (Incidentally one may ask whether it is significant for the provenance of the traditions behind Matthew and Luke respectively that in Matt. vi. 2 ostentatious prayer is in the synagogue, but in Lk. xviii. 10 in the Temple. In Matt. v. 23 f., however, there is no doubt about the Temple being in view.)

'In theory', then, the synagogue was secondary to the Temple. But it has to be admitted that 'in whose theory?' would be a legitimate question. For it is probably a mistake to imagine that there was any one Jewish 'orthodoxy' in the New Testament period. Rather, we have to imagine various types of thought and practice existing side by side.[1] No doubt the priestly aristocracy, mainly Sadducean, maintained that the Temple cult was essential, and alone essential. But equally, we have some idea, through the accounts of the Essenes in Philo and Josephus, and, recently, through the Qumran writings of how differently a sectarian, but still priestly, group might be behaving at the same time.[2] Evidently the Qumran sect maintained a priesthood and a ritual organization, but one which was independent and sharply critical of the Temple hierarchy. Although not in principle opposed to animal sacrifice as such, they seem to have regarded

[1] Cf. E. R. Goodenough, *Jewish Symbols in the Greco-Roman Period* (1953–), and A. D. Nock's review, *Gnomon* 27 (1955), 558 ff.

[2] Philo, *Prob.* 75; Josephus, *Ant.* xviii. 1. 5. The most important of the Qumran documents for this purpose is the so-called *Manual of Discipline* (designated 1QS in current notation), which may be conveniently read in the annotated translation by W. H. Brownlee in *Bulletin of the American Schools of Oriental Research, Supplementary Studies*, nos. 10-12 (1951).

the Jerusalem hierarchy as so corrupt that they must for the time being dissociate themselves from the system; and in the meantime, making a virtue of necessity, they were able to console themselves with the reflection that praise and prayer, 'the offering of the lips', was equal in value to the traditional sacrifice.[1] In addition to groups which held such an attitude, it is just possible that there were extreme movements within Judaism which were opposed to the Temple cultus on principle, and were content with a synagogue type of worship alone—a kind of 'Quaker' Judaism. (Isa. lxvi. 1-4 may represent something of the sort in the Old Testament.) Dr Marcel Simon has published interesting speculations about this in connexion with the Christian martyr Stephen and the so-called 'Hellenists' of Acts;[2] and it is possibly relevant to note that no lamb is mentioned in the accounts of the Last Supper itself (as distinct from its preparation, Mk xiv. 12 and parallels). It is possible that this is only because the accounts of the Last Supper are influenced by later Eucharistic practice; or it might be because the meal was no Passover; or, again, it might be (as Ethelbert Stauffer has suggested)[3] because Jesus had already been banned as a false-teacher by the officials of Judaism, and a heretic was not permitted a lamb. But might it, alternatively, be that Jesus was a non-sacrificing Jew? Or may it even be that Jesus, prescient in his anticipation of the fall of Jerusalem and the de-judaizing of the Gospel, deliberately attached his teaching not to the lamb

[1] See J. M. Baumgarten, 'Sacrifice and Worship among the Jewish Sectarians of the Dead Sea (Qumrān) Scrolls', *H.T.R.* xlvi (1953), 154-157; J. Carmignac, 'L'Utilité ou l'inutilité des sacrifices sanglants dans la "Règle de la Communauté" de Qumran', *R.B.* lxiii (1956), 524-532; M. Black, *The Scrolls and Christian Origins* (1961), 39 ff.

[2] M. Simon, *St Stephen and the Hellenists* (1958), and earlier studies there cited. (I do not by any means agree with all his conclusions.)

[3] E.g. in *Jesus, Gestalt und Geschichte* (1957), 86 (Eng. trans., *Jesus and His Story*, 1960). B. Gärtner, 'John 6 and the Jewish Passover', in *Coniectanea Neotestamentica*, xvii (1959), 46 ff., suggests that Jesus might the more easily have held a lambless but Passover-like meal on the day before the Passover if Jews of the dispersion were familiar with such celebrations when they could not come up to Jerusalem. Evidence that this was the case is scanty, but he cites Josephus, *Ant.* xiv. 214 for Jews in Delos, and Mishnaic evidence for the usage in Palestine outside Jerusalem. So M. Black, 'The Arrest and Trial of Jesus', in *New Testament Essays in mem. T. W. Manson*, ed. A. J. B. Higgins (1959), 32 refers to 'the [Passover] celebrations in the synagogue, especially in the Diaspora, without a paschal lamb'.

(whether there was lamb on the table or not) but to those elements of the food and drink which would always be available?

But that was a digression about varieties of attitude within Judaism. The important point for the present purpose is that the Christian Church was born within a context of Temple and synagogue; indeed, it has always been tempting to find already there the two components of Christian worship—the Sacraments, corresponding to the Temple, and 'the Word', corresponding to the non-sacrificial, non-sacramental synagogue, with its strong element of reading and instruction. Accordingly, there have been times when, for example, what is now represented in the Anglican Church by Matins and Evensong and by the 'Ante-Communion' has been traced to the synagogue service, while 'the Liturgy', the Holy Communion or Eucharist proper, has been treated as a kind of counterpart to the sacrificial and the cultic in Judaism. But in fact neither Judaism nor Christianity is so simple as to be fairly stylized in this manner; and it is better simply to note the Jewish setting and to see what picture of Christian worship emerges from such evidence as we possess, before we try to make rash generalizations or formulate principles

It is impossible to doubt that Jesus worshipped in the Temple. All four Gospels preserve allusions to this. According to Luke, he is found in the Temple as an infant when his parents bring him to be presented as their first male child, in accordance with the Law; and again when he goes up to Jerusalem as a boy for his first Passover. According to the unanimous witness of all four Gospels, it was when he had come to Jerusalem for the Passover that he was arrested and put to death. The Fourth Gospel expressly mentions his presence in the Temple also for the 'feast of tabernacles' (Jn vii. 2 f.) and for the winter festival of *Hannukkah* or Dedication (Jn x. 22).

What is not expressly evidenced is that Jesus himself ever offered an animal sacrifice. The nearest that the Gospels come to it is in sayings which might suggest approval of the sacrificial system (Mk i. 44 and parallels and Matt. v. 23 f.). But such sayings can hardly be pressed to mean positive approval of sacrifice. The meaning of Matt. v. 23 f., 'First go and make your peace with your brother, and only then come back and offer

15

your gift', is, in fact, almost identical with that of Christ's quotation from Hosea, 'I desire mercy and not sacrifice' (Matt. ix. 13, xii. 7); and although that only means that mercy is more important than sacrifice, one cannot help wondering whether (as has already been suggested) Jesus himself possibly worshipped without sacrificing.

However, that Jesus cared about the Temple worship, whether or not he actually joined in sacrifice, is evident enough, if only from the story of the expulsion of the dealers from its outer court. Whether this was an attack upon mercenary mindedness or a gesture towards the Gentiles, in either case it betokens a reckless zeal for the reform of the Temple. It is difficult to see it as an attack upon the Temple system as such.

Equally clearly, however, Jesus also saw that the Temple was doomed. The charge that he had said 'I will destroy this Temple . . .' was not, according to Mk xiv. 57-59, substantiated. But that he had indeed said something that might have been so interpreted, emerges from the taunts levelled at him in Mk xv. 29 (parallel to Matt. xxvii. 40). And in the introduction to the apocalyptic discourse (Mk xiii. 2 and parallels) he foretells the destruction of the Temple; while Jn ii. 19 has the saying 'Destroy this temple and in three days I will raise it'; and Matt. xii. 6, 'something greater than the Temple is here'. There is enough in these traditions to explain the attitude of Stephen (Acts vi. 14) who is accused of saying that Jesus is going to destroy 'this place'.

If there is no doubt that, despite these reservations, Jesus worshipped in the Temple, it is equally clear that he regularly went to synagogue on the Sabbath (cf. Acts xvii. 2, of Paul). In Lk. iv. 16 it is expressly described as his custom to do so; and even if we were to discount this as evidence, there is, all over the Gospels, a sufficient number of references to Jesus' teaching and healing in synagogues to leave us in no doubt on this score.

It is sometimes alleged that in synagogue Jesus would necessarily have recited the entire Psalter in the course of public worship. Of this there is no clear evidence. That the Psalter was at some period divided into sections corresponding with the lectionary cycles for other parts of the scriptures[1] neither proves

[1] See *T.B. Megillah*, and (e.g.) *The Jewish Encyclopaedia*, vi. 136.

that this held good for the time of Christ nor that, even if it did, all the Psalms in the sections were publicly used.[1] That Jesus was steeped in the scriptures, including the Psalter, is suggested by the sayings attributed to him in the Gospels. But the same evidence seems to suggest also a very considerable freedom in selection.

In sum, then, it may be said that, while Jesus used at least some of the Jewish institutions of worship, and apparently did so with ardour and great devotion, he refused to shut his eyes to the nemesis which was to overtake a Temple which had been made mercenary and exclusive; he saw in his ministry and in his own self the focal point of the 'new Temple'; and he was satisfied with nothing but the absolute sincerity and spirituality of which the Temple was meant, but too often failed, to be the medium: 'the time is coming when you will worship the Father neither on this mountain [in Samaria], nor in Jerusalem . . . those who are real worshippers will worship the Father in spirit and in truth' (Jn iv. 21, 23).

Coming now to the Acts, we find at once that the apostles in Jerusalem seem, as a matter of course, to have gone to prayer, at first, at any rate, in the Temple (Acts iii. 1; cf. Lk. xviii. 10, xxiv. 53, Acts ii. 46); and there are references to Paul not only worshipping in the Temple (Acts xxii. 17) but being ready to pay the expenses of sacrifice for a group of men, presumably poor men, as an act of Jewish piety (Acts xxi. 23-26). In the same way, contact is scrupulously maintained with the synagogue by such as Stephen (Acts vi. 9) and Paul (Acts *passim*), both in Jerusalem and outside Judaea in the dispersion, until they are expelled from it. Expulsion from the synagogue inevitably took place sooner or later (as Jn xvi. 2, cf. ix. 22, implies, and Acts xviii. 6 f. bears witness);[2] and it is likely that the final recognition that Christianity was incompatible with non-Christian Judaism had far-reaching influence on the shaping of Christian ways of worship.

---

[1] This is worth mentioning, since the indiscriminate use in certain branches of Christian worship of the entire Psalter, including the fiercely nationalist and bloodthirsty songs, is sometimes defended on the ground that Jesus himself used them all. One can only ask Did he? and, even if he did, would that necessarily be determinative (any more than the use, if that were substantiated, of animal sacrifices) for the post-resurrection practice of the Christian Church?　　　　[2] Though see p. 107, n. 1 below.

But that was not immediately; and in the meantime not only were the Jewish places of worship frequented by the Christian Jews but doubtless also the Jewish religious calendar was observed. Many, at least, of the early Christians are to be assumed to have gone on observing the Sabbath (Saturday) even if the next day of the week (Sunday) eventually came to occupy a dominant position as the day of the resurrection (Ignatius, *Magn.* ix. 1, Barnabas xv. 9, etc.; cf. Rev. i. 10 and the vision which follows). In any case, the Sabbath (Saturday) remained in Jewish societies the only day free for worship (in Gentile societies there was no *weekly* free day, only the pagan festivals at irregular intervals); and it is likely enough, as H. Riesenfeld suggests,[1] that the Christians began simply by prolonging the Sabbath during the night of Saturday-Sunday, by way of observing the accomplishment in Christ of the Jewish Sabbath. The rationalization of an *eighth* day—the day after the seventh—as marking the beginning of a new creation seems to be an idea brought in from Jewish apocalyptic (see Barnabas xv. 8 f.).[2] Rom. xiv. 5 f. bears witness to the existence, within the Christian community, of a diversity of views on the observance of holy days. Of the great festivals, the Jewish Passover probably continued to be kept by Christians long after they had found an existence of their own, especially as it lent itself so naturally to a Christian connotation and was bound up with the traditions of the death of Christ (cf. Acts xx. 6, 1 Cor. v. 7). Other Jewish festivals too must have persisted.[3] In Acts xx. 6 it is implied that Paul observed the Passover (so far as that was possible outside Jerusalem) before leaving Philippi; then, in Acts xx. 16, we find him hurrying so as to reach Jerusalem by Pentecost. Is this in order to celebrate with fellow Christians the Birthday of the Christian Church? Even if it was, it would of necessity have

[1] 'Sabbat et Jour du Seigneur' in *New Testament Essays* (as on p. 14, n. 3 above); cf. C. W. Dugmore, *The Influence of the Synagogue upon the Divine Office* (1948), 28, 30.
[2] Note also the possible implications of the Matthean genealogy (Matt. i. 17)—a new creation in Christ? See A. Farrer in *Studies in the Gospels* (ed. D. E. Nineham, *in mem.* R. H. Lightfoot, 1955), 87.
[3] See D. Daube, 'The Earliest Structure of the Gospels', *J.N.T.S.* 5. 3 (April 1959), 174 *fin.*; E. Lohse in *T.W.N.T.* vi. 49, n. 35 on the (? Christian) Passover of 1 Cor. v. 6-8; and (49) on the possibility of Christian Pentecosts outside Jerusalem. See also H. Kretschmar, 'Himmelfahrt und Pfingsten', *Zeitschrift für Kirchengeschichte*, 4th series, iv (1954–55), 209 ff.

meant also celebrating the festival publicly with the non-Christian Jews: how could that be avoided if one was actually at Jerusalem? There must have been a great deal of overlapping of Jewish feasts and Christian connotations, the one merging into and tending to colour the other. Passover and Pentecost, in their Christian forms as Easter and Whitsunday, were destined to form the basis of the 'Christian Year'.[1] Only when the observance of a certain calendar became bound up with views incompatible with the freedom of the Christian Gospel and the Christian estimate of Christ do we find Paul protesting against it, as in Gal. iv. 10 f., Col. ii. 16.

The same is true of circumcision. The practice of it alongside of Christian baptism by a judaizing party within the Church only becomes a matter of contention when it encroaches upon the essential Gospel and challenges the uniqueness and finality of Christ (Acts xv, etc.). Paul is prepared to circumcise Timothy so that he may be acceptable to the Jews (Acts xvi. 3); but he will not yield for an instant to those who want to treat circumcision as a necessary condition of membership in 'God's Israel', over and above incorporation in Christ (Gal. ii. 5, vi. 11-16).

Thus, whatever distinctive forms of Christian worship there were, sprang up side by side with Jewish worship or even within it. Take an instance. The cry 'Blessed is [? or be] the Lord!' is at the heart of Jewish adoration. As recent research has emphasized, there is something deeper here than even thanksgiving. Thanking God for specific mercies is only a special (and to some extent a man-regarding) expression of that deeper and even more extrovert adoration of God for his own sake, expressed by the Hebrew '*baruch Adonai*', 'blessed [is or be] the Lord!'; and the Old Testament furnishes plenty of stately examples of liturgies of adoration based upon this phrase—not, of course, confining themselves to this unspecified adoration, still less to this single word, but shot through with this attitude of adoration of God for his own sake, for his being, for his creation, and for his mighty works, as well as, in particular, for his work of rescuing his People. J.-P. Audet cites, as a good instance of this attitude (although here the actual phrase 'Blessed . . .' is reserved to

[1] A. A. McArthur, *The Evolution of the Christian Year* (1953).

the end), the great liturgy of 1 Chron. xvi. 8-36, which comprises parts of the Psalter:[1]

> O give thanks to the LORD,
> call on his name,
> make known his deeds among the peoples!
> Sing to him, sing praises to him,
> tell of all his wonderful works!
> Glory in his holy name;
> let the hearts of those who seek the LORD rejoice!
> Seek the LORD and his strength,
> seek his presence continually!
> Remember the wonderful works that he has done,
> the wonders he wrought, the judgments he uttered,
> O offspring of Abraham his servant,
> sons of Jacob, his chosen ones!
>
> .  .  .  .  .
>
> Blessed be the LORD, the God of Israel, from
> everlasting to everlasting!
> Then all the people said 'Amen!' and praised the LORD.

This attitude of 'benediction' is at the heart, then, of Jewish worship; and the rabbinic ejaculation, 'blessed be [or is] he!', still finds its way, here and there, into the phrases of Paul the converted Pharisee: Rom. i. 25, ix. 5, 2 Cor. xi. 31. But what is distinctively new about Christian expressions of worship is, of course, the reference to Jesus.

There were certain Jewish benedictions and prayers which made allusion to David the Servant of Yahweh. For instance, the prayer of a Passover *haggada* (exposition) contains the phrase 'David the son of Jesse thy servant, thine anointed'.[2] A Christianizing of this is strikingly illustrated in the *Didache* (ix) where next to thanks for 'the holy vine of *David thy Servant*', comes 'which thou madest known to us through *Jesus thy Servant*'. Here the replacement of 'thy Servant (παῖς) David', by 'thy Servant (παῖς) Jesus' can be seen actually in process of taking place: the non-Christian thanksgiving for King David, the Servant of the Lord, and for all the blessings promised for his

[1] J.-P. Audet, *La Didachè* (1958), 377 ff.
[2] See, e.g., W. Zimmerli and J. Jeremias, *The Servant of God* (Eng. trans., 1957), n. 184.

messianic line, becomes, on Christian lips, a thanksgiving for the fulfilment of that messianic promise in David's greater Son. Whatever the chronological position of the *Didache*, this represents a logically primitive stage in the Christian consciousness. In the New Testament itself παῖς is applied to Jesus only in two chapters, Acts iii and iv, and it seems probable that at any rate in Acts iv. 25 it is intended in just the same sense as when it was applied to David, and means not so much the suffering as the royal Servant of God. Acts iv. 24 ff. is undoubtedly liturgical. True, it is anything but formal. Quite apart from the fact that the Greek is chaotic and possibly corrupt, the occasion is represented as one of exultant spontaneity—an outburst of praise in the group of Jerusalem Christians, after the clash with the hierarchy in which the inflexible confidence and boldness of the apostles have been signally vindicated. But the interesting thing is that—whether (as seems quite possible) the writer has this from early oral tradition, or whether he is simply writing the kind of prayer that might have been used—the phrases fall into typically Jewish form:

*Address to God as Creator, and as the inspirer of prophecy:*
> Sovereign Lord, maker of heaven and earth and
> sea and of everything in them,
> who by the Holy Spirit, through the mouth of David
> thy servant, didst say,

*Quotation from Psalm ii about God's vindication of the Messiah:*
> Why did the Gentiles rage and the peoples lay
> their plots in vain?
> The kings of the earth took their stand and the
> rulers made common cause
> Against the Lord and against his Messiah.

*Allusion to God's dedicated Servant Jesus as the anointed King, and as vindicated against his enemies:*
> They did indeed make common cause in this very city against thy holy servant Jesus whom thou didst anoint as Messiah. Herod and Pontius Pilate conspired with the Gentiles and peoples of Israel to do all the things which, under thy hand and by thy decree, were foreordained.

*Prayer for continued help and championing, through the Name of God's Servant Jesus:*

> And now, O Lord, mark their threats, and enable thy servants to speak thy word with all boldness.
>
> Stretch out thy hand to heal and cause signs and wonders to be done through the name of thy holy servant Jesus.

Here are praise and prayer according to a familiar pattern, only with the difference that the centre of God's championing is identified—identified in Jesus, who is hailed as the anointed King, and as the medium of God's continued triumph.

Thus we are watching here, as we did in the words of the *Didache*, the bending of Jewish liturgy to the distinctively Christain standpoint. Where παῖς is used of Jesus in the preceding chapter (iii. 13) it is in explanation rather than in worship; and it seems, on the whole, more probable that there the reference is to the suffering Servant of Isa. liii. It is in the liturgical context of chapter iv that the royal note is dominant.[1]

Other examples in the New Testament of what purport to be spontaneous extemporizations of praise and worship are the Lucan canticles—the Benedictus, the Magnificat, and the Nunc Dimittis; but all these are, in the strict sense, pre-Christian.[2] In the Benedictus, indeed, it is difficult to resist the impression that John the Baptist is being hailed as *the* forerunner, *par excellence*, not of Jesus but of the Lord God—as the Elijah who was to precede the dawning of the final day, or (though this is not the term here used) as himself the Messiah.[3] At any rate, here again we have the allusion to David the Servant (παῖς) of God (Lk. i. 69), to the blessing of God, to God's work in actual history (the birth of the child), and to the aspiration and hope of

---

[1] For a discussion of the distinction in Christological vocabulary between worship and explanation, see C. F. D. Moule, 'The Influence of Circumstances on the Use of Christological Terms', *J.T.S.*, n.s. x (1959), 247 ff.

[2] Among much that has been written about the Lucan canticles as genuinely Semitic compositions, see R. A. Aytoun, 'The Ten Lucan Hymns of the Nativity in their Original Language', *J.T.S.* xviii (1916–17), 274 ff.; and P. Winter, 'Magnificat and Benedictus—Maccabaean Psalms?', *B.J.R.L.* 37 (1954), 328 ff., and 'The Proto-source of Luke I', *N.T.* i. 3 (1956), 184 ff. These studies, taking different sides in the Aramaic versus Hebrew controversy, should be read against the background of the studies referred to on p. 186, n. 2.

[3] See J. A .T. Robinson, 'Elijah, John and Jesus: an Essay in Detection', *J.N.T.S.* 4. 4 (July 1958), 263 ff.

a good time coming. Christians were able to assimilate this by interpreting κύριος of the Lord Jesus instead of God; and, since John preceded Jesus, if John is Elijah, then the coming of Jesus stands in the position of the final Day itself. Thus extempore pre-Christian liturgy is taken up and given a Christian direction, exactly as happened also to so many of the Psalms. Since the Magnificat is not a strictly messianic Psalm, but is mainly praise of God for his mighty deed in transposing the fortunes of low and high, Christians could use this, too, unaltered. Like the other fragments just examined, the Magnificat contains its allusion to God's παῖς, but this time it is his Servant Israel (Lk. i. 54).

The next most Psalm-like pieces among the New Testament ejaculations of worship are the songs of the Apocalypse. It is a familiar fact that students of the Psalter recognize certain 'enthronement Psalms'—Psalms such as xlvii, xciii, xcvi, xcvii, xcviii, xcix, which may have been used at an annual festival of the enthronement of Yahweh as divine King. There is no need here to debate the pros and cons of this theory,[1] but the Apocalypse certainly presents some splendid Christian enthronement Psalms:

> The sovereignty of the world has passed to our Lord and his Christ, and he shall reign for ever and ever! (Rev. xi. 15.)
> Alleluia! The Lord our God, sovereign over all, has entered on his reign! Exult and shout for joy and do him homage, for the wedding-day of the Lamb has come! His bride has made herself ready, and for her dress she has been given fine linen, clean and shining. (Rev. xix. 6-8.)

Even if these, and the other Christian Psalms and ejaculations in this extraordinary work, were composed by the seer expressly for the occasion or given him in ecstasy, it is hard to doubt that they represent the kind of poetry which Christians actually used in corporate worship. Again, therefore, it is to liturgy that we are able to trace the genesis of such parts of the New Testament —and to liturgy deeply influenced by Jewish forms.

Considerably further, in language and form, from any known

---

[1] For discussions see, e.g., A. Weiser, *Die Psalmen* (*Das Alte Testament Deutsch*, 1950), 17, 35 ff.; A. R. Johnson, 'The Role of the King in the Jerusalem Cultus', in *The Labyrinth* (ed. S. H. Hooke, 1935); H.-J. Kraus, *Psalmen* (*Biblischer Kommentar, Altes Testament*, 1960), I. xlii, lv.

Jewish antecedents are the little snatches of distinctively Christian hymnody (for such they are most naturally accounted) in Eph. v. 14 and 1 Tim. iii. 16. They therefore seem to take us one step further inside purely Christian worship: these, it would appear, are not mere adaptations of Jewish formulae but fresh creations of the Christian genius of worship. 1 Tim. iii. 16 provides, in this respect, an interesting parallel and contrast to the more Jewish enthronement-psalms of Revelation:

> He who was manifested in the body,
> vindicated in the spirit,
> seen by angels;
> who was proclaimed among the nations,
> believed in throughout the world,
> glorified in high heaven.

Its pattern, however—according, at least, to Jeremias' interpretation[1]—still links it with the ancient East, and it too is an 'enthronement-hymn'. Ancient oriental enthronement ceremonial (e.g. in Egypt) comprised elevation, presentation, and finally the actual installation on the throne. To these three movements, according to Jeremias, the three couplets of our hymn may be referred: (i) the vindication of the One who appeared in flesh; (ii) the presentation of his credentials to angels and men; (iii) his installation in the faith of the world and in the glory of heaven. A similar three-fold pattern is detected in Phil. ii. 9-11—elevation, proclamation, acclamation; and Matt. xxviii. 18-20 and Heb. i. 5-14 are invoked in the interests of the same theory. It requires, however, some degree of stretching to extract this particular pattern from 1 Tim. iii. 16, where, after all, the only *explicit* reference to elevation is at the end, not the beginning! It is, as a matter of fact, notoriously difficult to squeeze these six lines at all convincingly into conformity with any logical pattern, whether one takes them as a couple of triplets or a triplet of couplets; and perhaps we shall have to admit that the ardour of adoration is not always logical or even symmetrical. But, however it may be analysed or arranged, it remains highly probable that this really is a very early Christian

---

[1] J. Jeremias, *Die Briefe an Timotheus u. Titus* (*Das Neue Testament Deutsch*, 1953), *in loco.*

hymn: the very fact that it starts abruptly with a relative pronoun unattached (apparently) to any antecedent suggests a quotation from something that the reader already knew and would recognize; and, like many of the greatest Christian hymns, it is essentially credal—a great adorative confession, like the *Te Deum* after it.

As for Eph. v. 14, this is, if possible, even more elusive. In Acts xii, in the dramatic story of Peter's rescue from prison by an angel, we read (*v*. 6) that Peter was *sleeping* (κοιμώμενος) in chains between two soldiers; then (*v*. 7) 'behold an angel of the Lord came upon him and a *light* shone in the building; and striking Peter's side the angel aroused (ἤγειρεν) him saying "Get up (ἀνάστα) quickly!"' And here is Eph. v. 14:

> Awake, (ἔγειρε) sleeper,
> Rise (ἀνάστα) from the dead,
> And Christ will shine upon you.

Is this an ancient hymn built round the Peter-story? (Nowhere else in the New Testament, but only in these two passages, does the rare form ἀνάστα occur.) And was the hymn connected with the Passover (Easter) season, as the story certainly is (Acts xii. 3)?[1] And does this mean that it belongs to the greatest of baptismal settings—the great paschal baptisms after the scrutinies and the fasting of Lent? There is no doubt that baptism is closely associated with light—it soon came to be called 'enlightenment'; or that it meant life from death. We may have stumbled, then, on a fragment of the Church's most ancient baptismal hymn: indeed, the whole of Ephesians may be baptismal. These are common enough assumptions. But they remain speculation. All we can say with tolerable certainty is that, like 1 Tim. iii. 16, Eph. v. 14 is hymnic, and that 1 Tim. iii. 16 comprises an early Christian creed.

Many other passages have been claimed as hymns: Phil. ii. 6-11, Col. i. 15-20, 1 Pet. i. 3 ff., to mention only a few.[2] But in actual fact the criteria are inconclusive. These passages may or may not be strophic—i.e. symmetrical and balanced in their

---

[1] See A. Strobel, 'Passa-Symbolik und Passa-Wunder in Act. xii. 3 ff.', *J.N.T.S.* 4. 3 (April 1958), 210 ff.

[2] See literature in C. F. D. Moule, *Worship in the New Testament* (1961), 69 n. 4.

lines or their rhythms: nobody has conclusively demonstrated that they are. Even if they are not, as a matter of fact, they might still have been sung, just as Psalms and other irregular or metreless pieces in English can be sung. But who is to prove that they were hymns? Prose and poetry, adoration and statement, quotations from recognized liturgical forms and free, original composition, mingle and follow one another so easily in the mind of a Christian thinker that, without some external criterion, one can never be certain how much or how little of 'common prayer' one is overhearing. But we can be sure that parts of what a Paul or a Peter wrote or dictated for a letter he might equally well ejaculate in public worship; and the stately eulogies, beginning with the word εὐλογητός, 'blessed', in Eph. i. 3 and 1 Pet. i. 3 are undoubtedly liturgical in *type*, whether or not either is, in fact, a fresh composition not previously used.

Besides such snatches of actual hymns as can be recovered with more or less certainty, there are several allusions, in the New Testament, to the singing of psalms and hymns by Christians. There seems to be very little practical distinction, at this period or in this literature, between hymn ὕμνος (ὑμνεῖν), psalm ψαλμός (ψάλλειν), and song ᾠδή. So far as it is possible to test, the Old Testament Psalms are never described by any other noun than ψαλμός, though the verb ὑμνεῖν is certainly used of singing the *hallel* Psalms at the Last Supper (Matt. xxvi. 30, Mk xiv. 26). But it certainly does not follow that ψαλμός and ψάλλειν never refer to Christian compositions or, conversely, that ὕμνος necessarily means a Christian hymn. In 1 Cor. xiv. 26, Paul says that when the Christians come together for a meeting, each one has a psalm or a teaching or a revelation or a 'tongue' or an interpretation; and it seems unlikely that ψαλμός here, in the company of the other *ad hoc* items, means a Psalm from the Jewish Psalter which the worshipper comes ready to sing: it is more likely to be a Christian extemporization. Conversely, it is conceivable that Jewish Psalms are intended in Acts xvi. 25 where Paul and Silas προσευχόμενοι ὕμνουν τὸν θεόν—'prayed and sang [in praise of] God'. The only passages where anything like a clear distinction might be presumed are those in which all three words come together, in Eph. v. 19, Col. iii. 16; Christians are to sing (ᾄδοντες) with psalms and hymns and odes. But both passages are enthusiastic and effusive in style and it would be prosaic to insist that a conscious distinction is intended between (say) Jewish Psalms, Christian hymns, and perhaps more formal poems of praise. In any case, in both these passages the singing and psalming is to be done τῇ καρδίᾳ or ἐν ταῖς καρδίαις—that is, perhaps, silently and in the secret of the heart. The direct reference is thus conceivably not to audible, corporate worship but to the constant secret recollection of corporate praise which the Christians are to cherish—all unknown to their heathen masters or companions—as they go about their work (cf. especially Col. iii. 17).

At any rate, there is no doubt that the more jubilant moments of primitive Christian worship were marked by outbursts of song—generally, one assumes, unaccompanied, though one never knows whether a harper, or zither-player, κιθαριστής, might not sometimes smuggle in his instrument to the secret place of assembly. Incidentally, it is interesting that a vision of heavenly worship in the Revelation is accompanied (xiv. 2) by the sound of κιθαρῳδοί, which should strictly mean not mere instrumentalists (κιθαρισταί) who play the zither, but bards like the Homeric rhapsodists who also use their voices, and sing to their own accompaniment. Was the ᾠδή or song, perhaps, a solo performance of this sort?

But are there fragments of Christian liturgy in the New Testament besides the songs and psalms? Many scholars answer with a confident yes; and it has even been maintained that 1 Peter is virtually a Baptism Service (minus the 'rubrics', so to speak), complete with its exhortations and homilies, its hymns and prayers. This latter theory does not actually come out very well from scrutiny. The evidence, examined point by point, is rickety and must rely upon cumulative effect for whatever weight it carries; and—still more significant—it is not really easy to imagine a situation in which the substance of a baptism rite would naturally be dressed up in letter-form and sent to remote non-participants. It is far simpler to think of 1 Peter as a noble recall to former baptismal vows and promises, addressed to Christians who, facing the threat of persecution or actually undergoing it, needed just this bracing comfort. It is full of baptismal allusion, but need not be other than genuinely epistolary.[1] In any case, the language of Christian preaching and exhortation is virtually indistinguishable from what may be assumed to have been used at the administration of the sacraments; so that what we may describe as baptismal or eucharistic language is not necessarily to be associated with the moment of liturgical performance. The sacraments are evangelic and the gospel is sacramental: word and sacrament are in that sense one.

This is not, however, to imply that when, in 1 Cor. xi. 23 ff., Paul alludes to the words spoken by Jesus at the Last Supper, he is not quoting from traditions which were actually repeated at the eucharist; or, indeed, that the synoptic accounts of the Institution had not themselves been transmitted through repetition at the eucharist, long before they came to be written into the Gospels. Indeed, it is a familiar observation that the institution narratives in Mk xiv. 22-25 and Matt. xxvi. 26-28 show signs of accommodation to liturgical use. For, quite apart from details, there is a clear difference between the Pauline account and those others. In 1 Cor. xi. 25 Paul explicitly separates the cup from the bread by the phrase 'after supper'; and he presents the words over the cup in a form which is not parallel to those over the bread: over the bread 'This is my body . . .'; but over the cup, not 'This is my blood . . .', but 'This cup is the new covenant in [? i.e. sealed by] my blood'. In contrast to this, both Mark and Matthew indicate no interval between bread and cup, and both use the parallel phrases, 'this is my body . . .', 'this is my blood . . .' It is hard to resist the conclusion that—to this extent at least—Paul's version is the more historical, while the other two represent a modification arising from the sacramental use of the two sayings from the Last Supper in close juxtaposition. In all probability, the facts are not really so simple as that. A microscopic examination of the language and structure of the relevant passages by H. Schürmann[2] has led to the conclusion that in certain respects the Synoptists may be in closer touch than even Paul with original or very early forms of

[1] See C. F. D. Moule, 'The Nature and Purpose of I Peter', *J.N.T.S.* 3. 1 (Nov. 1956), 1 ff., with literature there cited; and criticisms of this in F. W. Beare, *The First Epistle of Peter* ([2]1958), 196 ff. See further T. C. G. Thornton, 'I Peter, a Paschal Liturgy?', *J.T.S.*, n.s., xii (1961), 14 ff.

[2] H. Schürmann, *Der Einsetzungsbericht* (1955).

the tradition; and in any case, the Lucan institution narrative presents peculiar problems of its own.[1] But it is enough here simply to illustrate the influence of liturgy on the formation of the New Testament by the undoubted signs of this process in the various forms of the words of institution, however delicate and complex a full statement might need to be.

A plausible case can be made, similarly, for detecting the echoes of the liturgy (perhaps in the Roman congregations) behind both Hebrews and 1 Clement, whose writers show certain significant traits in common.[2] Again, the guess has been hazarded that the 'farewell discourses' of Jn xiii-xvii owe their phrasing and form in considerable measure to the president's prayer at the Eucharist in the Ephesian tradition.[3]

Thus, much that we know about the words, and even deeds, of Jesus must owe its preservation to assemblies for worship. Even if only a scrap here and a scrap there can be recovered of the actual formulae of worship, this does not alter the fact that very much of what now constitutes the New Testament owes its existence to the requirements of worship. It will be argued, later in this book, that the Gospels were not primarily intended for use in worship, so much as for instruction and explanation and (in some cases) even for apologetic; but that is not to deny that the words and deeds of Jesus must have been recalled at worship, and that worship was a very important factor in the preservation and transmission of the traditions. D. Daube has suggested, indeed, that the Gospel-form may have grown out of the Christian Passover, as an extension and development of the Jewish practice of the Paschal *haggada*—the recitation of the story of salvation.[4] But on the whole, although we later have Justin's evidence for the reading of apostolic reminiscences (i.e. no doubt, Gospels) at worship (see p. 198), and although no Christian worship could have substance without some knowledge of the facts behind the faith, yet the written Gospels, from

[1] See C. F. D. Moule, *Worship in the New Testament* (1961), p. 25; and add H. Chadwick, 'The Shorter Text of Luke xxii. 15-20', in *H.T.R.* 50 (1957), 249-258.
[2] See A. Nairne, *The Epistle to the Hebrews* (1922), xxxiv.
[3] See the late A. C. Macpherson's thesis, shortly to be published.
[4] 'The Earliest Structure of the Gospels', *J.N.T.S.*, 5. 3 (April 1959), 174 ff.; *id. The New Testament and Rabbinic Judaism* (1956), there cited.

Mark onwards, seem to fit more naturally into the setting of instruction, explanation, and defence. Baptism and the Eucharist no doubt invited the recitation of certain words and deeds. Baptism is the most natural setting for early Christian Creeds whether the briefest of confessions, 'Jesus is Lord', or the slightly extended one, 'I believe that Jesus Christ is the Son of God' (Acts viii. 37D); and the Eucharist was the setting in which the Institution words and narrative lived on. But creeds, as we have just seen, are really hymns of praise; and it is for adoration, praise, and petition that one more reasonably looks to worship, rather than for narrative.[1]

It is possible, however, that worship early provided a matrix for the formation of Christian exhortation and ethical direction in the shape of the homily or sermon. Not that the primary *kerygma* need have been repeated in Christian sermons any less often than today; only, the assumption being that the congregation, by definition, knew and had accepted the *kerygma*, the speaker is more likely to have devoted himself to drawing out its ethical consequences. The *kerygma* is the right basis for praise and the ground of prayer; the homily would most naturally follow the line of exhortation to the congregation to *become* what, thanks to the Gospel-proclamation, they essentially *were*. It has been guessed that the Epistle of James may represent substantially some kind of Christian (or at least Christianized) synagogue sermon;[2] the homiletic quality of parts of 1 Peter

---

[1] See C. F. D. Moule, 'The Intention of the Evangelists', in *New Testament Essays, in mem.* T. W. Manson, ed. A. J. B. Higgins, (1959), 165 ff.

[2] See H. Thyen, *Der Stil der jüdisch-hellenistischen Homilie* (1955), 14-17; but see criticisms of his view below, p. 166, n. 2. Dr J. Adamson kindly informs me in a letter (11. xii. 60) that the idea that the epistle of James may have been originally a sermon seems to have been first suggested by Luther (Erlangen Ed. 63, 156 ff., Weimar Ed., Deutsche Bibel 7, 384 ff.), and taken up also by Jülicher (a penitential sermon), and Harnack (homiletic patchwork by an anonymous teacher), as well as by Moffatt, Goodspeed, Kennedy, J. Weiss, and H. F. D. Sparks. He calls attention to the short note by J. S. Stevenson, *E.T.* xxxv (1924), 44, imagining James the Lord's brother sending scraps from his addresses in Jewish and Christian synagogues to Jewish Christians in the dispersion. He also notes Paul Feine's valuable little book *Der Jakobusbrief nach'. Lehranschauungen und Entstehungsverhältnissen untersucht* (1893), where Feine argues for its origin in a synagogue homily by James himself (see, e.g., p. 95). (On p. 96 Feine cites, besides Luther, also Palmer, Weizsäcker, and Holtzmann for this view. But Luther does not really make a point of the sermon-form: he merely says that the Epistle may have been written by someone else, from James' preaching.)

has been observed;[1] and the rules for domestic and family life which the Germans neatly call 'household tables' (*Haustafeln*) in Colossians and Ephesians and (to some extent) in Romans and in other epistles, may owe much to sermons as well as to the more private instruction of catechumens.

The fact that apostolic letters were certainly designed to be read to an assembled house-church leads naturally to the assumption that they would, on such occasions, fulfil the function of a homily; and the closing words of 1 Cor. xvi. 20b-24:

> Greet one another with the kiss of peace.
> This greeting is in my own hand.—PAUL.
> If anyone does not love the Lord, let him
> be outcast.
> *Marana tha*—Come, O Lord!
> The grace of the Lord Jesus Christ be with you.
> My love to you all in Christ Jesus. Amen.

have ingeniously been linked with the Eucharist, and the conclusion has been drawn that Paul had actually designed this letter to lead into that act of worship, with its ban upon the excommunicate (*anathema*), its invocation (*maranatha*), its kiss of peace, and its salutation. But this latter refinement is less convincing, on closer examination, than at first sight, and is certainly not firmly established. The *maranatha* may reinforce the ban rather than open the Eucharist. There is remarkably little trace of anything clearly eucharistic at the end of any other New Testament epistles.[2]

This *anathema-maranatha* is, on any showing, however, a reminder of the remarkable legacy of Aramaic words and phrases which worship, in particular, rendered current among Greek-speaking Christians. Besides the (apparent) invocation *maranatha* ('Our Lord, come!'), there is the frequent *amen*, evidently used in worship in preference to such Greek alternatives as ναί, ἀληθῶς, γένοιτο, which sometimes occur outside worship; there is *alleluia, hosanna* (though in the New Testament this latter is not clearly used in Christian worship as it is in

[1] See commentaries, and B. H. Streeter, *The Primitive Church* (1929) 123 ff.
[2] For discussions of this point, see C. F. D. Moule, 'A Reconsideration of the Context of *Maranatha*', *J.N.T.S.* 6. 4 (July 1960), 307 ff., and the literature there cited.

*Didache* x. 6¹), and *Abba* (which seems to be the opening word of the Lord's Prayer as still recalled in Greek communities, Rom. viii. 15, Gal. iv. 6).

Whether worship has in other directions greatly influenced the choice of words in the New Testament is more questionable. But the striking way in which what we might describe as 'secular' words such as λειτουργεῖν (to render civic service) are applied also to 'divine service' provides a deeply Christian and very salutary reminder that worship is the be all and end all of Christian work; and that if worship and work are distinguished, that is only because of the frailty of human nature which cannot do more than one thing at a time. The necessary alternation between lifting up holy hands in prayer and swinging an axe in strong, dedicated hands for the glory of God is the human make-shift for that single, simultaneous, divine life in which work is worship and worship is the highest possible activity. And the single word 'liturgy' in the New Testament, like '*abodah*, 'work' or 'service' in the Old Testament, covers both.²

The Christian community at worship, then, must always stand in the very front of our search for the settings in which the component parts of the New Testament came into existence. Only, together with an enthusiastic recognition of this illuminating fact, it is important to bear in mind that there was necessarily an alternation between times of conscious worship and other activities; and it is even possible, in keeping with this distinction, that certain terms which were applied to Jesus in early Christian thought belong rather exclusively to these other contexts. The apparent location of the suffering servant idea in the context of explanation rather than of worship (hinted at in passing on p. 22 above) is an instance of this.³ We turn next, therefore, from adoration and worship to examine the more consciously rational activity of explanation.

---

¹ *Contra* H. Köster, *Synoptische Überlieferung bei den apostolischen Vätern* (1957), 196 f.
² See C. F. D. Moule, *Worship in the New Testament* (1961), 80.
³ See C. F. D. Moule as on p. 22, n. 1 above.

## CHAPTER III

# THE CHURCH EXPLAINS ITSELF:
# (1) STAGES OF SELF-AWARENESS

IT would be a mistake to attempt too precise a distinction, within the general term 'explanation', between the explanations offered by the Church to outsiders and the teaching and instruction offered to its own members or to definite enquirers. Or again, it is a faint line, in the last analysis, that divides explanations given to outsiders on the Church's own initiative, in the course of evangelism, and those given in reply to inquiry, criticism, or attack—explanations, that is, which constitute Christian apologetic. These various categories merge insensibly into one another. For the sake of clarity, however, the subject of 'catechesis'—the instruction of enquirers ('catechumens') or the newly baptized—and of 'edification' thereafter will be raised again in a later chapter; and for the present we turn our attention more generally to the Church's understanding of itself in the face of problems and pressures, whether from within or from without, so as to see the stages by which an awareness of its distinctive calling dawned.

It must be remembered at the outset that the Church in the first century, unlike the Church today, did not need to spend much time defending the existence of God. True, there were Epicureans, whose system relegated God to such a distance from the physical world as to constitute a virtual atheism; and there were one or two other brands of 'free thinking'. But for the most part everybody took some doctrine of deity and the supernatural as an axiom (it was the Christians who seemed atheists, with their lack of altar and shrine), and Christian explanation did not have to begin with God—least of all when confronted by Jewish monotheism—even if the distinctively Christian convictions did in fact involve a radically new conception of deity.

Chronologically, indeed, one of the earliest questions to be faced was what might at first seem far more pedestrian and less doctrinal—the question of the relation of the followers of Jesus to the rest of Judaism. This was forced upon the Church from within, as well as being pushed at it from outside; and, as we shall see eventually, it is really a major doctrinal issue. Even during the ministry of Jesus, onlookers had exclaimed in amazement, 'What is this?' and, in the same breath, had answered, 'New teaching!' (Mk i. 21 ff.). It was not long before the Christian community had to face a similar question: What was this that they were caught up in? What were they? Were they in fact something new and revolutionary or were they only an improved and expurgated version of the old? Were they a new race, a *tertium genus*, an addition to the familiar twofold classification into Jew and Gentile, or were they simply Israel, true Israel—a purified, inner nucleus of the one ancient People of God?

Unfortunately for the cause of simplicity and clarity, it proved to be unrealistic to come down exclusively on one side or the other, for there were senses in which both were true. God, by his purging of the old, had made a new creation. The message was at once both old and new (as 1 Jn ii. 7 f. says, though with a rather different connotation). Consequently, the New Testament contains evidence of both standpoints, and it is obvious enough that the emphasis is determined by the varying requirements of the circumstances and the tone in which the questions were asked.

On the side of the continuity of Christianity with Israel, a vigorous stream of thought issues out (like Ezekiel's stream from the Temple), and forks in two directions. As against anti-Christian Judaism, it stresses that the only real Jews are those who confess Jesus as Messiah: 'so far from not being Jews', Christians said in effect, 'we are the only Jews'. As against an anti-Semitic tendency in Gentile Christianity, it stresses that to become a Christian is necessarily to be growing, whether naturally or by grafting, on the stock of Israel: 'so far from not being Jews, Christians cannot be Christians unless they are Jews'. There is little room for doubt that Jesus himself began by appealing to Israel—and, so far as his earthly ministry goes, virtually ended with Israel also. He addressed his message to Israel, and saw his own mission and vocation in terms of the fulfilment of Israel's destiny. Even if one sets aside the question whether or not he accepted the title of Messiah, the anointed King of Israel, his use of the term 'the Son of Man' was related at the very least to God's plan for Israel through him—probably to his very self as the epitome and representative of loyal Israel. That he chose a body of twelve men to be his messengers and intimates (unmistakably suggesting the twelve patriarchs representing the twelve tribes, cf. Matt. xix. 28, Lk. xxii. 30), and that he virtually restricted his ministry to Israelite territory, are themselves significantly Israelite gestures.

Correspondingly, in the Acts, not only are the earliest Palestinian Nazarenes represented (as we have seen) as going on worshipping in the Temple and practising Judaism, but scrupulous care is taken to show even Paul both as making a regular practice of going first to the Jewish community whenever he was beginning to preach the Gospel in a new area (Acts xiii. 5 and *passim*; cf. Rom. i. 16), and also as claiming himself to be still a good, Pharisaic Israelite (Acts xxiii. 6, xxiv. 12-15, xxvi. 5-7). And it is well known that the Acts represents Christianity as acceptable to the Roman government, which it would not have been (so the implied argument seems to run) had it been a totally new religion. It appears from Gal. v. 11 that there were even some (possibly the most radical, anti-Semitic Christians)[1] who complained that, in effect, Paul (of all people!) was 'still' proclaiming the need for circumcision (contrast Acts xxi. 21!). What he did proclaim, in Rom. xi. 13 ff. especially, was that *salus extra Israel non est* (to adapt the Cyprianic phrase, *Ep.* 73, 21). If the Gentiles are to be given wholeness, salvation, they must be grafted into the original stock, they must become Jews by adoption. Similarly, Eph. (ii. 11-iii. 7) speaks of the salvation of the Gentiles in terms of fellow-citizenship with Israel. *A fortiori*, those who are already Jews by birthright will—even if temporarily excluded because of obstinacy—be brought back in the end into the community to which they belong by birth. The ecclesia of Christ *is* the assembly of Israel. As J. Munck remarks, Paul never turned his back on Jerusalem; or, at least as

---

[1] Or was it rather the Judaizers, who tried to argue that the *logic* of Paul's position, whatever his *practice*, was that he still maintained that circumcision had much profit in all directions (Rom. iii. 1 f.)?

H. Chadwick points out, he moved in an ellipse, with Jerusalem as one of the foci. He did not think of a *tertium genus*, but rather of the Covenant renewed by God with the children of Abraham.[1]

If one branch of the stream of 'identity' flows out to cut off those who try to by-pass the spiritual heritage of Israel on the way to salvation, its other branch, as we have seen, is directed against the anti-Christian Jew who denies that the Church is Israelite at all, or against the extreme Judaizing Christian who will only allow that it is Israelite if it is marked by a rigorous observance of circumcision. Here there are all the sayings of Jesus about the rejection of the children of the Kingdom in favour of better members—a line of attack reaching its climax in the bitter controversies of the Fourth Gospel and the great tirade of Matt. xxiii and the fierce strictures of Rev. ii. 9 ('. . . who call themselves Jews and are not, but are a synagogue of Satan'). And in the Pauline Epistles there are passages such as the following: Gal. i. 6-9 (Judaizing Christians are actually pronounced excommunicate for making circumcision a *sine qua non*):

> I am astonished to find you turning so quickly away from him who called you by grace, and following a different gospel. Not that it is in fact another gospel; only there are persons who unsettle your minds by trying to distort the gospel of Christ. But if anyone, if we ourselves or an angel from heaven, should preach a gospel at variance with the gospel we preached to you, he shall be held outcast. I now repeat what I have said before: if anyone preaches a gospel at variance with the gospel which you received, let him be outcast!

iii. 16, 29 (the 'seed of Abraham' is Christ, and therefore it is those who are 'in' Christ who alone are true Israel):

> Now the promises were pronounced to Abraham and to his 'issue'. It does not say 'issues' in the plural, but in the singular, 'and to your issue'; and the 'issue' intended is Christ. . . .
> But if you thus belong to Christ, you are the 'issue' of Abraham, and so heirs by promise.

[1] J. Munck, *Paul and the Salvation of Mankind* (Eng. trans., 1960, of *Paulus und die Heilsgeschichte*, 1954), especially ch. 10 (see p. 277); H. Chadwick, *The Circle and the Ellipse* (Oxford Inaugural Lecture, 1959), esp. 13 ff.; W. C. van Unnik, 'La Conception paulinienne de la Nouvelle Alliance', *Recherches bibliques* v (1960), 122 f.

vi. 15 ff. (God's Israel is all those, whether circumcised or not, who have been brought inside the new creation):

> Circumcision is nothing; uncircumcision is nothing; the only thing that counts is new creation! Whoever they are who take this principle for their guide, peace and mercy be upon them, and upon the whole Israel of God.
>
> In future let no one make trouble for me, for I bear the marks of Jesus branded on my body.
>
> The grace of our Lord Jesus Christ be with your spirit, my brothers. Amen.

## Phil. iii. 3:

> We are the circumcised, we whose worship is spiritual, whose pride is in Christ Jesus, and who put no confidence in anything external.

## Col. ii. 11:

> In him also you were circumcised, not in a physical sense, but by being divested of the lower nature; this is Christ's way of circumcision.

(i.e., baptism into Christ achieves that total surrender of the body which transcends and includes mere circumcision). Again, all over the Epistle to the Hebrews there is the argument that Christians, so far from being deprived and 'unchurched' from Israel, are the only ones to whom belong, in an absolute degree, the priesthood, the sacrifices, the altar, and the sanctuary. In 1 Pet. ii. 9 f., Christians are the real, worshipping People of God

> But you are a chosen race, a royal priesthood, a dedicated nation, and a people claimed by God for his own, to proclaim the triumphs of him who has called you out of darkness into his marvellous light. You are now the people of God, who once were not his people; outside his mercy once, you have now received his mercy;

and similarly in Rev. i. 5b, 6 it is they who are the royal and priestly people:

> To him who loves us and freed us from our sins with his life's blood, who made of us a royal house, to serve as the priests of his God and Father—to him be glory and dominion for ever and ever! Amen.

Yet, conversely, with this stout defence of the position that Christianity is Israel and that there is no salvation without

37

inclusion in this Israel, there dawned very soon, if not simultaneously, the realization of its *difference*, its newness. It is probably true to say that this was not sought, still less fought for by argument: all the instincts of Christians were on the other side—that of claiming continuity and antiquity. There was no desire to break away or to form a new sect or religion. It was only that the quality of the Christian experience, and the centre of gravity in Christian teaching, were so different that, sooner or later, they simply had to be acknowledged. Many in the past have spoken of the Hellenizing of Christianity; but it has become more fashionable recently—and with good reason—to speak rather of its 'de-judaizing' or its 'catholicizing'.[1] And the seeds of this revolutionary differentiation were sown by Jesus. His ministry was marked by an attitude to the religious authorities, and a manifestation of his own personal authority, which were entirely unacceptable to the most influential exponents of Judaism at the time. They sought authority in tradition or written documents rather than in the personal encounter, the dialogue, between the living God and man. For guidance, they looked to the precedents of past authority, or to recognized techniques of scriptural exposition, rather than to the divine encounter within the worshipping community. In a word, the most authoritative spokesmen of the Israel of Jesus' day were 'authoritarian', not 'prophetic'. Jesus himself, by contrast, reached out a hand—so far as he reached backwards at all and was not altogether forward-looking, new, and different—not to the authoritarian scribes' religion of the post-prophetic period but to the mighty prophets of Israel. His ministry, heralded by the prophetic ministry of the Baptist—the only great prophetic voice since the ancient prophets fell silent—went on, and went still deeper, into the ancient prophetic tradition. Unlike the rabbis, he went straight behind legislation and casuistry to the great controlling principles and motives—to the creation of man and wife by God (Mk x. 6); to God's call to love, to love of God and of neighbour (Mk xii. 28 ff.); to the supreme dignity of man

---

[1] It is a mistake to identify 'catholicizing' with Hellenizing. See G. Dix, *Jew and Greek* (1953), 109; E. Stauffer, *Die Botschaft Jesu damals und heute* (1959), takes the extreme position that Jesus' own 'de-judaizing' of religion was almost immediately 're-judaized'—even by Paul! (See, e.g., p. 45.)

within creation, and his accountability before the living God (Mk ii. 27). It was in the framework of these fundamental, personal categories that Jesus found his own direct contact, in prayer and converse, with his Father, and in this living, personal contact that he found and followed his Father's will and purpose. The outward manifestation of this absolute harmony of will between Jesus and the Father was the creative power that showed itself with unprecedented majesty in deeds of healing. When he spoke, it was with the Creator's words of power.

All this is only another way of saying that the ministry of Jesus pointed to such a new covenant as is described in Jer. xxxi—a relation between God and man not of propositional statement such as may be written and engraven on tablets of stone, but of personal obedience in the realm of heart and conscience: a relation properly belonging to the new age of which those same deeds of power were harbingers (see Paul's exposition of this theme in 2 Cor. iii). And one more way of expressing this is to say that the community which Jesus formed round himself was the community of the new age: it was Israel, indeed, but it was the Israel of the latter days; and in committing their loyalty to Jesus, the Twelve and others with them were constituted in that sense a new community.[1]

Thus, if the very number twelve bears witness to the Israel-consciousness of Jesus, and if (as we have seen) he scarcely began to extend his ministry beyond the confines of Israelite territory, yet his teaching and his attitude no less clearly bear witness to the radical, the 'eschatological', newness of this Israel: here are contained the germs of its universal expansion. True, it is a well-known (though often forgotten) fact that the New Testament nowhere countenances the term 'New Israel'—indeed, the very term 'New Testament' (i.e., New Covenant) implies continuity with the recipients of the earlier covenants; yet the fact remains that *God's* Israel, *true* Israel, was so radically different from what counted as Israel in the contemporary world, that there is an undeniable sense in which it is 'new'.[2]

[1] See L. Goppelt, *Christentum und Judentum im ersten und zweiten Jahrhundert* (1954), 74 f., W. C. van Unnik, *loc. cit.* on p. 36, n. 1, *passim*.
[2] It is interesting, as E. Schweizer, *s.v.* σάρξ, *T.W.N.T.* vii. 126 f., points out, that 'Israel according to the spirit' is not found, as a contrast to 'Israel according to the flesh', in 1 Cor. x. 18.

We have seen how even the radical sayings of such epistles as Galatians and Romans fit into the 'continuity' side of the argument, and we have observed that discontinuity (or at least startling newness) was not argued for and defended, so much as (almost reluctantly) accepted and recognized. But those radical passages in Paul's letters do argue clearly enough, if not directly, for this newness also. To be in Christ is, as he acknowledges, to be part of a new creation: and though this new world is indeed that to which the apocalyptic of Israel looked forward, it is strikingly different from the ordinary Israelite conception of it.

Another way of putting the same point is to look back once more at the traditions of the ministry of Jesus. Here there is evidence that, long before the climax, he had begun to fall foul of the religious leaders, who regarded him as a dangerous false teacher, and that he was warning his disciples to expect the same sort of opposition, leading to excommunication (Mk iii. 6, vii. 1 ff., viii. 15, x. 29 ff.; cf. Matt. x. 17, 25, Jn xvi. 2, etc.). It is true, there is no sign that Jesus ever set up his own authority against the books of Moses or any other scriptures regarded at that time as authoritative. But his way of using the scriptures and of selecting from them, and the conclusions he drew, were so subversive to the rabbinic scheme of life that it is not surprising if he was regarded as a breaker of the law. It was of small avail if, in breaking the Sabbath law as the rabbis had defined it, he appealed behind the rabbis to scripture. It is true that this may not have greatly disturbed the Sadducees; indeed, it is noteworthy[1] that only once before his trial is Jesus recorded to have had any clash with them (Mk xii. 18 ff. and parallels), while, if the story of the temple tax in Matt. xvii. 24 ff. is any reflection from the actual period of his ministry, it shows Jesus scrupulously avoiding offence to the Temple hierarchy. It was not until the end of the ministry that the political interests of the Sadducees came into conflict with Jesus: thereafter, they were going to play a prominent part, in the very early days of the Church, in attacking the Christians as upsetters of the peace (e.g. Acts iv. 5 ff., and contrast the comparative friendliness of the Pharisees in Acts xxiii. 9). But all through the ministry, the genuinely

[1] Cf. G. Stählin, *T.W.N.T.* *s.v.* σκάνδαλον.

religious leaders of Judaism—the Pharisees and especially their rabbis and scribes—did recognize the threat to their system presented by this revolutionary and subversive teacher. Luke, it is true, alludes to some degree of friendliness from Pharisees (vii. 36 ff., xiii. 31 ff., xiv. 1 ff.); but, for the most part, they are the real antagonists. Jesus' way of authority simply did not square with theirs. For instance, when he pronounced love of God to be the first commandment, he did not mean that from it could be deduced all the rabbinical régulations, but that it must take priority over, and, if necessary, nullify any others.[1] And Jesus not only saw the implications of this attitude for himself, but, as we have seen, seems to have warned his followers of impending excommunication and persecution for them. If E. Stauffer is right, there was even systematic spying and collecting of incriminating evidence against Jesus by the scribal authorities long before he was actually indicted, and when he came to Jerusalem for the final Passover he was already a marked heretic, already, perhaps, excluded from normal participation in the festival.[2]

Thus, when the Christians claimed (Acts iv. 11, etc.) that Jesus was the foundation-stone or the corner-stone of God's Israel, they were inevitably proclaiming the radical newness, the essential *differentia* of their faith. For this was the very stone which the accredited builders in Israel had decisively rejected. Either the experts of Israel must confess to a vast mistake or the Christian edifice must be branded as something new and alien to Israel. It is this stone which becomes the touchstone: you either fell foul of it and found it a *skandalon*, or you discovered in it the one foundation of the whole building.[3]

[1] E. Stauffer, *Die Botschaft Jesu damals und heute* (1959), ch. 5, argues that the Marcan form (Mk xii. 31) alone preserves this radical and revolutionary sense: the other versions reduce it to precisely the rabbinic 'deduction' form. I cannot go with him in all his further strictures on other New Testament writers (including Paul!); but here he has put his finger on a striking fact. *Contra* G. Barth in G. Bornkamm, G. Barth, and H. J. Held, *Überlieferung und Auslegung im Matthäus-Evangelium* (1960), 70 ff. See below, p. 66.

[2] E. Stauffer, 'Neue Wege der Jesusforschung', *Wissenschaftliche Zeitschrift der Martin-Luther-Universität Halle-Wittenberg (Ges.-Sprachw.* vii. 2, 451 ff. (March 1958)); *Jesus: Gestalt und Geschichte* (1957) = Eng. trans., *Jesus and his Story* (1960) chh. 6, 7; *Jerusalem und Rom* (1957), ch. 10.

[3] See also R. Swaeles, 'L'Arrière-fond scripturaire de Matt. xxi. 43 et son lien avec Matt. xxi. 44', *J.N.T.S.* 6. 4 (July 1960), 310 ff., arguing that (a)

But this newness did not become immediately evident, and the evolution of the Christian writings may, in part, be traced in terms of the gradual dawning of this very consciousness. About the time of Christ, there were already Jewish sectarians who, eager to separate themselves from the corruption of Judaism, had styled themselves 'the community of the New Covenant'.[1] And no doubt the early Christians too believed themselves to be no less Israelite than a reforming group of this kind—a kind of religious confraternity (a *haburah*[2]) within Israel. As we have seen, their very habits of worship bore witness to their assumption that they were truly Israelite. Yet their one distinctiveness was so fundamental that their extrusion from Judaism could only be a matter of time. It turned on the vital question of the seat of authority. For Judaism, the keeping of the Law, loyalty to the divine Wisdom, was believed to be the ultimate test on the day of judgment;[3] and for the extreme Judaistic wing of Christianity itself, Jesus was only one stone in the building: the Law, circumcision, and the rest were equally vital; 'justification'—that is, a right relation with God—might be *either* by Law *or* by faith.[4] But for Christians such as Paul and John, Jesus was the supreme and unique test: he was the keystone of the building, the only door into the sheepfold; and the one decisive test was loyalty to him and trust in him. He was of necessity either foundation-stone (Isa. xxviii. 16) or *skandalon* (Isa. viii. 14). Decision was inescapable. And inevitably, therefore, the cleft occurred. Rather like the Methodists

Matt. xxi. 44 is genuine; (b) both *vv.* 43, 44 are reminiscent of Dan. ii and vii (θ); (c) Matt.'s use of ἔθνος (LXX) rather than θ's λαός is due to Matt.'s own deliberate choice: he wants to oppose the new ἔθνος to the λαός from whom the Kingdom is taken. This last step is not very convincing; but it may be important for the development of the 'third race' concept.

[1] See J. Jeremias, *Jerusalem zur Zeit Jesu* (²1958), ii. 116 ff., appealing to the Damascus 'Community of the New Covenant' (see *CD* viii. 21, in, e.g., C. Rabin, *The Zadokite Documents*, (²1958), 37), and to evidence in the Talmud which he interprets as pointing to the existence in Jerusalem in the first century A.D. of a Pharisaic purist group calling themselves 'the holy community of Jerusalem'. Cf. Goppelt, *op. cit.* 72 n. 7, on the use of haeresis (αἵρεσις) for Jewish groups.        [2] For *haburah* see Jeremias, *loc. cit.*

[3] See *T.W.N.T. s.v.* σοφία, citing Eth. Enoch v. 8, xci. 10, cf. xxxii. 3-6, xlviii. 1, xlix. 1 (lxi. 11), xc. 35; Syr. Baruch liv. 13, 2 Esdras viii. 52; Test. xii Levi 18.

[4] See 2 Esdras ix. 7, cf. xiii. 23; and C. H. Dodd, 'À l'arrière-plan d'un dialogue johannique', *Rev. d'Hist. et de Philos.* 37 (1957), 5 ff. (especially p. 9 discussing Gal. ii. 15 f.).

in England, the Christians found themselves squeezed out by the logic of their position, even when they were themselves reluctant to go.

A factor which must have accelerated the process of segregation was the implication of blame in the Christian declaration that the rebel condemned and handed over to execution by the Jews was in fact Israel's divinely-chosen King—that the expert builders had made the great mistake of all time. On top of the conservative Sadducean fear that the Nazarenes might upset the political equilibrium, on top of the scorn of the Zealots, at the opposite wing, for revolutionaries who refused to revolt,[1] on top of the Pharisaic belief that they were purveyors of dangerous heresy, this implication of blame (coupled with sheer jealousy at the Christians' success with the common people) must have helped to awaken a fierce resentment and antagonism.

But in this there seem to have been degrees of intensity, corresponding with degrees of provocation. There is no evidence, in the Acts at any rate, that the apostles in the early days in Jerusalem took the line that all but a small 'remnant' or nucleus within Israel had always gone wrong. That was Stephen's argument. It is Stephen (and cf. Matt. xxiii. 31) who calls the Jews sons of the murderers of the prophets (vii. 52); Peter calls them sons of the prophets (iii. 25 f.).[2] It seems to have been Stephen's argument which precipitated the first serious persecution. Thereafter there followed two consequences. One was that even the Jerusalem apostles began to be suspect as disloyal to the heart of Judaism, so that Herod Agrippa I (41–44) was able to execute the apostle James, and, finding this acceptable to the Jews, to make an attempt on the life of Peter (Acts xii. 1 ff.). The other was that among those actually scattered by the Stephen persecution were some bold enough to preach about Jesus to non-Jews (Acts xi. 20).

Boldness it needed; for the ministry of Jesus had virtually confined itself, with resolute concentration, to the People of Israel, while the teaching of Jesus about the rejection of Israel and the coming into the Kingdom of aliens from afar (Matt. viii. 11 f., Lk. xiii. 28 f.), if not actually forgotten for the time being, might have been construed as applying to the Jewish

[1] See Goppelt, *op. cit.* 98.     [2] Goppelt, *op. cit.* 78.

43

diaspora and not to Gentiles (perhaps cf. Jn vii. 35). It was a courageous application of Stephen's arguments, then, coupled with sheer eagerness to share the good news, which led to the beginnings of the Gentile mission. And once begun, it had to be reckoned with. The Jerusalem leaders sent Barnabas to investigate (Acts xi. 22 ff.). He approved, and fetched Paul to help to consolidate the gains. So the greatest mind of the early Church was lent to the advance of the Gospel beyond the limits of Judaism, and thus prepared the way for a step which, however, Paul did not himself take, the definition of the Church as a *tertium genus* over against Jew and Gentile.[1]

And then the breach was no doubt clinched by political circumstance. In the disastrous war of A.D. 66–70, the 'Nazarenes' (a term by then applied to the Jewish Christians) refused to participate in the Jewish resistance movement, the Zealot insurrection (see p. 43, n. 1). If the crisis of A.D. 40—Caligula's threat to the sanctity of the Temple—might have closed the ranks of world monotheism, the crisis of 66 decisively separated Jew from Christian. The Epistle to the Hebrews is plausibly placed at this point[2] (though an even earlier crisis is conceivable —see p. 53 below)—when intense political and psychological pressures must have been exerted on Jewish Christians to show their loyalty to their ancestral religion and their nation by sinking differences and helping to present a united front in the bitter struggle for existence. But it is exactly such a situation that forces the distinctiveness of Christianity agonizingly into view. And the heroic and the percipient, like the writer to the Hebrews, then see it their duty to say: Now is the eternal crisis: to go back into Judaism (even Judaism of a liberal, Philonian type) is to desert the Crucified and to join the ranks of the crucifiers.[3] The only way to life is the way forward, not back:

[1] Eph. iii. 5 ff. can claim that the inclusion of the Gentiles is a divine revelation to God's dedicated apostles and prophets (the early Church's media of authority). For St Paul's own refusal to take this step, see W. C. van Unnik, *loc. cit.* (p. 36, n. 1), 122, and n. 2, where he cites the *Kerygma Petri* ap. Clem. Alex. *Strom.* vi. 41 (fr. 2, in E. Klostermann, *Apocrypha* i (1933), 15) for this conception of the *tertium genus*.

[2] See especially A. Nairne, *The Epistle of Priesthood* (1913), and his commentary on Hebrews in the *Cambridge Greek Testament* series (1918); though his is not the first exposition of this view.

[3] C. H. Dodd, *loc. cit.*, 9 (n. 10), 10 (comparing Jn viii. 37).

we must go outside the camp, bearing Christ's reproach. And, he adds, do not be deflected from your purpose by the ignorant taunts of Jews and pagans, who, both alike, say that Christians are atheists because they have cut themselves adrift from priesthood, altar, sacrifice, and shrine: all these we *have*, and have them on the heavenly level of the absolute (Heb. viii. 1, x. 19 ff., xiii. 10 ff.). We alone are citizens of that true Jerusalem, the city which, as the Psalmist puts it, has the foundations:

> . . . he was looking forward to the city with (the) firm foundations, whose architect and builder is God (Heb. xi. 10);

apparently a reminiscence of:

> His foundations (plural) are on the holy hills . . . (Ps. lxxxvi. 1, LXX);

cf. Gal. iv. 26,[1] Phil. iii. 20.

Thus there emerges, in succession to the primitive, unexamined assumption, 'of course we Christians are Jews', a polemical and carefully reasoned apologetic for the Church of Christ as alone the real Church of Israel. Ultimately, this logically involves also the paradoxical conclusion that the scriptures of Israel not merely belong, but belong exclusively to Christians.[2] But long before this ever became explicit, and before the Jewish war had precipitated the split on a large scale, the tools of thought had already been sharpened by Paul[3] in his personal conflicts; and

---

[1] C. Gore, *The Reconstruction of Belief* (one-vol. edn., 1926), 770, pointed out that in this verse Paul appears to be quoting Ps. lxxxvi. 5 LXX, Μήτηρ Σιων, ἐρεῖ ἄνθρωπος.

[2] G. Schrenk, *s.v.* γράφω etc., *T.W.N.T.* i. 759, cites Rom. iv. 23 ('those words were written, not for Abraham's sake alone, but for our sake too'), 1 Cor. ix. 10 ('Do you suppose God's concern is with oxen? Or is the reference clearly to ourselves? Of course it refers to us . . .'), x. 11 ('these things . . . were recorded for our benefit as a warning'), as pointing to the conclusion (in the mind of Paul) that the old Testament scriptures were written for the Christian community. But this, of course, is not the same thing as to claim that they belong *exclusively* to Christians (as Tertullian, *De Praescr. Haeret.* 19, argues that [Christian] scripture belongs only to the orthodox). The Epistle of Barnabas (iv etc.) is a fairly early example of this claim,

[3] Cf. E. Meyer, *Ursprung und Anfänge des Christentums*, iii (1923), 584. cited by S. G. F. Brandon, *The Fall of Jerusalem* (²1957), 12 (but my translation): 'It is a widely held opinion that the destruction of Jerusalem in the year 70 was of decisive importance for the development of Christianity, and that it was this which first definitely emancipated Christianity from Judaism and decided the victory of Gentile Christianity. But the facts do not correspond to this view; rather, the break away from the Jerusalem moorings

he had begun to use two contrasting terms—'Jews' for those
who are externally or by birth Jews, 'Israel' for the religious
community, the People of God as such. The latter is constituted
by all, whether circumcised or uncircumcised, who put their
trust in Jesus and are baptized into his Name. Of the former,
only they belong to 'Israel' who are in the latter category.[1]
Sooner or later, as a result of this distinction, 'Jews' came to be
used in certain Christian writings almost exclusively for antagonistic, anti-Christian Judaism, and nowhere more strikingly than
in the Fourth Gospel.

John only twice uses 'Israel' (i. 31; iii. 10); but the term 'the
Jews' is used often, and in a remarkable way, always as though
by a non-Jew or an outside observer, for the benefit of non-Jews
or outside observers. The writer is at pains to explain that the
Passover and the Feast of Tabernacles are festivals of 'the Jews'
(vi. 4, vii. 2, xi. 55); Jewish customs are alluded to as though
requiring explanation (ii. 6, xix. 31, 40, 42); the Jews are regularly the opponents of Jesus, except when a section of them is
expressly distinguished as those Jews who had come to believe
him (viii. 31, xi. 45, xii. 11). Once Jesus himself is described as a
Jew, but only by the Samaritan woman who is distinguishing
his race from her own (iv. 9). 'The term "the Jews"', writes
Dr J. A. T. Robinson, 'is found overwhelmingly in polemical
contexts: they are the representatives of darkness and opposition
throughout the Gospel.'[2] The significance of this for the milieu
of the Fourth Gospel is a matter which must be discussed elsewhere (see pp. 93 ff. below); but meanwhile, the usage well illus-
trates the terminology of separation, and corresponds with

had already been achieved by Paul. The further events which took place
there naturally aroused the interest of Christians, and the destruction of city
and temple appeared to them like the fulfilment of prophecy and the condign
punishment for a stiff-necked people; it was the establishment of the position
that the Jews had in fact wholly misunderstood revelation and scripture, that
the Christians were alone true Israel, the chosen people and the bearers of
the divine promise. But, actually, this brought no further significance to the
claims of Christianity; these had been established long before by Paul.' Cf.
Chadwick, *The Circle and the Ellipse* (as above). Yet see pp. 121 ff. below.
[1]  This statement has been challenged in an important article by D. W. B.
Robinson, 'The Salvation of Israel in Romans 9-11' *The Reformed Theological
Review* (Australia) 26 (1967), 81 ff. (See 83, n. 6).
[2]  J. A. T. Robinson, 'The Destination and Purpose of St John's Gospel',
*J.N.T.S.* 6. 2 (Jan. 1960), 118. Relevant here is also the discussion by C. H.
Dodd already referred to on p. 42, n. 4, and see Goppelt, *op. cit.*, 101 f.

Paul's use as just described. One other example of the same tendency worth mentioning here is Matt. xxviii. 15, where the false story of the theft of the Lord's body is described as current among the Jews. This is the only occurrence of this usage in Matt., though in iv. 23 Jesus is described as preaching 'in *their* synagogues', as though the narrator felt himself standing outside Judaism.

But if such writings bear witness to the sharpening of the consciousness of the gulf, how did the Christians explain and rationalize it? Was such a situation anticipated in scripture? Could it be fitted into the purposes of God? There were sufficient scriptures about the Gentiles coming into Israel and bringing their wealth and glory into the Temple (Isa. lx., etc.). But did not that mean as *proselytes*? And ought not converts from the Gentiles therefore to be circumcised and made true Jews? The logic of the question is obvious enough. To secure membership in 'God's Israel', true Israel, what was to be the minimum requirement? Surely circumcision, and all else that went to the full instatement of a proselyte, in addition to the distinctively Christian confession of Jesus of Nazareth as the King of Israel. If the Christians were true Jews, distinguished from others only in that they identified Jesus as Messiah, surely this was the logic of the situation.

The Church as a whole answered, No, and therein enunciated far-reaching Christological decisions. Within Judaism, R. Joshua ben Ḥananiah had claimed that baptism alone was sufficient to make even a male Gentile a proselyte; but even he did not deny that circumcision was a duty; and the orthodox position, championed by Eliezer ben Hyrcanos had prevailed.[1] But the Christian debate did not turn simply on the issue 'liberalism *versus* rigorism', nor did it rely upon an inward and spiritual interpretation of circumcision (though Paul does allude to this in Rom. ii. 28 f.): it was (implicitly) a Christological controversy. And Paul is the fullest and most explicit spokesman of—not liberalism but high Christology. It was probably his influence, also, in the Christian world generally which turned the scale.

[1] See *T.B. Yebamotn* 46a, adduced by J. Klausner, *From Jesus to Paul* (Eng. trans., 1946), 39, 339, 367, and H. J. Schoeps, *Paulus* (1959), 60 (Eng. trans., *Paul* (1961), 66), and D. Daube, *The New Testament and Rabbinic Judaism* (1956), 109, whose formulation has in part been copied here.

His argument was this. The distinctive form of initiation into the Christian community as such was by baptism into the Name of Jesus. This meant incorporation into the Messiah. According to Paul, it actually involved the 'stripping off' of one's whole 'body'. When Jesus died, he 'stripped off', he parted with, he surrendered his body: obedient to God, he handed over his very self to death. And being baptized 'into Christ' meant being identified with just that act of total surrender: it meant death and burial with Christ:

> In him also you were circumcised, not in a physical sense, but by being divested of the lower nature; this is Christ's way of circumcision. For in baptism you were buried with him, in baptism also you were raised to life with him through your faith in the active power of God who raised him from the dead. And although you were dead because of your sins and because you were morally uncircumcised, he has made you alive with Christ. For he has forgiven us all our sins; he has cancelled the bond which pledged us to the decrees of the law. It stood against us, but he has set it aside, nailing it to the cross. On that cross he discarded the cosmic powers and authorities like a garment; he made a public spectacle of them and led them[1] as captives in his triumphal procession.

(Col. ii. 11-15, on which see the commentators.[2])

But circumcision was the symbolic stripping off of only a small part of the body. Christ's total stripping, as shared by the Christian in baptism, was thus the greater which included the less (cf. Jn vii. 23, contrasting circumcision with health to the *whole* body). Accordingly baptism included and obviated circumcision; and to demand circumcision in addition would have been to pronounce on the insufficiency and non-inclusive nature of baptism. Besides, once incorporate in the Messiah, how could one go further inside Israel? To add to baptism would therefore also have been to pronounce upon the non-inclusiveness of Christ (cf. Gal. ii. 5, v. 4). In a word, if Jesus had been only an individual and his death only a noble martyrdom, things might have been different. The vehement Pauline refusal to require circumcision in addition to baptism implies an estimate of

---

[1] *N.E.B. margin:* or '. . . he stripped himself of his physical body, and thereby boldly made a spectacle of the cosmic powers and authorities, and led them. . . .'

[2] Criticisms of the exegesis represented by the text are to be found in E. Schweizer, *s.v.* σάρξ, *T.W.N.T.* vii. 137 n. 292.

Christ's person and work which sees them as all-inclusive and as absolute.[1]

This line of argument involved Paul's viewing Abraham rather than Moses as the true symbol of Israel. The great Pauline manifesto on it is the Epistle to the Romans, gathering up and ordering the results, no doubt, of prolonged and widespread controversy. That the Sabbath controversy (which of course has left very clear marks in the Gospels—the Beza logion, Lk. vi. 5 (D), in particular looking like a polemic 'reply' to Nu. xv. 32 ff.[2]) does not figure in Acts xv, nor even at all prominently in the Pauline epistles, must presumably be due to the fact that, whereas circumcision would have been practicable for Gentile converts, Sabbath observance simply was not. Unless they came inside the Jewish ghetto, where there was an ordered life adjusted to the cessation of work on the Sabbath, they could not earn their living or subsist while observing the Sabbath. If they were slaves, Gentile masters would not release them from work; and if they were independent and earning their own living, they would still have had to pursue their trade on a Sabbath. It was no doubt because circumcision was a practical possibility for Gentile Christians as the Sabbath was not that it was the centre of controversy.[3]

But, in addition to the great Christological argument against requiring circumcision, there were other considerations also. Since it concerned males only, it was bound to become less and less significant in communities where women were becoming far

---

[1] Cf. Justin, *Trypho* xlvii. 1-4 (Stevenson No. 43).

[2] D (Codex Bezae), in place of Lk. vi. 5, which it transfers to follow *v.* 10, has: 'the same day, seeing someone working on the sabbath day, he said to him: "My man, if you know what you are doing, you are blest; but if you do not know, you are accurst and a law-breaker".'

If the significance of the Beza logion is that it is a deliberate reversal of Num. xv. 32 ff., it is comparable to the deliberate alteration of fast-days in *Did.* viii (so as not to be like the 'hypocrites'); and another possible parallel may be 1 Pet. iii. 19 ff., if it is deliberately aimed against Mishnaic strictures on the flood-generation (see Mishna, *Sanh.* 10, 3; *Test. Benj.* 10, 6; Iren. *Adv. haer.* i. 27. 3; Epiphan. *Pan. Haer.* 42. 4 (S.-B. i. 964, iv. 1185 f.)). See also J. Jeremias, *Jesus' Promise to the Nations* (Eng. trans. 1958, of German 1956), 47, and Eldon J. Epp 'The "Ignorance Motif" in Acts and Antijudaic Tendencies in Codex Bezae', *H.T.R.* lv (1962), 51 ff.

[3] For the prominence of the Sabbath law in the Damascus Sect, see E. Lohse, *s.v.* σάββατον etc., *T.W.N.T.* vii. 9 f. Curiously, there is no mention of it in the *Manual of Discipline* (1QS): see *ibid.* Note 61.

more prominent than in non-Christian Jewish communities.[1] Also, besides being, for adults, a drastic step, it was open to fierce obloquy and contempt and would therefore make a great rift between the convert and his pagan friends:[2] was it right, then, to require it? And finally—and more seriously still—it carried with it the obligation to keep the whole law and brought the proselyte under the influence of the Jewish authorities who were themselves antagonistic to Christianity. It might thus afford a route leading straight past Christianity into anti-Christian Judaism. In Acts xv. 10, Peter is represented as arguing that even Jews themselves could not keep the Law, and that the Law had thus failed to prove itself a means of salvation (cf. Gal. vi. 13). Now that, by faith in Jesus, a new means of salvation was offered, why burden converts with this additional and unnecessary obligation? Christ had opened a new way into Israel, bringing freedom and power, not frustration.

The Jerusalem Council was thus persuaded (according to the narrative of Acts xv) that, while the call of the Gentiles into membership was in accordance with God's design (Amos ix. 11 f. (LXX) and Isa. xlv. 21 were cited in support), to force circumcision upon them would be wrong. But they did lay down certain stipulations by way of securing a *modus vivendi* with Jewish Christians—namely, the avoidance of technical 'contamination' from idolatry, the avoidance of meat with the blood in it (which to Jews was ritually abhorrent) and the avoidance of fornication. The question of how far this was based upon the so-called Noachic rules is an interesting one, and is duly discussed by the commentators (see, e.g., C. S. C. Williams, *in loc.*, and literature there), but need not delay us here.

It seems likely that before long the ritual food-clause became a dead-letter. The further Christianity went from Judaism, the less necessary became its accommodation to table-fellowship with orthodox Jews. As Goppelt points out (e.g. *op. cit.* 96), the

[1] So H. H. Rowley, cited by A. Gilmore in *Christian Baptism* (1959), 24, and *E.T.* lxiv (1952–53), 362; lxv (1953–54), 158; and D. Daube, *The New Testament and Rabbinic Judaism* (1956), 106, 113.
[2] See R. Meyer, *s.v.* περιτέμνω etc., *T.W.N.T.* vi. 78, and references there. The 'God-fearers'—Gentiles who admired Judaism but had not taken the step of becoming proselytes—seem to have provided a ready field for Christian evangelism; and it may be that one of their reasons for avoiding full Judaism was objection to circumcision.

change seems to have taken place between the writing of Galatians and Romans. In Galatians there is need for strenuous defence of Christian freedom against Judaizing claims; by the time Rom. xiv is written, the scruples of the Jewish Christian (as a 'weak' person) have to be protected against harsh treatment. Romans (as Goppelt shows, *op. cit.* 124 f.) is the very centre of the history of the early Church's response to this question of Christianity *vis-à-vis* Judaism.

But the other two clauses, broadly interpreted as the avoidance of idolatry and sexual immorality, were basic religious and ethical demands which of course had permanent relevance. It is noteworthy (Goppelt *op. cit.* 125 f., 138) that in the Corinthian correspondence and Colossians it is not strictly legalistic Judaism but rather syncretism that is the object of attack. Indeed, in Corinth there was no tendency to Judaism, so far as our evidence goes. Thus, Jewish antagonism pushing from one side, and Gentile conversions pressing in from the other, led to the Church's definition of itself as true Israel because baptized into the Messiah, rather than because circumcised into the Law of Moses. It is simplest to assume that when Paul deliberately circumcised Timothy (Acts xvi. 3), it was because, in his case, there was no question of circumcision being a *sine qua non* of Christianity. It was only 'to make an honest Jew' of him, so that he might preach to Jews as one of them. If Paul resisted the circumcision of Titus (if that is what Gal ii. 3 does mean), it was because in his case the implication would indeed have been that circumcision was a *sine qua non*.

It is against the background, then, of the gradual hammering-out of Christian self-consciousness that much of the New Testament writing becomes intelligible; and the very genesis of certain sections of Paul's letters and of an entire document such as the Epistle to the Hebrews may credibly be traced to this process. The Epistle to the Ephesians, again, whoever was its author, is rightly interpreted as concerned to show that the Christian Church is indeed continuous with Judaism, and, at the same time is not limited by the limitations of Judaism: it is (as has been well said)[1] a splendid *apologia* in the face of the 'scandal of

[1] See H. Chadwick, 'Die Absicht des Epheserbriefes', *Z.N.T.W.* 51 (1960), 145 ff.

particularity': its claim that the Church has existed always in the mind of God, and is cosmic in its range and embraces the entire human race, is an answer to the objector who sees only a particular group of persons in a particular setting in time and space. Thus it is to non-Christian Judaism as a whole that the much-used words of Isaiah come to be applied:

> And he said, 'Go, and say to this people:
>  "Hear and hear, but do not understand;
>  see and see, but do not perceive".
> Make the heart of this people fat,
>  and their ears heavy,
>  and shut their eyes;
> lest they see with their eyes,
>  and hear with their ears,
>  and understand with their hearts,
>  and turn and be healed.'

(Isa. vi. 9 f.; cf. Mk iv. 12 and pars., Jn. xii. 40, Acts xxviii. 26, Rom. xi. 8.)[1]

We turn, next, to the consideration of a special aspect of the process—the use of scripture by the Christian Church.

---

[1] There is an important discussion of the various stages of Christian apologetic to which this quotation bears witness in its various applications, in Barnabas Lindars' *New Testament Apologetic* (1961); and see the full treatment in J. Gnilka, *Die Verstockung Israels* (1961).

## CHAPTER IV

# THE CHURCH EXPLAINS ITSELF:
## (2) THE USE OF THE JEWISH SCRIPTURES

AMONG the writings that have been passed in review, the Epistle to the Hebrews is clearly one for which some specific setting may be postulated, and such a setting, it has been suggested, may be found in the ardent Jewish nationalism which the opening of the Jewish war (A.D. 66) precipitated: or perhaps in some other situation independent of this crisis, when Christian Jews were persecuted: the converted synagogue, which (as is suggested later, p. 75) may be implied by the Epistle to the Hebrews, might have begun to suffer immediately after the Neronian persecution.

For the birth of much else in the New Testament, however,—and, indeed, for the antecedents of the Epistle to the Hebrews itself—it is natural to postulate a prolonged process of gestation. Thus, to take an example, the formulations of St Paul's arguments in his epistles represent, no doubt, the results of much debate, preaching, and instruction that had preceded these crystallizations. It is one of the merits of 'form-criticism' that it has forced us to strain our eyes—though we generally have inadequate illumination—to see these antecedent stages in the formation of the Christian scriptures; and the Acts offers us some sufficiently convincing pictures of the process. Its very last scene (xxviii. 23 ff.) portrays an intensive debate between Paul and representatives of the Jews in Rome. Scriptures in hand, they hammer away from dawn till dusk: and this is only a more extended description of what is lightly sketched in earlier chapters also (xiii. 16 ff., xiv. 1 ff., xvii. 2 ff., 11, xviii. 4, 11, xix. 8 ff.). Accustomed to think of Paul as the apostle to the Gentiles, we too easily forget his extensive ministry in the synagogue, and the heroic courage that it must have required. The passing allusion in 2 Cor. xi. 24 to five occasions when he had received the Jewish penalty of scourging (see Deut. xxv. 3, where forty strokes is the maximum, and the Mishnah, *Mak.* 3, 10, where this is interpreted so as to mean thirty-nine) reveals how often he must have come within range of synagogue jurisdiction. Admittedly the offences for which scourging was a penalty mentioned in *Mak.* 3. 1 ff. are scarcely relevant, except that a scholar might be scourged instead of suffering excommunication (see S.-B. iii. 530 and iv. 293 ff.). But in Acts v. 40 the apostles are beaten (δείραντες, and cf. xxii. 19), and it seems reasonable to conclude that, at any rate in St Paul's day, the penalty was more widely imposed. At any rate, there is no doubt about Paul's extensive ministry within Judaism.[1] The usual pattern of events is probably that of Acts xiii. 15 ff.—first, a polite hearing, but later (*vv.* 44 ff.) a deeper realization of the implications of this teaching, accompanied by jealousy, resentment, and a fiercely antagonistic reaction. There is plenty of scope here for the development of scriptural debate.

Again, Acts xv draws a (perhaps stylized) picture of a scriptural discussion within the Church. Here is a wider than the Pauline circle debating, still with scriptures in hand, about the conditions for Gentile membership of Christ's Israel—sinister echoes of the debate, still unconcluded, returning in Chapter xxi. Much of the story of the Church's explanation of itself has to be deduced by attempting to read between the lines of the New Testament—the end-product of the oral process; and later, we shall see how the Gospel parables bear traces of such controversy, and how the Fourth Gospel contains polemic with a similar stamp. But at the moment we are more particularly concerned with the use of Jewish scripture in these discussions, and we must only pause now to note, in passing, that of course a great deal of other material besides scripture entered in. Controversy about the Sabbath law, for instance, would no doubt be conducted not only by reference to scripture but also by recalling incidents and sayings from the life of Jesus. This is exactly (we may presume) how such sections of our Gospels originally began to take shape. Christians in a ghetto, living shoulder to shoulder with non-Christian Jews, would daily be driven into controversy

[1] Might not 2 Cor. iii. 4 ff. have been constructed out of the substance of a daring synagogue sermon?

over their unorthodox ways, their novel standards of reference, their altered scale of values. What was more natural than that they should recall and recite traditions (or, if they were eye-witnesses, personal reminiscences) about Jesus healing on the Sabbath or pronouncing about its ultimate purpose? How, again, could they help recalling sayings of Jesus bearing on the clean and the unclean—foodstuffs, leprosy-laws, and so forth? Christians in the great pagan centres, correspondingly, would have their own particular problems: they would be faced with difficult decisions about what constituted idolatry, what latitude might be allowed in sexual conduct, how far pagan institutions might be 'baptized' into use for Christians; and might Jewish Christians and Gentile Christians fraternize and participate in an *agape* at the same table? It is not difficult to imagine how self-contained units of Christian teaching came to be hammered out, first orally, then as written fly-sheets or tracts—often in several differing though related shapes, according to the contexts in which they were used.

When, therefore, John Mark (for example) sharpened his reed pen and dipped it in the ink to write, he had already behind him a considerable tradition of Christian speaking and possibly writing,[1] by Peter and many others,—recognized patterns of argument and exhortation, of defence and attack, of instruction and challenge—from among which he might select his narrative material and his sayings. The earliest Christian writers were probably already heirs to a considerable body of tradition.

Within this, we now turn especially to the early Christian uses of Jewish scripture. 'Jesus is Messiah!' the Christians asserted. But what in the world had led them to find the King of Israel in this Jesus of Nazareth, and how could they hope to support such a claim? By the orthodox Jerusalem Jews—and especially, one suspects, any who had never seen or heard Jesus personally—he must have been thought of as a popular prophet who had taught dangerously subversive doctrines such as to undermine the very structure of rabbinic Judaism; who had

---

[1] It is worth while to ask whether the celebrated phrase (Euseb. *H.E.* iii. 39) ἑρμηνευτὴς Πέτρου γενόμενος may not mean, not that Mark accompanied Peter as his oral interpreter, but that, *in the act of writing* in Greek, he became the interpreter of what Peter had written in Aramaic. See *J.N.T.S.* 2. 2 (Nov. 1955), 115.

even made some maniac claims to a unique relationship with God; who had perhaps been a sorcerer;[1] and who, in the end, had been brought to book by the Jewish High Court who had managed to get him ignominiously executed, by the degrading torture of crucifixion, as an insurgent against the Emperor's authority.[2] By Jewish law a dangerous false teacher and heretic, by Roman law guilty of treason, disgraced and made an object-lesson: how could Jesus of Nazareth conceivably be argued to be the Lord's Anointed?

In the earliest days, the Christians' convictions seem, as a matter of fact, to have been expressed less as a statement about who Jesus was than as evidence about what God had done in him and to him.[3] God had anointed him with Spirit, they said: that is, Jesus had received the spiritual equivalent of an en-thronement ceremony or at least some sort of special commis-sioning, like the speaker of the words in Isa. lxi. 1, 'The spirit of the Lord GOD is upon me; because the LORD has anointed

---

[1] For the conception of Jesus as a dangerous false teacher, see E. Stauffer, (as on p. 41, n. 2). There are passages relating to Jesus in the Talmud and in later Jewish literature. The Talmudic texts are edited by G. Dalman as an appendix to H. Laible's *Jesus Christus im Thalmud* (1891); the later Jewish writings are in S. Krauss, *Das Leben Jesu nach jüdischen Quellen* (1902); see also J. Klausner, *Jesus of Nazareth* (Eng. trans. 1929). 'Klausner' (writes T. W. Manson, *B.J.R.L.* 27 (1942–43), where the subject is briefly discussed, 330) 'did succeed in distilling out enough [from these sources] to make a short narrative paragraph', which contains the statements 'that [Jesus] "practised sorcery" [i.e. performed miracles, as was usual in those days] and beguiled and led Israel astray'.

[2] The details of the charge against Jesus in his trial before the Jewish court are widely debated Among recent discussions see E. Lohse *s.v. συνέδριον*, *T.W.N.T.* vii, and P. Winter, *On the Trial of Jesus* (1961). Whether or not one agrees with a sceptical conclusion about the New Testament accounts of this, the charge attempted before the Roman court seems to remain com-paratively undisputed. Lohse and Winter impugn the historicity of the New Testament account of the charge of blasphemy, and hold that it reflects the later conflict between Church and synagogue or the motive of exonerating Rome. Is it not conceivable that Jesus was indeed condemned, in the Jewish court, for blasphemy, for claiming to be 'the Son of Man with clouds' (an exalted, supernatural figure), but that the Jews preferred not to put him to death by stoning for this (as might have been possible, according to some authorities) but to shift the responsibility and get him crucified by the Romans for treason?

[3] 'To the first Church Jesus Christ was not an idea but a sum of events'— E. Schweizer, *Lordship and Discipleship* (Eng. Version, 1960, of *Erniedrigung u. Erhöhung bei Jesus u. seinen Nachfolgern*, 1955), 96. But he rightly adds that the *events* were (so far as significant) all *interpreted*, and depended for their significance on the Christian interpretation.

me to bring good tidings . . .' There were witnesses who could describe the baptism of Jesus as just such a spiritual 'Christing' (Ps. ii, 'You are my son', was a messianic address, and something like it was associated with the baptism of Jesus, even if actually it was even more reminiscent of the suffering servant); they might even have heard Jesus himself applying Isa. lxi to his ministry (Lk. iv. 18; cf. Acts x. 38). Besides, the exceptional deeds of power accompanying his ministry were evidence that 'God was with him' (Acts x. 38); Jesus himself, when asked by the Baptist's followers whether he was the one they were hoping for, had pointed to these events, and again had linked them with such Isaianic passages (Isa. xxxv. 5, lxi. 1, Matt. xi. 2 ff., Lk. vii. 18 ff.). Once, in controversy with the educated religious men of Jerusalem, Jesus, the Christians recalled, had invoked Ps. cx—a Psalm seemingly referring to a royal (and priestly) personage of even higher dignity than David himself (Mk xii. 35 ff.). Such were the passages most naturally appealed to, to locate in the scriptures, so to speak, the divine *imprimatur* upon Jesus of Nazareth during his lifetime—scriptures which, according to tradition, Jesus had himself appropriated.

But there was much more even than his ministry. After his death, God had not allowed his dead body to become corrupt (that was just like Ps. xvi—'. . . thou wilt not abandon my soul to Hades, Nor let thy loyal servant suffer corruption', Acts ii. 27); he had raised him from the tomb to a position of supreme honour (Ps. cx again!). In view of these overwhelming events—and the Christians had been convinced of them, despite their own despair and loss of all confidence, by the inescapable evidence of their eyes—was it not clear that they were living in the midst of a divine fulfilment of all the hopes of Israel?[1] The Christians began from Jesus—from his known character and mighty deeds and sayings, and his death and resurrection; and with these they went to the scriptures, and found that God's dealings with his People and his intentions for

---

[1] It is very striking, that, with all the parallels between the New Testament use of scripture and its use in the Qumran writings and in other Jewish literature, the note of *fulfilment* seems to be peculiar to the New Testament. *CD* vii. 10-11 is not far off, but אלמ appears not to occur in this connexion. See J. A. Fitzmyer, 'The Use of Explicit Old Testament Quotations in Qumran Literature and in the New Testament', *J.N.T.S.* 7. 4 (July 1961), 297 ff.

them there reflected did, in fact, leap into new significance in the light of these recent happenings. Sooner or later this was to lead, through a definition of what God had done, to something like a definition of who Jesus was.

But first we must look more closely at the circumstances controlling the early Christian use of scripture. Three main factors are discernible. *First*, pre-Christian Judaism (drawing partly on Gentile traditions) had already developed certain ways of interpreting scripture. *Secondly*, Jesus himself, during his ministry, had used scripture with great originality, and yet with an understanding of traditional methods. And *thirdly*, the early Christians were conscious that the voice of inspired prophecy, long silent, had begun once more to be audible; and they therefore used both scripture and the memories and traditions of the words of Jesus with the creative freedom of the inspired. This third factor, as a matter of fact, interlocks in a striking manner with the second; for the historical Jesus whose exegesis of scripture they recalled was at the same time found to be far more than a teacher of days gone by: as the Lord of faith, he was still with and in and among his people as they continued to expound the scriptures in his name. Thus, early Christian exegesis of scripture (in keeping with what we have already discovered about early Christian worship and the character of the early Christian community as a whole) was a new and creative thing, albeit rooted also in an antecedent Jewish tradition. Christ was found to be more authoritative than scripture, but in the sense of fulfilling and transcending, not of abolishing it.

We must examine these three factors.

(i) What methods of handling scripture were current in the days of Jesus? For all devout Jews alike, it was axiomatic (says R. Loewe) 'that the channel of divine Revelation is Torah—Torah as explicitly set forth in the inspired text of the Bible, but also, in regard to anything not explicitly found therein, deducible by the application of human reason to the text, provided only that human reason acknowledges its dependence upon divine grace'.[1] But within this assumption it seems possible, broadly speaking, to distinguish two main attitudes. One attitude at-

[1] 'The Jewish Midrashim and Patristic and Scholastic Exegesis of the Bible', *Studia Patristica* i = *T. und U.* 63 (1957), 492 ff.

tached a good deal of importance to the traditions of the great rabbis—to traditional interpretations of particular passages handed down communally, by which rules of conduct and other rulings were extracted from the scriptures. 'Extracted' is not an unfair word for some of these performances, though the best rabbis knew the dangers of arbitrary word-juggling, and only used it when it seemed absolutely necessary to sanction some much-needed ruling by Mosaic authority. To Rabbi Eleazar of Modin (a contemporary of the mighty Aqiba, about A.D. 120) is attributed the saying, 'He who discloses aspects in the Torah which are not in accord with rabbinical teaching has no portion in the world to come'.[1] Indeed, it was the strength of this position that sufficient weight was attached to the traditions of the great exegetes to prevent an irresponsible individualism in interpretation. The other attitude to the text of the Torah was essentially more individualistic (even if its adherents would not have acknowledged this). Viewing the actual written words as themselves a constant source of inspiration,[2] it made it possible for any individual, provided only (to repeat the proviso from Loewe's article) that he acknowledged his dependence upon God's grace, to expect direct divine guidance from his private study of them. The former attitude tended to locate authoritative interpretation in rabbinic leaders of learning and in the communally transmitted traditions of their wisdom; the latter in the individual's own use of the very words of scripture (often, it must be confessed, in a wildly inaccurate Greek translation).[3] Christian readers will recognize here, *mutatis mutandis*, the respective tendencies of Christian 'Catholic' and 'Protestant' exegesis. In the article already cited, Loewe seems to characterize what underlay the latter attitude when he says that the exegetical principle stressed by R. Aqiba 'points to the inspired quality of the text, asserting that no jot or tittle in it can be

---

[1] Mishnah, *Pirke Aboth* 3. 12, quoted by P. Winter, 'Marginal Notes on the Trial of Jesus' *Z.N.T.W.* 50 (1959), 12. For a lighter vein, see *ibid.* n. 38 (according to one Talmudic story, Moses descended to earth to visit Aqiba's school and was bewildered by the erudite arguments; his confidence was restored, however, when Aqiba assured a pupil asking for his authority for a ruling that it 'was given to Moses on Mount Sinai').

[2] *T.W.N.T.* i. 755, ll. 1-14.

[3] D. W. Gooding, *The Account of the Tabernacle* (1959), shows how little sacrosanct were the *ipsissima verba* to the LXX translators.

without significance for deductional exegesis' (*loc. cit.* 505). Loewe contrasts with this Ishmael ben Elisha's insistence (at about the same period) 'that Torah speaks in human language': but that is perhaps simply a stress upon reasonableness in interpretation, and is not quite the equivalent of the traditionalist attitude that is here being contrasted with the essentially individualist. There was a time when the verbal inspirationist type might have been called the more Hellenistic—and it is certainly well represented by Philo of Alexandria. But it has been observed by P. Katz,[1] that it is also represented in the (Palestinian) Wisdom of Sirach (Ecclesiasticus). Geographical generalizations are thus dangerous. But the traditional type of exegesis was undoubtedly well established in Palestine by the time of Christ, and Jeremias[2] traces the influence of the scribes to their esoteric knowledge, often of an apocalyptic character. This, no doubt, is the key of knowledge which they professed to possess but would not use for the benefit of others (Lk. xi. 52). Whatever its origin and milieu may be, 2 Pet. i. 20 f. seems to be making a very interesting pronouncement on the nature of inspiration, though its meaning would be clearer if one could be certain of the situation to which it is addressed:

> But first note this: no one can interpret any prophecy of Scripture by himself. For it was not through any human whim that men prophesied of old; men they were, but, impelled by the Holy Spirit, they spoke the words of God.

Presumably it means 'the original prophets, whose words are now part of scripture, were themselves speaking not of their own human choosing but under the compulsion of the Spirit of God; therefore the present-day reader, correspondingly, must not expect to understand them by his private, unaided judgment'. But whether the opposite of 'private, unaided judgment' is, in this case, private, inspired judgment, or not private judgment at all but only what the authoritative Church leaders say, is another matter.

It is to be noticed, at any rate, that both the attitudes just defined worked on the assumption that the voice of prophecy had fallen silent. Divine authority must be sought not in the

---

[1] 'The Old Testament Canon in Palestine and Alexandria', *Z.N.T.W.* 47 (1956), 191 ff.　　[2] *Jerusalem zur Zeit Jesu* ([2]1958), 106 ff.

living, contemporary utterance of contemporary inspired men, but in the interpretation of a past inspiration—the inspiration of scripture.[1] As a matter of fact, however, the voice of prophecy was not as silent as might appear. There was apocalyptic writing to be reckoned with. Apocalyptic usually purported to be inspired prediction by some ancient sage of the prophetic period, preserved to be divulged to a later generation on the eve of its destined fulfilment. In fact, however, it was generally a contemporary writer's work, masquerading under the ancient name. Thus, there were contemporaries, though they did not declare themselves, speaking original messages of hope or consolation: seldom voicing the social righteousness of the great prophets, but at least uttering, under their measure of direct inspiration, a message for the times. And so popular was the outlook of the apocalyptists that it in some measure controlled also the exegesis of the earlier writings: the Law, and (so far as they were used as authoritative) the Prophets and the other scriptures too, tended to be interpreted along the lines of the apocalyptic message—supernatural rescue is imminent for the People of God. For this was the burden of apocalyptic. The old Prophets had looked for God's purposes to be achieved in righteous kings and rulers of integrity; but now, under the alien domination of Rome, it was in the main easier to hope for some supernatural intervention and to reinterpret even ancient moral and political messages along these lines. The so-called 'commentary' on the Book of Habakkuk in the Dead Sea Scrolls represents an interesting combination of the political and the apocalyptic. For the most part (so far as one may judge from the defective manuscript) it was an effort to apply the words of the prophet, perhaps some 500 years before, to the pressures of secularism and all the alarums and excursions of the period just before Christ. 'The interpretation (*pesher*) of (such-and-such a phrase) is. . . .' So runs the formula of the Habakkuk commentary,[2] like the Aramaic equivalent in the interpretation of

[1] For formulae of quotation (many closely parallel to the New Testament) in Qumran writings, see J. A. Fitzmyer as on p. 57, n.1 . But (*ut sup.*) note the absence of the idea of '*fulfilment*'.
[2] For details of the Qumran exegetical methods, see O. Betz, *Offenbarung und Schriftforschung in der Qumransekte* (1960); also F. F. Bruce, *Biblical Exegesis in the Qumran Texts* (1960).

the dreams or the writing on the wall in Daniel (iv. 6 (*M.T.* iv. 3), v. 15, 26, vii. 16, etc.); and generally the interpretation is in terms of persons and peoples contemporary with the interpreter—the wicked priest, the teacher of righteousness, the Kittim. But the contemporary period is believed to be the closing days of the age; and now and then the expectation of supernatural intervention breaks in àlso: 'in the day of judgment God will destroy all the worshippers of idols and the wicked from the earth' (the last words, in Millar Burrows' translation). Stauffer is probably right in saying that in the latter years of Judaism apocalyptic was the dominant factor in biblical interpretation. In the paintings in the synagogue at Dura on the Euphrates (excavated in 1934 and following years), figures tentatively identified as Enoch and Ezra (apocalyptists) enjoy a place of honour side by side with Moses and Joshua.[1]

Yet even so we must not lose sight of messages of individual piety which were also current at the same time. To look at Philo's writings is to be reminded that there were at least some (and why not many?) who were interested in the scriptures chiefly as an allegory of Mansoul, and who found in them the ideal for individual self-culture in religion and piety.

(ii) Thus it was into a long and varied tradition of scriptural exegesis that Jesus came. How did he use his Bible? One striking example of contemporary application at once springs to mind: 'Today . . . in your very hearing this text has come true', he says (Lk. iv. 21), as he expounds Isa. lxi. Here is Qumran-like *pesher*—the interpretation of an ancient passage so as to apply to current events; but the idea of fulfilment, unlike the Qumran usage, holds in it an eschatological intensity. This passage is peculiar to Luke, though that is, in itself, no reason for doubting its authenticity. Both Matthew and Mark have what is almost a *pesher*-application of Zech. xiii. 7 after the last supper:

[1] E. Stauffer, *Theologie* (⁴1948), 3 (Eng. trans., *New Testament Theology*, 1955, 20 f.), and references to literature there; cf. Jeremias, *Jerusalem zur Zeit Jesu*, (²1958), 107 f. The Ezra-painting is reproduced in *Atlas of the Early Christian World*, by F. van der Meer and C. Mohrmann (1959), plate 68. It must however, be admitted that the identification of Enoch is very doubtful. For a full and authoritative account see *The Excavations at Dura-Europos*, Final Report VIII part 1, *The Synagogue* by C. H. Kraeling (1956), where the plates are in colour.

Tonight you will all fall from your faith on my account; for it stands written: 'I will strike the shepherd down and the sheep of the flock will be scattered'.

(Matt. xxvi. 31, Mk xiv. 27). But even more securely embedded in the traditions—in all four Gospels—is Jesus' use of the term 'the Son of Man', which is most simply explained (despite all arguments to the contrary) as the use of a symbol from Dan. vii which is both historical and eschatological. It is the symbol of the loyal martyr-people of God (embodied, in the first instance, by the Maccabaean martyrs)—the human figure who, for all his unprotected weakness before the bestial empires of tyranny, is divinely vindicated in the end, and, because of his readiness to suffer, is crowned with glory and honour, and seen exalted to the presence of God. Jesus applies this symbol to his own ministry, and to himself as the initiator and representative of the loyal and obedient people of God, now on earth in humiliation, but destined to be exalted with the clouds of heaven.[1]

To the same paradoxical denouement Jesus is said to have applied also the figure of the 'stone' of Ps. cxviii which, rejected by the expert masons who ought to have known better, turns out after all to be the most vital stone of the whole edifice (Mk xii. 10 and pars.).

Again, Jesus seems to have applied the expectations of the coming Elijah (Mal. iv. 5) to the mission of John the Baptist— perhaps intending the startling corollary that his own ministry must be identified with the Day of Yahweh (Mk ix. 13, Matt. xvii. 12).[2]

[1] Out of the vast literature on 'the Son of Man', the following short list, including most of the various theories, may be of value: F. J. Foakes-Jackson and K. Lake (eds.), *The Beginnings of Christianity* i (1920), 368 ff.; T. W. Manson, *The Teaching of Jesus* (1935), 211 ff.; R. Otto, *The Kingdom of God and the Son of Man* (Eng. trans., 1938); J. Knox, *Christ the Lord* (1945), 32 ff. reprinted in his *Jesus Lord and Christ* (1958), 90 ff.; E. K. T. Sjöberg, *Der Menschensohn im Äthiopischen Henochbuch* (1946); G. S. Duncan, *Jesus, Son of Man* (1947); J. Y. Campbell, *J.T.S.* xlviii (1947), 145 ff.; T. W. Manson, *B.J.R.L.* 32. 2 (1950) 171 ff.; A. Farrer, *A Study in St. Mark* (1951), 247 ff.; C. F. D. Moule, 'From Defendant to Judge—and Deliverer', *S.N.T.S. Bulletin* iii (1952), 40 ff.; V. Taylor, *The Names of Jesus* (1954), 25 ff.; J. Knox, *The Death of Christ* (1958; English ed. 1959), 87 ff.; G. Bornkamm, *Jesus of Nazareth* (Eng. trans., 1960), 228 ff.

[2] See J. A. T. Robinson, 'Elijah, John and Jesus: an Essay in Detection', *J.N.T.S.* 4. 4 (July 1958), 263 ff., for some very penetrating observations on this question.

On one occasion, too, Jesus is represented (Mk xii. 35 ff. and pars.) as appealing to Ps. cx to convince his antagonists that their messianic expectations were too superficial. The argument seems to run thus. David, who is assumed to be the speaker, alludes to a divine promise, addressed to some unnamed person, that this person will be given a position of royal majesty at God's right hand until all his enemies are subdued. The person is commonly identified (evidently by Jesus' antagonists, among others) as the hoped-for divinely-chosen King of Israel (the anointed one, messiah). But in this very Psalm David calls him 'my Lord': how can he, then, be junior to David,—be David's descendant, as the Messiah is commonly expected to be? There is the dilemma. And the moral might be (as some commentators hold) that the true Messiah is not Davidic at all; but more likely it is that the Messiah, even if Davidic, is also of supernatural status, 'David's greater Son'[1]. It is curious that the latter part of the Psalm, in which the person is addressed as a priest (cf. Heb. v. 7), seems to cause no embarrassment in this context, although the Evangelist clearly intends the Psalm to apply to Jesus (who was no priest), whether or not Jesus himself so intended it. Ps. cx. 3, which seems to describe a miraculous divine birth, ('. . . from the womb of the morning, thou hast the dew of thy youth' ( ? )), was not used in New Testament *testimonia*, but Ps. ii came in for this purpose instead.[2] 'You are my son; this day have I begotten you' (Acts xiii. 33). At any rate, here is an instance of the use by Jesus of an exegetical process which is not straightforwardly historical (still less 'critical' as to the authorship and original setting of the Psalm), but which depends on the suggestive quality of words in the context of certain assumptions and

---

[1] 'The term "Son of David" signifies the same as a new David. The Messianic Florilegium [ =4Q Florilegium; the part in question was published by J. M. Allegro in *J.B.L.* 75 (1956), 176 f.; see also F. F. Bruce, *Biblical Exegesis in the Qumran Texts* (1960), 52] from Cave IV, however, interprets the prophecy of Nathan to David (2 Sam. vii. 11-14) as meaning that the messianic scion of David of the last days will be the one of whom God said "I will be his Father, and he shall be my son". . . . The messianic son of David was therefore to be identical with the pre-existent Son of God. Thus the question which caused difficulty for Pharisaism is readily understood when we understand the particular presuppositions of the Qumran doctrine of the Messiah.'—Kurt Schubert, *The Dead Sea Community* (Eng. trans. of *Die Gemeinde vom Toten Meer* (1958), by J. W. Doberstein (1959)), 139 f.

[2] See H.-J. Kraus, *Psalmen* (*Biblischer Kommentar*, 1960), on Ps. cx.

presuppositions—Davidic authorship, messianic reference—
entertained by his hearers and probably also by him.

But this is rare in the Synoptic tradition of Jesus' teaching.
The only other synoptic instance of the attribution to Jesus of
what might be deemed strained exegesis, dependent on merely
verbal detail, is the refutation of the Sadducees' disbelief in an
after-life by the citation (Mk xii. 26) of 'I am the God of
Abraham and the God of Isaac and the God of Jacob', leading
to the conclusion that, since God is not the God of the dead but
of the living, these patriarchs must all be still alive.' The actual
words of Exodus of course need mean no more than 'I am the
God who was formerly worshipped by Abraham, Isaac, and
Jacob'. Again, therefore, the lesson depends on something
extraneous to the bare meaning of the words. The real authority
for the conclusion is the conviction that if God establishes contact with a man and is willing to be called his God, then that
relationship is such that death cannot break it: the appeal,
beneath and behind the words of scripture, is to an otherwise
known quality in the character of God and therefore of his
relations with men. If the prediction that Jesus would rise in
three days, or after three days (Mk viii. 31 and pars., ix. 31 and
pars.), were based on Hos. vi. 2, here again would be a seemingly
forced reading of scripture; but it is by no means clear that, even
if these are genuinely dominical words, they were related by
Jesus himself to Hos. vi. 2 in precisely this way (see below,
p. 85). And the strained application of the tale of Jonah to the
resurrection is attested only in the Matthean version of that
saying (Matt. xii. 40), and is far from secure as a genuine *logion*
of Jesus. Apart from these few, practically all the uses of direct
quotation from scripture attributed to Jesus himself in the
synoptic tradition—we are not thinking now of the application
of scriptural figures to his mission—are the straightforward
moral or religious ones which depend upon no straining or
subtle word-play or allegorizing, and which anyone today
would recognize as valid: worship and love of God; love of
neighbour; the ideal of life-long wedlock; and the design of God
through the obedience of his people as against worldly scheming
and materialistic values (see Matt. iv. 10 and par., Mk xii. 30 f.
and pars., Mk x. 2 ff. and par., Matt. iv. 4 and par., and *passim*).

In the Johannine tradition there is one argument from scripture on the lips of Jesus that seems unacceptable to the modern reader, namely that in Jn x. 34, where the obscure words from Ps. lxxxii, 'I said: You are gods', assumed to be addressed by God to men, or, at most, to lesser gods or 'angels',[1] are appealed to in defence of Jesus' own claims. Men (or other beings) to whom God's word came—so runs the argument—were called gods; how much more may he be called God's Son who is expressly sanctified and sent into the world by the Father! It is very probable that the whole dialogue reflects the Christian Church's conflict with the Synagogue rather than the original words of Jesus—especially in view of the literalist phrase, 'Scripture cannot be set aside', so unlike anything that we can gather about Christ's attitude to authority. Incidentally, it has been argued (see p. 41, n. 1, above) that even the Matthean form of the 'great commandment' itself shows a rabbinical tendency to *deduce* morals from scripture ('on these two commandments hang all the Law and the Prophets', Matt. xxii. 40), over against the Marcan form (Mk xii. 31) which seems to set the basic law of religion—love of God and neighbour—above any other commands, whether scriptural or not. If so, here, too, may be traced the echoes of later Christian misunderstanding and adaptation of the Lord's words to more literalist ways of thought. But none of this is absolutely demonstrable; and if the arguments in Jn x and Matt. are sound traditions, we are driven to accepting that Jesus himself, on occasion, used, *ad hominem*, the verbal casuistry of rabbinic techniques. Elsewhere in the Fourth Gospel (vii. 23) we find him using the *a fortiori* method of deducing the greater from the less: if circumcision is permitted on the Sabbath to avoid breaking the Law, how much more the restoration of health to an entire man! But in general the Jesus of the Fourth Gospel uses scripture in an allusive, poetic, evocative way— Jacob's ladder (?), the brazen serpent, the manna, the living streams of water (see Jn i. 51, iii. 14, vi. 49, vii. 38): it is the picture-writing, the symbols of scripture that he uses, almost as embryonic parables. Once in John he applies a scriptural phrase to current events in the *pesher*-manner: the allusion to the

---

[1] See J. A. Emerton, 'Some New Testament Notes', *J.T.S.*, n.s., xi (1960), 329ff.

treachery of a close friend in Ps. xli is all too relevant (Jn xiii. 18).

It is only Luke who depicts Jesus after the resurrection as clinching the process of exposition by expounding in all the scriptures the things concerning himself (Lk. xxiv. 27, 44 ff.). And the phrase 'that the Messiah had to suffer' (Lk. xxiv. 46, Acts iii. 18, xxvi. 23) may be Luke's own summary.[1] But, if so, it does express in a nutshell the whole emphasis of the ministry of Jesus—the suffering, the service, the vindication, the transmission of the achievement to others. When Luke represents Jesus at the last supper as saying 'all that is written of me is being fulfilled' (Lk. xxii. 37), he is at any rate pointing to a principle of interpretation compatible with the whole Christian understanding of scripture, and apparently rooted in Christ's own use. The use or non-use of Isa. liii will come up for further consideration later. What is important and original is that Jesus seems to have taken not so much individual proof-texts as the whole sweep of God's dealings with his People and of God's design for them, and interpreted his mission in the light of it.

(iii) The originality of Jesus' use of scripture is strikingly confirmed when we consider the early Christian use of scripture and its implications. It is true, as has already been pointed out, that the use of the Old Testament scriptures by the New Testament writers does include a considerable element of verbal play and literalism which are much less characteristic of the traditions about Jesus' own use. But the remarkable phenomenon is not that artificial uses persisted (or even were freshly coined) but that the dominant use was—as compared with its Jewish antecedents—a quite new and convincing one: and the best explanation for this is that it was derived from the Lord himself. This new use has been described as a use of scripture 'in the round', in contrast to its use—for instance by Philo—as a flat, two-dimensional area.[2] As long as scripture is viewed primarily as an inspired device for yielding divine pronouncements, it is reasonable enough to go to any part of it indifferently with an

[1] See J. A. T. Robinson, 'The Most Primitive Christology of All?', *J.T.S.*, n.s. vii (1956), 177 ff. (esp. 183).

[2] See C. H. Dodd, *The Old Testament in the New* (The Ethel M. Wood lecture for 1952), and *According to the Scriptures* (1952).

equal expectation of extracting, from the words of whatever verses are chosen for interrogation, a hint or an oracle; and, if so, it is almost inevitable that techniques should be devised for ensuring that the words do yield up a message even when they are intractable and unpromising. As has already been said, such devices may be in the hands of authoritative exponents, heirs of a long tradition, like the rabbis; or, in another tradition or situation, they may be applied by an individual like Philo in his private studies and devotions. But this is not the distinctively New Testament use of scripture. Whatever New Testament specimens there may be of rabbinic and Philonian interpretations, these are not the most characteristic. What marks the New Testament use as new is precisely this treatment of scripture 'in the round', as a three-dimensional entity—indeed, one ought to say four-dimensional, for time is a very important factor. The most characteristic New Testament use of scripture is 'modern' in that it treats the Old Testament as a *record* of revelation—as a historical narrative of God's dealings with his people, to be listened to as a whole and learnt from as a continuous story. There is a world of difference between this and the use of scripture as a divining-medium.

And the reason why the Christians began thus to use scripture 'historically' (as we should say) was that they had actually found in Jesus of Nazareth the climax of the long story of God's dealings with his people. In Jesus *par excellence* was exhibited the age-long principle of God's way with men: it is the loyal, devoted minority in whom God's purposes are fulfilled. And chosen individuals—anointed king, anointed priest, prophet, and sage—these representative figures were, all through the history of God's people, the rallying-points summing up this principle of response to God in the teeth of a disloyal, self-seeking majority. Thus, while material wealth and worldly success might temporarily pass to the majority, it was along the course of disinterested loyalty that the pure stream of God's purpose had run. Now, it is precisely this principle that was not only epitomized but perfectly achieved in Jesus—Jesus, who, for all his vivid individuality, turned out also to be so far more than an individual; and it was inevitable, therefore, that the great biblical passages about the ideal people of God, as well as those about their ideal representatives, should begin to be drawn together round Jesus, as a magnet collects iron filings. It was not only Jesus' own use of scripture (though that was probably normative), but also his person, his character, and the mighty work of God in him that gave a new coherence to scripture and led to a new use of it. The result was a new grouping of the passages. A non-Christian Jewish rabbi, if asked about the scriptures relating to God's purposes for his people, would almost certainly not have offered exactly the same anthology as a Christian. For one thing, it would have been less comprehensive. Jewish expectation ran along different lines at different times and in different places. The messianic expectation was only one—and not always a prominent one—among many forms which it took. The anointed one, messiah, is a figure more appropriate to literal, political hopes of a Kingdom than to a period of indefinitely prolonged domination by an alien empire. Kingship—the Lord's anointed—is prominent enough in the Psalms of Solomon written about 60 B.C.; but by the time of Christ such hopes lingered mostly among the fanatic revolutionaries, whereas other forms of expectation filled less violent minds. One of these was the apocalyptic hope that, if only Israel were loyal, God would dramatically intervene; and a specially noble form of this hope was the other-wordly conviction that, though the loyal minority were extinguished in martyrdom, yet on the spiritual level this 'human figure' would be vindicated over the bestial oppressors. The anointed priest was another embodiment of hope. He had become a reality in the best days of the Maccabees. The most spiritual form of all might have been the creative and redemptive suffering of the anonymous martyr of Isa. liii, whose loyal death mysteriously converted and redeemed his very enemies; but the extent to which pre-Christian Jews exploited this is obscure.[1]

But the new and exciting phenomenon is the convergence of all these figures upon Jesus; and that in him they became coherent was due to the fact that upon Jesus converged the whole history of Israel in the past, and from him deployed the

[1] See W. Zimmerli and J. Jeremias, *The Servant of God* (Eng. trans., 1957), for a generous estimate of pre-Christian use; *contra* M. D. Hooker, *Jesus and the Servant* (1959).

whole future of the People of God. It was the coherent organiz-. ing of all this into a single inclusive personality that made a completely new thing of Old Testament exegesis.[1] And although, as has been said, Jesus' own expositions no doubt set a precious example and began a lasting tradition, it was his living person even more than his remembered words that conditioned its course. To have lived responsively through the events of the ministry, death, and resurrection was to have gained a completely new angle of approach to scripture: or, to change the figure, it meant viewing the map of scripture for the first time as a genuinely three-dimensional relief map illuminated centrally by a brilliant light.

It was from this experience—though doubtless without a clearly articulated account of its implications for scripture—that the apostles and their companions first set out upon their witness, and their task of explanation. And this has brought us back to the point from which we began: the distinctiveness of the early Christian use of scripture is part of the conviction that, in Jesus, God had spoken directly to his people: that thus the voice of 'prophecy'—the immediate witness to the behest of God—had begun to sound again; that God had visited and redeemed his people and that a new understanding of his purposes had been vouchsafed. Therefore the Christians were no longer dependent upon rabbinic traditions for discerning the mind of God or upon the importuning of jots and tittles to yield up a message: they came to scripture from an already given experience, and had only to read in its main contours and its living story the confirmation that what they had experienced was not alien, though so new: it was the climax, the culmination, the 'Amen' to all God's purposes (2 Cor. i. 20).

As has been said already, they had intensely difficult questions to answer: it must have seemed a quite preposterous story that they had to vindicate—'Christ nailed to the cross . . . a stumbling-block to Jews and folly to Greeks' (1 Cor. i. 23). And it was inevitable, that, in the course of controversy, 'proof texts' should be invoked—in some cases, they had already been used by Jesus himself. But behind all such adventitious uses of scripture, the Christians had their solid, impregnable experience.

[1] Cf. F. F. Bruce, *op. cit.* p. 61, n. 2, 77.

Whatever this verse or that might mean (or be tortured into meaning) they now had the key to the whole purposes of God —to sum up all things in Christ (Eph. i. 10). When Luther affirmed this principle of scriptural interpretation, he was going back to the primitive Church.

With this behind us, we may go forward to see the various forms taken by the Christian argument from scripture—some, as we might judge today, retrograde, some over-ingenious, but all controlled by this new, overruling conviction: Christ the ultimate authority, the key to the scriptures.

We are, we must remember, pursuing the genesis of Christian writings. What, then, for a start, lies behind such a passage as Rom. ix-xi, St Paul's extended defence of the Christian Gospel in the face of its rejection by the bulk of Judaism? Here we are immediately reminded of a persistent argument against Christianity. If the Gospel is really God's word, how comes it, its antagonists were continually asking, that God's own Israel have rejected it? According to the traditions, Jesus himself met the problem of unresponsiveness by the recognition that, as a matter of fact, this always had been the pattern in Israel. Was not the prophet warned that his message would be rejected? (Isa. vi); was it not the expert builders who rejected the most vital stone? (Ps. cxviii); is there not a famous passage about a stone that would cause downfall in Israel? (Isa. viii). And equally, the scriptural conviction of God's ineluctable purposes affirmed their ultimate vindication: the vital corner-stone did, in the end, come into its true position; the stone for stumbling over turned out, after all, to be a sure foundation (Isa. xxviii); the stone hewn by no human hands eventually came to shatter the fragile empires of the godless (Dan. ii); the despised and rejected human figure was vindicated (Dan. vii). And it was along these lines that debate developed in the apostolic age. Its results, pro and con, are expressed in almost lyrical terms, in 1 Cor. i. 22-25:

> Jews call for miracles, Greeks look for wisdom; but we proclaim Christ—yes, Christ nailed to the cross; and though this is a stumbling-block to Jews and folly to Greeks, yet to those who have heard his call, Jews and Greeks alike, he is the power of God and the wisdom of God. Divine folly is wiser than the wisdom of man, and divine weakness stronger than man's strength.

Peter is shown in Acts iv. 11 appealing to the corner-stone saying:

> This Jesus is the stone rejected by the builders which has become the key-stone—and you are the builders.

At the end of the Acts Paul's last word to the unconvinced Jews as they leave the long debate is to quote the passage from Isa. vi (Acts xxviii. 25-28):

> How well the Holy Spirit spoke to your fathers through the prophet Isaiah when he said, 'Go to this people and say: You will hear and hear, but never understand; you will look and look, but never see. For this people has grown gross at heart; their ears are dull, and their eyes are closed. Otherwise, their eyes might see, their ears hear, and their heart understand, and then they might turn again, and I would heal them.' Therefore take notice that this salvation of God has been sent to the Gentiles: the Gentiles will listen.

But sooner or later the thoughtful Christian disputant is bound to attempt to piece together these fragments of defence. If Israel was all along 'meant' to be unresponsive, then what of its future? If the Gentiles are now invited in, has God's election passed to them? And, if so, what of the constancy of God's promises? A major problem of 'theodicy' has developed; every Christian missionary is confronted by it in some form or another; but no one meets it in such an acute form, or is so well equipped to wrestle with it, as Paul, the rabbinically trained disputer with the Jews on behalf of the Gentiles. And we are fortunate to have, in Rom. ix-xi, the deposit of his conflicts. Gal. iii. 7-iv. 31 is an earlier specimen. The correlative to the *testimonia* for the obduracy of Israel is in the scriptures about God's welcome to the Gentiles. There is little evidence that Jesus appealed much to this during his ministry. Matt. viii. 11, 'many shall come from the east and west . . .' may be a reminiscence of Isaianic phrases; but, in the main, a case can be made[1] for a deliberate reserve in this respect, and an application of the 'Gentile' scriptures rather to the post-resurrection situation. Acts xv. 16 f. affords one example; but it is Paul, especially in Rom. ix-xi and xv, who provides them in profusion.

[1] J. Jeremias, *Jesus' Promise to the Nations* (Eng. trans., 1958).

But not all were travelling evangelists or skilled disputants. What of the humble Christians whose circumstances brought them into constant touch with non-Christian Jews—the Jewish Christians still living within the ghetto, or the Gentile Christians just outside it? It looks as though St Matthew's Gospel may represent the end-term of a long process of evolving catechetical instruction designed for just such circumstances. It is possible that the Evangelist himself was not a Jew.[1] But in any case, it seems designed as an apologia, to be used by Christians in reply to curious or critical Jews. And its burden is that Jesus of Nazareth can be shown to have fulfilled the scriptural pattern, that he did not undermine the righteousness of Judaism, but, on the contrary, enhanced and completed it, and that to belong to Christ is truly to belong to Israel. And if members of Israel rejected him, so did their forefathers reject the prophets: true Israel has always been a remnant within the larger, degenerate mass. Nowhere in the New Testament is so extreme an acceptance of rabbinic Judaism enunciated as in Matt. v. 18, 19:[2]

> I tell you this: so long as heaven and earth endure, not a letter, not a stroke, will disappear from the Law until all that must happen has happened. If any man therefore sets aside even the least of the Law's demands, and teaches others to do the same, he will have the lowest place in the kingdom of Heaven, whereas anyone who keeps the Law and teaches others so will stand high in the kingdom of Heaven.

It is perhaps (see further pp. 88, 90 f. below) intended to show that Christ had no intention to lower the highest standards of Israel but rather to heighten them:

> I tell you, unless you show yourselves far better men than the Pharisees and the doctors of the law, you can never enter the kingdom of Heaven (v. 20).

Yet nowhere is a self-regarding 'priggish' righteousness more ruthlessly exposed than in Matt. xxiii—the great onslaught on

---

[1] See, especially, P. Nepper-Christensen, *Das Matthäusevangelium: ein juden-christliches Evangelium?* (1958).

[2] On which, in addition to plentiful earlier discussion, see H. Ljungman, *Das Gesetz Erfüllen* (1954); P. Nepper-Christensen, *op. cit.*; G. Barth, as on p. 5, n. 1.; H. Schürmann, '"Wer daher eines geringsten Gebote auflöst ..." wo fand Matthäus das logion Mt. 5, 19?' *Bibl Zeitschr.* 2 (1960), 238 ff.

the doctors of the law and the Pharisees. These two factors well
suit a Christian 'ghetto' within or near the Jewish ghetto. And
it is hardly surprising to find here also, in addition to the uses of
scripture which have been described as characteristic of Christianity, other uses which can only be described as artificial,
forced, and literalistic. A plausible case has been made for the
interpretation of Matthew as the result of a 'school' of exegesis.[1]
It is quite conceivable (though it cannot be demonstrated) that
the better educated Christians, in such circumstances as have
been described, should get together as a study-group to see
whether they could not, for the benefit of themselves and of less
well-educated members of the community, draw up a reply to
their critics in their own language and with their own techniques. And if indeed the writer of this Gospel, or (if he was not
himself a Jew) one among his circle, was a trained rabbinic
scribe who had become a disciple in the Kingdom of Heaven
(xiii. 52)—a converted scribe—here is at least a partial explanation of the phenomena. The only problem is to explain the
inclusion, here and there, of mistakes about Judaism. Perhaps,
even if the writer was himself not a Gentile but a converted
scribe, there were, in this scribe's group, at least some who did
not know their way about Judaism as well as he did. A large
number of Christian converts were from among the σεβόμενοι,
the Gentiles who reverenced the God of Judaism. It is far from
unlikely that these had a hand in the compiling and using of
such a document. Or may it be, instead, that the final editor was
not a rabbinic but a 'secular' scribe (exactly as Matthew himself,
if a tax-collector, would have been)?

If much that went to the compilation of Matt. is correctly
placed in the context of strenuous conflict between Church and
synagogue, the same may well be true of St John's Gospel.
But its use of the Old Testament is less direct, and its consideration therefore scarcely belongs here. Returning to indications of
public debate in the Acts, we are reminded that, besides the
debates of Peter and of Paul, a vivid description of a different
type of Jewish-Christian apologetic is offered in the account of
Stephen in Acts vi, vii. Here is a man, who, like Jesus himself, is
accused of a traitorous attack upon the very heart of Judaism—

[1] K. Stendahl, *The School of St. Matthew* (1954).

Moses and the Temple. His defence is of an arresting character. Instead of replying directly, he simply begins to recount the familiar story of the origins of Israel, from Abraham onwards. But he does it in such a way as to indicate that every advance involved the rejection of the traditional and the static; and that at every point the Holy Spirit is the Spirit of advance, of movement, of the refusal to be static; so that the heroes of Israel are all people of gigantic faith, exchanging the known for the unknown, abandoning the security of the familiar in blind obedience to the call of God. Abraham, Joseph, Moses—these are the three mighty men who laid the foundations of Israel by coming out, or going away, and by serving God in the dangerous and the unfamiliar. Accordingly, it is the portable tabernacle rather than the solid Temple that Stephen chooses as his symbol for the true worship of God; and it is Moses, foretelling a future Prophet, and David, debarred from building a static Temple, who are his pointers forward.

In other words, here is a lively defence of the Christian position by carrying the attack behind the enemy's lines: read your scriptures, Stephen is saying in effect, and you will find that it is the scriptures themselves that tell you to look beyond Moses and beyond the Temple (cf. Jn v. 39). Stephen was in all probability a 'Hellenist' (Acts vi. 1 ff.)—that is, a Jew who read his scriptures in Greek translation and who could not or did not speak Semitic languages; and he probably belonged to a synagogue of similar traditions (Acts vi. 9, cf. xi. 19 f.); and it seems entirely possible (although this is only a guess) that his successful disputing and his courageous death may have led to the conversion to Christianity of a group of like-minded Hellenistic Jews from this synagogue. May it not, then, be precisely such a group who are addressed by one of their number in the Epistle to the Hebrews? Its main argument runs in part along the very same lines as Stephen's—that true Judaism lies in advancing forward to Christ, not in retreating back to an entrenched position; that the tabernacle is the sketch (or rather copy!)—not of the Solomonic or any other material Temple, but of the true sanctuary in heaven; and that Moses is the pattern of that greater Moses who was to come. It is certainly not impossible, in view of this, that the apparent allusion in Heb. xiii. 7 to martyr-leaders may include Stephen himself.[1] At any rate, this epistle affords us a fascinating example of the end-product, the written form, of precisely the kind of debate which is represented as in progress in the trial of Stephen; and it bears witness to yet another 'school' of interpretation, besides what may be postulated behind Matthew. Here is the carefully—indeed brilliantly—constructed apologia of an educated, Alexandrine-type Jewish Christian.[2] He is concerned to help his friends to meet the extreme temptation to relapse back into Judaism, perhaps under nationalist pressure;[3] and he is using all his (or perhaps their joint) resources of scriptural exegesis to show the finality of Christ and his absolute superiority over Moses and all Jewish approximations. In Num. xii. 8 Moses is described in superlative terms, as the only one with whom God spoke mouth to mouth. It looks uncommonly as though Heb. iii. 1 ff., with its quotations from this very context, reflects conflict with the proof-text mind of a Jewish opponent, who had been saying 'Your claims for Jesus, even if they are soundly established, place him at best no

---

[1] As a matter of fact, it is not impossible to fit Heb. ii. 3 f. into the same guess. This says that the Christian message was confirmed to the writer of the epistle and his readers by those who had heard it from the Lord himself, and that God added his own witness in signs and portents and various deeds of power and apportionings (μερισμοῖς) of the Holy Spirit, in accordance with his will. All this is entirely appropriate as a description of Pentecost, as we find it in the Acts story, by one who, though not an original disciple of Jesus, had been drawn into the Christian Church at that time—exactly as Stephen and his fellow-worshippers in his synagogue might have been. See Acts ii. 3 ('tongues' apportioned or distributed) 19 ('portents . . . and signs'), 36 ('let all Israel then accept as certain . . .').

[2] In Heb. vi. 13 ff. much emphasis is laid upon the assurance provided by the divine oath in the passage about the promise to Abraham (Gen. xxii. 16 f.). The argument leads straight on, however, into the Melchizedek theme (vi. 20 ff.), and one might have expected immediate reference to the divine oath in the Melchizedek Ps. cx. This, however, is reserved until vii. 20 f. This suggests, I think, very careful and thoughtful arrangement. The writer wishes to introduce the Melchizedek theme and to follow up first its Genesis-symbolism; he will not allow himself to be diverted to the oath of Ps. cx until he is ready. Then, and not until he has finished with Genesis, this second oath-passage occurs impressively, to pick up that earlier reference to the Genesis oath. Incidentally, why does Heb. vi. 13 refer to God's oath in indirect speech rather than citing the words of the oath in the direct quotation in the next verse?

[3] Another motive for such a move, operative at times of persecution for Christians, was to come under the protection of Judaism, like that Domnus, to whom Serapion of Antioch addressed a treatise, 'who had fallen away from the faith of Christ, at the time of the persecution [of Severus], to Jewish will-worship' (Euseb. H.E. vi. 12. 1).

higher than Moses'. Such an argument is reminiscent of the
artificial proof-text method alluded to by a modern writer[1] who
says that in face of the Christian doctrine of the virgin birth a
Muslim will sometimes appeal to Melchizedek's mysterious
origin, and urge therefore that Jesus was no better than Melchizedek—thus taking a subsequent leaf out of this epistle's very
argument and reversing it! At any rate, it is a familiar fact that
this writer does indulge in a good deal of the 'Alexandrine' type
of exegesis—depending on words and hints to make his points.[2]
Perhaps the most perplexing of all these to the modern reader
is the astonishing application to Christ in Heb. i. 10-12 of a
Psalm (cii) which seems manifestly to be addressed to God
almighty as Creator, and which (one would think) could therefore have no cogency whatever as a scriptural proof about the
status of Christ.[3] It is one thing to read Ps. cx as an address
by David to his Lord the Messiah (Mk xii. 36, etc.); it is surely
quite another to lift a passage addressed by a worshipper to God
and to use it without more ado as evidence for the qualities of
the Christ. Even when Paul (or a Christian hymnwright quoted
by Paul?) takes Yahweh the Creator's description of himself in

---

[1] J. Crossley, *Christian Witness* (Lee Abbey journal) xiii, 2 (June 1960),
18. Cf. K. Cragg, *The Call of The Minaret* (1956), 284 f.
[2] An unpublished PhD Thesis for Manchester University by K. J.
Thomas (borrowed, by kind permission of the University Librarian of Manchester) on *The Use of the Septuagint in the Epistle to the Hebrews* (June 1959)
seems to establish that the writer knew certain (a few) of Philo's tractates,
and indeed was directly opposing Philo's interpretations in some instances.
[3] K. J. Thomas (*ut sup.*) does not meet this difficulty when he says (p. 28),
'According to this quotation, the Son is associated with the creation of the
world. This idea has both New Testament and Old Testament parallels',
and goes on to allude to Jn i. 2 f., Col. i. 15 f., 1 Cor. viii. 6, and Jewish ideas
about Wisdom and Torah as instrumental (*only* instrumental incidentally)
in creation. The difficulty remains that, in order to prove Christ's supremacy
to a Jew from this Psalm, one has to be able to assume that it would be recognized as addressed to Christ; and Thomas does nothing to show this. In
his bibliography he has Bacon's article (see p. 79, below), but makes no
reference to it in this section, nor on p. 186, where he deals with variations
in the LXX text of this part of the Psalm.
See further: F. Bleek, *Theologische Studien und Kritiken* viii (1835), 441-
446 and J. van der Ploeg, 'L'Exégèse de l'Ancien Testament dans l'Épître aux
Hébreux', *R.B.* liv (1947), 187-228, taking a view very different from mine;
and L. Venard, *L'Utilisation des Psaumes dans l'Épître aux Hébreux* (1945),
id. 'Citations de l'Ancien Testament dans le Nouveau Testament', *Dict. Bibl.*
Suppl. II (1934), 23-51, which I note from K. J. Thomas' bibliography. Add,
from P. Seidensticker, *Lebendiges Opfer* (1954), 299, n. 24, G. Harder, 'Die
Septuagintazitate des Hebräerbriefes', *Theologia viatorum* (1939), 33-52.

Isa. xlv (that every knee shall bow to him, and every tongue swear by him) and applies it to Christ in Phil. ii. 10 f., he is still not using it as a *proof* that these are the attributes of Christ: he is (on other grounds) affirming these divine attributes and borrowing ready-made phrases to describe them. But here in Heb. i. 10 ff., apparently in the course of an argument from scripture intended to strengthen the Christian convictions of readers who know Judaism from the inside, and to arm them with arguments against non-Christian Jews, is the application to Christ of words which a Jew, one might have assumed, would simply claim to be irrelevant to Christ:

> By thee, Lord, were earth's foundations laid of old,
> And the heavens are the work of thy hands.
> They shall pass away, but thou endurest;
> Like clothes they shall all grow old;
> Thou shalt fold them up like a cloak;
> Yes, they shall be changed like any garment.
> But thou art the same, and thy years shall have no end.

Most commentators follow the lines of B. F. Westcott (*in loc.*): 'The application to the Incarnate Son of words addressed to Jehovah . . . rests on the essential conception of the relation of Jehovah to His people. The Covenant leads up to the Incarnation. And historically it was through the identification of the coming of Christ with the coming of "the LORD" that the Apostles were led to the perception of His true Divinity.' That may be: but it goes no way towards explaining how *in an argument from scripture for the divinity of Christ* a passage which an opponent would presumably have assumed to belong not to Messiah but to God[1] could be used as proof of qualities claimed by the Christian apologist to belong to Christ. Whatever the obscurities of the quotation from Ps. xlv, which in Heb. i. 8 f. precede this one, it at least does not present this problem, for it is demonstrably intended as an address by God to some man (even if he be a God-man).[2] It is in this respect comparable to

[1] There is nothing surprising in the detachment of the phrase from its true context: F. F. Bruce (*op. cit.* p. 64, n. 1), 12 notes how Hab. i. 13 ('thou art of purer eyes . . .') is simply transferred, in the Habakkuk Commentary, from God to a group of men. The surprising feature of Heb. i. 10-12 is the use of this passage in argument, where it might seem to be so easily refuted.

[2] K. J. Thomas (*op. cit.*) adopts the view that ὁ θεός is nominative, not vocative, and paraphrases (typescript 26): 'God is thy power for ever and

Ps. lxxxii ('I said: You are gods') used, as has already been noted (p. 66, above) in Jn x. 34. B. W. Bacon seems to be the only scholar who has attempted a thoroughgoing explanation. He maintains[1] that Ps. cii (LXX ci) in the LXX version (whose variants can here be explained as misreadings or mis-interpretations of the Hebrew), had already turned these verses into an address by Yahweh to his Messiah. They thus become Yahweh's reply to the Messiah's complaint; they admonish him not to be impatient, for God's planned delay is only half completed; the Messiah must be patient, for in due course he will be vindicated and shown his own eternity. In the course of this exalted reply the Messiah is understandably addressed by the Lord himself as 'Lord', κύριε (although, if the argument of Mk xii. 37 from Ps. cx were pressed, it would mean that a greater than God was being addressed!). Now, admittedly, there is much here that is speculative and seems far fetched. But it is perhaps the only intelligible explanation of the use—here, in what is manifestly an apologetic sequence—of such a passage. If Greek-speaking non-Christian Jews did already recognize Ps. cii (LXX ci) 24b-29 as God's answer to his Messiah's appeal, then it does become a strong argument in the hands of the Christian apologist who is trying to demonstrate the superiority of Christ over all other intermediaries. He may then justly say, See in what supernal, divine terms God himself addresses Christ!

One other passage, Heb. ii. 13, presents a comparable problem. The quotation in the preceding verse from Ps. xxii is not too difficult to understand, for the Psalmist may without too much strain be assumed to have been, in the eyes of the ancient reader, 'Messianic':

> . . . he says, 'I will proclaim thy name to my brothers; in full assembly I will sing thy praise';

But why should words from Isa. viii,

> . . . and again, 'I will keep my trust fixed on him'; and again, 'Here am I, and the children whom God has given me',

ever and the scepter of uprightness is the authority of his kingdom'. But see J. R. Porter, *J.T.S.*, n.s., xii (1961), 51 ff.

[1] B. W. Bacon, 'Heb. 1. 10-12 and the Septuagint Rendering of Ps. 102, 23', *Z.N.T.W.* 3 (1902), 280 ff.

be tacitly assumed to be spoken by 'Christ'? The answer may possibly be, once more, that the Greek Bible had already, in pre-Christian days, made them Messianic. For 'the Greek text of Isaiah viii has the words καὶ ἐρεῖ ("and he will say") inserted before verse 17, which give the impression that another speaker than the prophet is introduced':[1] 'and he will say: "I will wait for God. . . . Behold, I and the children. . . ."' If this is the right explanation, here are two non-Christian Messianic intrusions into the Greek Bible, requisitioned by our writer for his Christian purposes.

These passages and the Moses-passage in Heb. iii have been singled out for special mention here as pointers (which have not always received so much attention as other citations) to the situation behind this epistle. Taken with all the other uses which are made of the Old Testament in the course of its argument, on which the commentaries have plenty to say, they point to a body of readers used to subtle exegesis of the Greek Bible, and they make it plausible to postulate for Hebrews, as K. Stendahl has postulated for Matthew, a 'school' of Christian apologetic: a systematic re-examination and re-application of the Greek scriptures by educated Christians in debate with scripture-searching non-Christians.[2] And if one of them—their leader—is writing to the rest (cf. xiii. 19), it is natural that he should go over again the ground that they had traversed in their joint studies, reiterating, reapplying, and working them into an ordered whole.[3] It is true that he addresses them throughout as though their leader and father in God; and that once (v. 11 ff.) he complains that they are sluggish in understanding and are still children when they ought to be mature enough to teach others. But that still does not make it impossible to postulate previous concerted study under his leadership.

[1] K. J. Thomas, op. cit. 14, after Bleek, Lünemann, and Moffatt.

[2] H. Kosmala (Hebräer-Essener-Christen, 1959) has very learnedly and ingeniously renewed the argument for Hebrews being written for non-Christian Jews as a missionary tract. No doubt this helps to explain the seemingly non-Christian allusion to βαπτισμοί in vi. 2, but it leaves much unexplained. For the use made in Heb. of Ps. cx, see some important observations in A. J. B. Higgins, 'The Old Testament and some Aspects of New Testament Christology', Canad. Journ. of Theol. vi (1960), No. 3, 200 ff.

[3] The great preponderance of citations is from the Pentateuch and the Psalter. But there are also some from the Prophets and from the Writings other than the Psalms, and signs of a knowledge of apocryphal writings.

Of all the scriptures that Christians of the present day might have expected to be prominent in early Christian apologetic, Isa. liii is the chief: but in fact it is curiously seldom used in the New Testament. It would appear to combine, as has already been observed, the finest conception of the vindication of the martyr (herein comparable to the vindicated human figure of Dan. vii) with the even finer conception of the redemptive power of the martyr's death, even for his tormentors and oppressors. And, *a priori*, one would have expected that Isa. liii would have been prominent both in Jesus' own interpretation of his mission and ministry and in early Christian evangelism and apologetic.

But in fact the only definite quotation from Isa. liii on the lips of Jesus in the Gospels is the allusion, peculiar to Luke, to his 'being reckoned among the lawless' (Lk. xxii. 37)—not a redemptive allusion. Whatever other allusions we may detect in the words of Jesus are in phrases not demonstrably dependent on the words of Isa.: Mk x. 45 and the words of Institution.[1] And even the New Testament writers themselves make startlingly little use of the Servant Songs. Outside the New Testament, but within the first century, 1 Clement xvi cites Isa. liii at length, though even then, it is related only to Christ's example of humility; and Barnabas v. 2 cites the 'redemptive' passage. But within the New Testament, how little it is used! Matthew applies Isa. liii. 4 to Jesus' ministry of healing (viii. 17); Acts iii. 13 probably uses παῖς in this sense (Acts iv less probably: see p. 21, above); Philip the evangelist applies Isa. liii. 7 f. (about the humble submission to injustice) to Jesus according to Acts viii. 32 f.; Acts xiii. 47 applies another Servant Song (Isa. xlix. 6) to the apostles; 1 Pet. ii. 24 has a definite application to the death of Christ of the redemptive words (the solitary instance in the New Testament). But in Paul's writings, where one would expect much, there is little. Unless Phil. ii contains allusions to the Hebrew text of Isa. liii (and this, though certainly possible and even probable, is not demonstrable), the only other allusions are in Rom. iv. 25 and x. 16. The former is a definitely redemptive

---

[1] As well as M. D. Hooker, *op. cit.* p. 69, n. 1, see C. K. Barrett, 'The Background of Mark 10: 45' in *New Testament Essays, in mem.* T. W. Manson, ed. A. J. B. Higgins (1959), 1 ff.

allusion (but how fleeting!); the latter is a citation of Isa. liii. 1 in the interests of showing that Israel's obduracy was all along recognized by scripture as something to be expected and reckoned with.[1]

Thus, a passage of scripture that might have been expected to contribute signally to the formation and shaping of Christian apologetic is singularly rare. One can only surmise that it had somehow been vitiated for this purpose—that it had already been spoilt or blunted as an argument directed to the Jews, by some circumstances no longer clearly discernible to us. Jeremias has argued that Isa. liii had in pre-Christian times been applied by some to the Messiah (or to God's chosen Deliverer in some form), and that it was because the Jews realized too clearly its applicability to Jesus that they reacted against this and began to impose on the passage a quite different interpretation. Later rabbinical interpretations show how the suffering had, by then at least, been applied to the Jews' enemies, and only the exaltation and glory to their own nation or its representative.[2] If such interpretations began to be used very early in the Christian period, it is possible to imagine why Christian apologists seldom appealed much to Isa. liii: they knew in advance how their exegesis of it would be countered by their opponents. But this would still go only a little way towards explaining why the traditions about the words of Jesus himself show so little direct trace of its use by him; for the contents of these traditions are at other points by no means wholly conditioned by what the Church seems to have found useful or interesting for itself; and if Jesus had often quoted Isa. liii, one would expect that, even after it had been largely abandoned by Christian apologetic, it would still survive among his words. Jesus' life, death, and resurrection were clearly recognized by the Church (and, the evidence seems to suggest, by himself also) as redemptive: this is the Gospel of Paul, of Peter, of the Epistle to the Hebrews,

---

[1] Jeremias, reviewing M. D. Hooker (as cited on p. 69, n. 1) in *J.T.S.*, n.s., xi (1960), 140 ff., complains that 'she treats the New Testament like a mosaic and examines each stone separately', and that she ignores the allusions over and above the direct quotations, such as πολλοί, ὑπέρ, or ἀντί etc.

[2] See W. Zimmerli and J. Jeremias, *op. cit.* p. 20, n. 2; and note especially the apparently messianic interpretation of Isa. lii. 14 implied by one of the Qumran texts (1Q Isa. A): see F. F. Bruce, *op. cit.* p. 64, n. 1, 56.

and of the Johannine writings, even if one leaves out of account the Synoptists and Acts. Yet the only clearly redemptive-suffering passage in the Jewish scriptures is only sparingly used. Here is a phenomenon that still awaits explanation.

Enough, however, has perhaps been said to indicate, by a few selected examples, how the scriptures entered into early Christian apologetic, until sooner or later whole tracts, such as Rom. ix-xi and the Epistle to the Hebrews and Matthew were the result.

Outside and beyond the New Testament one finds other extended examples, such as the *Epistle of Barnabas*, Cyprian's work on testimonies, and Justin's Dialogue with Trypho. Comparison of these with the New Testament serves to throw into sharp relief the prevailing sanity and reserve of the New Testament.

But the mention of Cyprian is a reminder that it is relevant to our enquiry to ask whether we are to imagine the Christians of the New Testament period already, like Cyprian and Melito before him (Euseb. *H.E.* iv. 26), using 'testimony books'—anthologies of such Old Testament passages as were regarded as significant for Christians. J. Rendel Harris answered in the affirmative.[1] Working back from Cyprian's treatise on the Testimonies (*c.* A.D. 249), and observing such phenomena as the juxtaposition of the 'stone-passages' from Isa. viii and xxviii in Rom. ix and 1 Pet. ii, he suggested that the evidence pointed to the very early use of such testimony-books. More recently C. H. Dodd, followed by J. W. Doeve and others,[2] has argued that the New Testament data may be satisfied by postulating simply that, without necessarily using written anthologies at all, the Christians learnt to use whole sections of scripture in the light of the events they had experienced, and that these sections thus came to be associated together in their minds and on their lips. It is difficult, even so, to see, *prima facie*, any reason why written collections should not also have been in circulation, and M. D.

[1] J. R. Harris, *Testimonies* (1916, 1920).
[2] C. H. Dodd, *According to the Scriptures* (1952); J. W. Doeve, *Jewish Hermeneutics in the Synoptic Gospels and Acts* (*c.* 1953); E. E. Ellis, *Paul's Use of the Old Testament* (1957), 98 f. See also T. W. Manson, 'The Argument from Prophecy', *J.T.S.* xlvi (1945), 129 ff.; and B. Lindars, *New Testament Apologetic* (1961).

Hooker, *Jesus and the Servant* (1959), 21 ff., has questioned whether Dodd's claims can be upheld, at any rate, in the case of the Servant Songs.

If written testimony-collections were used, we are confronted once again with the long-debated suggestion that the Hebrew *logia* attributed by Papias to Matthew (Euseb. *H.E.* iii. 39. 16) were Old Testament *testimonia*. On the whole, however—even if we allow the probability that testimony-books circulated in early days—the likelihood is that Papias meant by *logia* sayings of Jesus, and that what he is describing is something like what critical scholarship has labelled 'Q'—a collection, or a group of collections, of sayings of Jesus, drawn upon in the compilation of the Gospels according to Matthew and Luke.[1] That such a sayings-collection should have been associated with Matthew the apostle is not *a priori* unlikely. At any rate, whatever answers are given to the questions whether there were testimony-books and whether the *logia* were Old Testament testimonies or sayings of Jesus, the important fact remains that early Christian writings took shape under the influence of Christian interpretation and application of Jewish scriptures. When it is claimed that whole sections in the Gospels were spun out of Old Testament material, this is far out-running the evidence. In the main, the evidence points to the Gospel events as the controlling and decisive factor, to which the Old Testament material is almost always subordinate. Here and there an Old Testament passage may have contributed some circumstantial detail in the recounting of a

[1] For the origin of the symbol Q, see W. F. Howard, *E.T.* 1 (1938–39); 379 ff. It is generally said to be derived from the German Quelle, 'source', but R. H. Lightfoot, *History and Interpretation in the Gospels* (1935), 27 n., relates how J. A. Robinson claimed that the symbol was first used by himself, chosen simply because (lecturing in Cambridge in the 'nineties) he was in the habit of using 'P' to denote Mark's Gospel as the reminiscences of Peter, and 'Q' was the natural symbol to use for the next document. W. F. Howard, however, points out that J. Weiss, as early as 1892, in *Die Predigt Jesu*, was using the symbol; and that there is a hint (though not a demonstration) that he borrowed it from his father Bernhard Weiss, since J. Weiss, in an essay contributed to *Studien und Kritiken* in 1891, writes (p. 248) of 'The Apocalyptic discourse, which we with Weiss and others derive from the Logia (Q) ...' J. A. Robinson's claim to be the inventor would thus, Howard maintains, fall to the ground; but the *reason* for the choice of the symbol still need not be assumed to be (the rather improbable one) that it stands for Quelle. It would not be specially natural in English to designate an unknown source 'S', merely because it was a source.

tradition about Jesus—the two beasts in Matthew's triumphal entry (Matt. xxi. 2, 5) provide a standard instance. Similarly, A. Guilding attributes the name Malchus in Jn xviii. 10 to the Old Testament lection which her theory finds behind this passage.[1] But it is questionable whether any story of Jesus in the New Testament has been generated, from start to finish, by nothing but an Old Testament passage.

On the contrary, the fact is rather that the choice of Old Testament passages is determined by the Christian events and their interpretation dictated by Christian tradition. Indeed, it is plausibly suggested (by Fr Barnabas Lindars[2]) that it was (for instance) the literal fulfilment of what he believes may have been Christ's own prediction that he would rise again 'on the third day' that the Christians first fastened upon; and that it was only secondarily that they attached it to Hos. vi. 2, although it may have been from here that Jesus himself drew the phrase (using it idiomatically to mean 'very soon').

The Christians thus found themselves pushed by the pressure of events into a new way of selecting, relating, grouping, and interpreting what we call 'Old Testament' passages;[3] and, while the scriptures of the Jews undoubtedly exercised a great influence upon the form in which they presented their material, and ultimately upon the very writing and collecting of the Christian scriptures, this influence was evidently subordinate both to the influence of the apostolic witness to Jesus and to the living inspiration of Christian prophets in the Church.

[1] A. Guilding, *The Fourth Gospel and Jewish Worship* (1960), 232.
[2] Barnabas Lindars, *New Testament Apologetic* (1961), 59 ff.
[3] There was as yet, of course, no defined 'canon' of scripture; and the books used by (e.g.) St Paul evidently included some that we now know as 'apocrypha' and even 'pseudepigrapha'.

## CHAPTER V

# THE CHURCH EXPLAINS ITSELF:
## (3) THE GOSPELS AND ACTS

IT has become fashionable to relate the Gospels of Matthew and Mark primarily to Christian worship, and Luke-Acts to apologetic.[1] But there is much to be said for finding apologetic as a prominent motive in all three Synoptic Gospels and perhaps also in St John's Gospel, in the sense that they constitute works of 'explanation'. Not that Matt. and Mk are at all likely to have been written as tracts for the unbeliever to read: they are undoubtedly Church-books. But even so they are most easily explainable as instruction, certainly for believers in the first instance, but with special reference to unbelievers: aids to Christians in explaining their faith and defending it when occasion offered.[2]

The attempts to relate Matt. and Mk primarily to worship are not wholly convincing. Carrington's theory that Mk follows a lectionary system does not seem to stand up to closer scrutiny; and although Kilpatrick makes possible the thesis that Matt. represents the adaptation of Christian traditions for reading at worship, Stendahl's thesis that it represents rather the work of a school of exposition is more plausible.[3] And, when one comes to think about it, it is obvious enough that, once someone had accepted the *kerygma*, he would need a filling out of it and (as it were) an 'embodiment' of the Jesus who had been thus

[1] See, e.g., G. D. Kilpatrick, *The Origins of the Gospel according to St. Matthew* (1946) (*contra* K. Stendahl, *The School of St. Matthew* (1954)); P. Carrington, *The Primitive Christian Calendar* (1940) (*contra* W. D. Davies in *The Background of the New Testament and its Eschatology*, (*in hon.* C. H. Dodd, 1956), 124 ff.) and *According to Mark* (1961); B. S. Easton, *Early Christianity: the Purpose of Acts and Other Papers* (ed. F. C. Grant, 1955).
[2] See C. F. D. Moule, 'The intention of the evangelists' in *New Testament Essays in mem. T. W. Manson*, ed. A. J. B. Higgins (1959).
[3] There are very wise reviews of the possibilities in S. E. Johnson's commentary on Mark (1960) and in F. V. Filson's Commentary on Matthew (1960).

briefly proclaimed as Lord. The evangelistic message of Paul, as we deduce it from references in his epistles, would have lacked the power to hold the affections and loyalty of the believer if it had never been reinforced by a portrait of the Lord in his words and deeds;[1] and, what is more, it would have been virtually impossible to explain Christianity to an enquirer or defend it against an antagonist without some circumstantial account of 'how it all happened'. It is all very well to say to the Jerusalem crowd very soon after the crucifixion that the Jesus whom they crucified has been made Lord and Christ (Acts ii. 36); but hearers remoter in time or place would necessarily ask, Who is this Jesus, and how came he to be crucified by his own people? And even the already converted would very soon ask, What is known about his story? What sort of words and deeds are connected with him? Why did he fall foul of his own people? It is in the context of such enquiry that the Gospels seem most likely to have taken shape.

Matt. has again and again been called the Gospel for the Jews. But it might more truly be called the Gospel against the Jews:[2] so much of it reads like ammunition for Christians to use when attacked by non-Christian Jews who say, Your Master was no Messiah (answer—yes, he was: of Davidic descent, fitting into the pattern of prophecy (Matt. i. 1 ff., and *passim*)); or,

[1] Cf. C. H. Dodd in E. H. Sneath (ed.), *The Evolution of Ethics* (1927), 300 ff., pointing out that Paul's ethics gain their concreteness and find a ready point of attachment in the figure of the historical Jesus, who loved us and died for us and is to be imitated. (It is worth while, in passing, however, to recall how little interest there appears to have been in antiquity in a *literal* portraiture of persons—whether pictorially or by description. The famous description of Paul's appearance in the *Acts of Paul and Thecla*, iii, is exceptional, and in any case, is comparatively late. Is the lack to be traced primarily to the Hebrew antipathy to visual representation?)

[2] '. . . A historical apology for the Nazarene and his Community as against Judaism'—Zahn, *Einleitung*, ii, 294, cited by P. Nepper-Christensen, *Das Matthäusevangelium* (1958), 13. n. 3. Similarly, Feine-Behm, *Einleitung*, 53, cited *ibid.*; so J. Schmid, *Das Evangelium nach Matthäus* (²1952), 24 f. and 27, describes it as a weapon for the readers to save them from falling too easy a victim to the Jews (also *apud* Nepper-Christensen, p. 35). Here Zahn takes the opposite view, holding it likely that 'Matthew chiefly wished to see his book read by non-believing Jews'. He thinks *also*, however, of Jewish Christians (more Jewish than Christian perhaps!) who would be flustered in debate with non-Christian Jews and would need this support (Nepper-Christensen, 15. n. 11). See also the fresh discussion by E. P. Blair, *Jesus in the Gospel of Matthew* (1960), e.g. '. . . it is obvious that the church was locked in bitter struggle with the synagogue . . .' (161).

Your Master was no true rabbi—he undermined the Law (answer—on the contrary, he set more rigorous standards than the Jewish rabbis (Matt. v. 17-20)); or, the Nazarenes' claim to be true Israel is false (answer—no, it is on the confession of Jesus as Christ that the assembly of Israel is built (Matt. xvi. 18)); or, What business have you to be going out to the Gentiles? (answer—the Lord, it is true, kept carefully within Israel during his own ministry, and directed his disciples accordingly; but his long-term sayings and his commission were universalist (Matt. viii. 11, x. 5, 23, xv. 26, xxviii. 19)). Here are just the sort of arguments that might have been used in such conflict, and it is easy to see Matt. as a text-book for Christians living very near (if not in) a Jewish ghetto: possibly 'near' rather than 'in', for it has been questioned whether the Christians from whom it springs were themselves Jewish. It is very clearly aimed *at* Jews: is it as clear that it is aimed *by* Jews? There are one or two details that seem surprising if they are assumed to have been written by one who knew the inside of Judaism.[1] On the other hand, admittedly, there is the famous allusion to the scribe turned Christian (Matt. xiii. 52), and a respect for the ideals of scribes (Matt. xxiii. 2, 34). Is it possible that Matt. represents the work of a thoughtful group of Christians (Stendahl's 'school')—a kind of 'study-group' (cf. p. 74, above)—comprising both Jews and Gentiles, who had together assembled the traditions (including Mark) and formulated the arguments and presented a portrait of Jesus such as would help them and their community in standing up to non-Christian Jews? Here is a body of Christians 'explaining' themselves as true Israel, *vis-à-vis* near neighbours who spit out their name as unclean. The target of attack is the 'hypocrite' which (for this community), means the non-Christian Pharisaic Jew, just as the *ethnikos* is the non-Christian Gentile.

No doubt we are bound to find room, in any account of how

---

[1] Matt. xxvii. 62: is it possible that the high priests and Pharisees would have gone to Pilate on the day after the Preparation—whether this means that the day in question was Passover day or Sabbath? Matt. iii. 7, xvi. 1, 6 ff: is this combination of Pharisees and Sadducees really plausible? Contrast the parallels in the other Gospels (where there are any).

See also K. W. Clark, 'The Gentile Bias in Matthew', *J.B.L.* lxvi (1947), 165 ff.

Matt. came to be and what it was for, for the persistent early tradition of a Semitic writing by the apostle Matthew.[1] The most often quoted form of that tradition is that in Papias (*apud* Euseb. *H.E.* iii. 39. 16), which speaks of 'the oracles' (τὰ λόγια), translated from the Semitic original by each reader as best he could. It seems to be widely agreed that the Gospel as we know it does not offer any clear evidence of being, as a whole, and in its more distinctive parts, a translation, and includes material which it is difficult to attribute to one of the Twelve. But it is difficult to see how the tradition of a Semitic and apostolic original sprang up at all if there is absolutely nothing behind it. It is simplest, probably, to postulate a Semitic apostolic sayings-collection—perhaps (as was said above, p. 84) the very one (usually called 'Q') which it appears Luke also used; and to assume that, at however many removes from the original, this contributed to the traditions drawn into our present Gospel. It still remains possible to see the Gospel as it now stands as a collection of 'explanations' for Christians to use among themselves for edification and in conflict with opponents.

If 'the oracles' are identified with some such early Semitic source lying behind both Matt. and Lk., then it is conceivable that Papias' allusion to diverse Greek versions ('each reader translated them as best he could') may help to explain some of the differences between Matt. and Lk. in these parallel passages.[2] This is not, of course, to deny that many differences—perhaps the majority—may be traced to the theological and other predilections of the editors or collectors (in their common use of Mk this is demonstrable); it is only to suggest that some of them may be accounted for as variant renderings of a common Semitic original. This would hold good in some measure at least, even if an extreme position were adopted, postulating (as is the tendency in Scandinavian scholarship) oral traditions rather than anything so rigid as a document ('Q').

One thing is clear about the enigmatic Gospel according to Matthew as we now have it: it embraces a considerable breadth

---

[1] See the texts collected by Nepper-Christensen, *op. cit.* p. 73, n. 1, pp. 210 f. (Euseb. *H.E.* iii. 24. 6, 39. 16; v. 8. 2, 10. 3; vi. 25. 4; Jerome, *De vir. ill.* iii, *In Matt.* II. xii, *Adv. Pelag.* iii. 2).

[2] See Excursus I: *Translation Greek and Original Greek in Matthew.*

of tradition, and no one absolutely consistent outlook can be extracted from it. It may be that the actual writer himself (or writers, if it was a group) had a consistent policy and outlook—for instance, approval of the evangelization of the Gentiles and a defence of the Christian Church as true Israel without making them proselytes. But respect for the traditions, and a desire to preserve them even when they could not be fitted into the scheme, have evidently weighed heavier than the desire for consistency. Hence particularist or rigorist sayings stand side by side with liberal and universalist ones. Perhaps the most glaring discrepancy is constituted by the presence within this Gospel of the famous saying in Matt. x. 23 'before you have gone through all the towns of Israel the Son of Man will have come'. Either the evangelist identified the coming of the Son of Man here with the Resurrection, despite other passages in which it seems clearly to relate to the remoter future; or he is interpreting the mission-charge of Matt. x without any relation to the context in the ministry of Jesus in which he has himself placed it, and applying it instead to his own contemporary situation; or he is faithfully preserving a saying found in his traditions, which (whether genuinely dominical or not) had ceased to have any relation to his own day; or, finally, the saying originally related to the 'coming of the Son of Man' in the crisis of the Jewish war.[1] Of these difficult choices, the last is perhaps the least difficult to believe.

There is another Matthean saying, already touched on (above, pp. 73, 89), which is notoriously difficult to fit convincingly into the scheme—the 'rigorist' one in v. 18 about the permanence of the law and the prophets: 'I tell you this: so long as heaven and earth endure, not a letter, not a stroke, will disappear from the Law until all that must happen has happened' (or, N.E.B. margin, 'before all that it stands for is achieved'). But it is possible that this was deliberately retained by the Evangelist from his traditions, in order to rebut charges levelled by Jews against Christians of undermining the high standards of Pharisaic Judaism. It would be as much as to say, Jesus himself set a maximum, not a minimum standard. Is not this a more likely

---

[1] See A. Feuillet, 'Les Origines et la signification de Mt 10, 23ᵇ', *Cath. Bib. Quarterly* xxiii. 2 (April 1961), 182 ff.

explanation than the one more usually offered [1] that it reflects strictures on antinomianism within the Matthean community? Is it not rather ammunition brought out from the armoury of the *logia* (though in this case not also used by Luke) against non-Christians who are attacking the Christians (as St Paul was attacked) for ruining Judaism?

If we view Matt. as a collection of traditions by a Christian group who may have had a definite view-point of their own and a definite defence to maintain against Jewish antagonists, but who yet were more anxious to preserve the traditions than to observe consistency everywhere, we shall perhaps be seeing it in its true light. It need hardly be added that its careful arrangement in topical sections makes plausible the idea that it was planned for the instruction of believers in their faith and its vindication. This is a manual (in this respect something like the *Didache*), a catechist's book: but it is for instruction in apologetic quite as much as in religion and morals. [2]

Mk, on a simpler scale, also furnishes material for explanation and defence. It shows how jealousy and antagonism arose; it points to the recognition of Jesus by the few as Christ and Son of God, and explains his rejection by the many. It contains a nucleus of the stories of his mighty deeds and words. It is not nearly so pointedly anti-Judaic as Matt.: it is suitable for the training of Christians generally, in explaining, whether to Jews or Gentiles, how it all began, and why they hold Jesus to be Christ and the Son of God. It opens with a *pesher*-style application of scripture (for which see pp. 61 f., above)—including the very scripture in Isa. xl ('the voice of one crying . . .') which we now know was being used also in the Qumran circles (1QS,

---

[1] E.g. recently by Gerhard Barth in *Überlieferung und Auslegung im Matthäus-Evangelium*, by G. Bornkamm, G. Barth, and H. J. Held (1960), 149.

[2] See W. Trilling, *Das wahre Israel* (1959), for a very interesting presentation of the thesis that Matthew's aim is to present the Christian Church as the true Israel, for whom the Lordship of God is the Lordship of Christ, and whose mission is to all the world. Trilling takes the closing words of the Gospel as normative for its whole outlook. E. P. Blair, *op. cit.* p. 87, n. 2 above, makes the tentative suggestion that Matt. might be a sort of revision of Mk by one of the Hellenists, while Jn represents the Hellenists' tradition in purer form (157). But it is questionable whether O. Cullmann's speculations about the Hellenists (here presupposed) will support this construction.

viii. 12-16), combined with another scripture (Mal. iii. 1 or Exod. xxiii. 20); these are declared to apply to the circumstances of John the Baptist. And throughout this Gospel Old Testament *testimonia* occur. Mk is the apostolic *kerygma*—Old Testament evidence and all—built up into a vivid, narrative form.

Lk. and Jn, each in its own way, are different again. It is easier to imagine them as devised actually to be put into the hands of an opponent or a doubter, and not as dependent on verbal mediation by the Christian. If Matt. and Mk are instructions to help Christians to explain themselves, both to themselves and to others, Lk.-Acts, at any rate, is a single individual's direct address to a catechumen (as Theophilus may have been) and to others of his type—the people on the fringe, the outsiders who are looking enquiringly within; possibly even, through them, to really antagonistic readers also.[1] Not that it does not contain magnificent material for the building up of the Christian body; but if we are looking for primary purposes, it looks like something outward-aiming. It is most improbable that it would have been produced in many copies. Most likely the single autograph was handed to a single individual, Theophilus, only later to be copied (and perhaps embellished, as in the d-text). It is possible, admittedly, to exaggerate the apologetic character of Acts. From time to time it is described as though its one object was to prove to the Roman authorities (through His Excellency Theophilus) that Christianity has as much right to exist as Israel—or rather, that Christians alone *are* true Israel. It is doubtful (cf. p. 122, below) whether Luke would have done exactly what he has done if that had been his single aim. Without denying this motive as a contributory element, it is nearer the mark to see the Acts as, in the main, a grand vindication of the will of God. It is the story of the minute but mighty mustard-seed; it is the narrative of the Holy Spirit championing and vindicating the cause of Christ in such a way that prison-bars

[1] C. H. Roberts, in his Sandars Lectures at Cambridge, February 1961, pointed out that the first Christian books found on rolls, in contrast to the usual Christian codex, are Luke and Acts—pointing, possibly, to their design for a non-Christian public. He hazarded the guess (contrary to my guess later in this paragraph) that the d-text might represent this 'public' edition, and the b-text a more restrained revision for Christian use. M. Dibelius, *Studies in the Acts of the Apostles* (Eng. trans., 1956), 89 f., traces the wide variations in the text of Acts to its 'secular' currency.

go down like clay before the divine decree; or, if a witness of the Gospel does lay down his life, then it turns out positively to be to the furtherance of the very cause that the enemy is putting to the sword. The whole story runs to its climax through storm and shipwreck, the plotting of evil men and the attack of the serpent: nothing can prevent the 'chosen vessel' from achieving God's design.[1]

Here, then, in the Synoptic Gospels and Acts, each with its peculiar emphasis, may be found the deposit of early Christian explanation: here are the voices of Christians explaining what led to their existence—how they came to be: telling the story to themselves, that they may tell it to others, or even telling it directly to those others.

What may be said about the genesis and purpose of St John's Gospel, the great enigma? It declares of itself that its object is to aid belief (xx. 31). Does that mean to strengthen belief in the already believing, or to create belief in the unbelieving? This is a familiar problem, and almost certainly cannot be settled on purely grammatical grounds. The clause (in either of its two variant forms) could, if need be, mean either or both.[2] If we are to find an answer at all, it must be in the character of the Gospel (and its related epistles) as a whole. Recently, some strong bids have been made to have it as a Gospel for Jews—diaspora Jews, who are offered a brilliant representation of early Palestinian traditions of high historical worth in such form as to speak to their needs and hesitations and compel their attention.[3] But it is almost impossible to explain certain phenomena if it was meant for Jews exclusively: that the Passover was a Jewish Festival is

---

[1] H. Chadwick, *The Circle and the Ellipse*, 16. A very valuable estimate of the purpose of Luke-Acts is to be found in C. K. Barrett, *Luke the Historian in Recent Study* (1961).

[2] See a discussion of the issue in C. H. Dodd, *The Interpretation of the Fourth Gospel* (1953), 9.

[3] W. C. van Unnik, 'The Purpose of St. John's Gospel' in *Studia Evangelica* (papers at 'Four Gospels Conference' Oxford, 1957, *T. und U.*, 73, 1959); also in *The Gospels Reconsidered* (a selection from the above, 1960), 167 ff.; J. A. T. Robinson, 'The New Look on the Fourth Gospel', *ibid.* 338 ff.; 'The Destination and Purpose of St. John's Gospel', *J.N.T.S.* 6. 2 (January 1960), 117 ff.; and, for a survey of views, A. J. B. Higgins, *The Historicity of the Fourth Gospel* (1960). For arguments which, while recognizing much material appropriate to Jews, lay considerable emphasis also upon a Gentile apologetic, see C. H. Dodd's *The Interpretation of the Fourth Gospel* (1953).

scarcely a gloss that such would need. It is easier to see it as meant for Jew and Gentile alike, and to read the glosses—so painfully elementary even for Jews of the dispersion—as put in for the benefit of Gentiles.

More important is its general outlook and approach. This Gospel, unlike the others, answers the question, 'What must I do to be saved?' The others mainly confine themselves to the story of discipleship; the Fourth Gospel speaks in terms not only of following and imitation, but of belief and incorporation. What is less often noticed is that it also answers the question 'What must *I* do . . .'—it is an extremely individualistic message. Whereas St Paul sees Jesus as the New Humanity, the incorporative Body in which all are organically connected limbs, the one in whom the resurrection of all mankind has actually taken place, St John sees Jesus as the source of life, to be connected with whom is, for each individual, life eternal. He sees the Holy Spirit in each heart as the presence of the Lord, and he can speak already of fulfilment in this realm precisely because he does move on the individual level. He does not deny a general resurrection at the last day or a coming of the Lord at the end. But he is concerned with the individual's faith and contact with the Lord of life now. Here is a Gospel that—to that extent—could be readily accepted by the Gentile mind. Perhaps it is the evangelist's explanation of Christianity to the cosmopolitan people of Ephesus, Jew and Greek alike.[1]

Yet it also contains tough polemic against Jews. The conflict of Jesus with his antagonists, especially in Chapters vii, viii, and ix, is reminiscent of the sternest Jewish controversy of other parts of the New Testament, including some of the Pauline Epistles, and Matt. In Chapter ix the story of the man born blind seems to be told in such a way as to typify the consequences of Christian baptism in an antagonistic Jewish setting. The human condition of being born in sin (*v.* 34) is equivalent to being (spiritually) blind from birth (*v.* 1). Enlightenment (or Baptism) comes from washing in water which is (like Christ himself) divinely 'sent' (*v.* 7). Perhaps even baptismal anointing is hinted at by the ἐπέχρισεν ('smeared') of *v.* 11 (though in *v.* 6 it is

---

[1] See C. F. D. Moule, 'The Individualism of St John's Gospel', *Nov.T.* (*Festheft* for E. Stauffer) (1961), forthcoming.

ἐπέθηκεν, simply 'applied'.) There follows the simple Christian witness, 'once I was blind, now I can see' (v. 25); and ultimately this is found to imply the basic Christian confession—belief in Jesus as Son of God (? or Son of Man, the reading is uncertain) and Lord (vv. 35-38). The inevitable result of 'enlightenment' is ostracism and excommunication from the synagogue (vv. 22, 34). Thus, although the order of events is not accommodated precisely to the pattern of baptism, the scattered phrases and the total picture add up to an irresistible impression that a genuine piece of dominical tradition is being retold in the light of the prevailing conflicts. And it is easy to believe the same of Chapters vii and viii, as well as of other less extended passages here and there.[1]

Here, then, may be good traditions of the actual controversies of Christ's own life-time, preserved and re-set in such a way as to be entirely topical to the evangelist's own circumstances. In a city like Ephesus, the mystic and the rabbinic Jew, the gnostic and the ebionite jostled one another: and the story of the Word of God incarnate, with his mighty words and luminous deeds had messages for all.

In all four Gospels, the passion narrative is a prominent and proportionately large component part. In none of them is it told in such a way as to make the redemptive aspect of the death of Christ particularly obvious, although the Old Testament allusions make it clear that the whole story is treated as the fulfilment of God's design of salvation for his people—so much so that its very opponents unconsciously help to weave the pattern. Once again, then, it is an explanatory or an apologetic purpose that seems to underlie the telling; and this indeed seems to be served not only by the Old Testament allusions but also by what is ostensibly straight narration. It is precisely the apologetic purpose that has, according to one of the latest of the numerous reconstructions, grossly distorted the trial narratives of the Gospels. P. Winter argues[2] that Jesus was really condemned by the Roman Governor as an insurgent, and that the Gospels, in declaring Jewish complicity in his death, only reflect a period

[1] See C. H. Dodd, 'A l'arrière-plan d'un dialogue johannique', *Rev. d'Hist. et de Philos.* l (1951), 5 ff.
[2] P. Winter, *On the Trial of Jesus* (1961). Contrast J. Blinzler, *Der Prozess Jesu* (³1960).

when the Christians were trying to ingratiate themselves with the government by as far as possible exonerating the Romans. This, quite apart from the difficulty of dismissing so much that is circumstantial as though it were mere fabrication,[1] does less than justice to the evidence, indicated above (pp. 40 f.), that Jesus' way of life and teaching were already recognized during his ministry as dangerous to Pharisaic Judaism; and, in its measure, the story of St Paul also, as it is presented in the Acts, is extremely difficult to discount as evidence that the Christian position is basically such that it must rouse opposition from the Jewish side. It makes much better sense of the trial narratives— whatever their undeniable difficulties and discrepancies in detail —to accept the motive of Jewish antagonism as historical. A credible story emerges if only we may assume that the Jewish gravamen was 'blasphemy' (or some form, at any rate, of false teaching), but that the Jews did not choose (even if they had it in their power)[2] to execute the sentence of death, but preferred instead to get Jesus crucified by the Romans as a rebel. This would be intelligible as a very skilful attempt on the part of the Jewish leaders to remove a popular but dangerous figure without incurring unpopularity for themselves. At any rate, one of the primary motives behind the stories of the trials and the crucifixion is likely enough to have been simply that of explaining how Jesus came to be crucified although Son of God and Messiah.

[1] See an interesting and sympathetic review article, 'Neue Forschungen über den Prozess Jesu', by H. van Dyen, *Christlich-jüdisches Forum*, 26 (May 1961), 1 ff.

[2] For a recent discussion of this problem, see P. Winter, *op. cit.*

## CHAPTER VI

# THE CHURCH EXPLAINS ITSELF:
## (4) THE REIGN OF CHRIST

'BUT where is your Messiah?' Just as the grosser idolaters had pointed derisively at the Jews' empty shrine until they were forced to exclaim 'As for our God, he is in heaven' (Ps. cxv. 3), so the non-Christians, both Jew and Gentile, naturally asked the Christians what had become of the King whom they alleged to have been raised from death. And, within their own hearts, the Christians had to meet the same question. If Christianity was to explain itself, one of the foremost difficulties that it had to explain was the invisibility of the Christians' Lord, and the patent fact that his reign of peace was not yet implemented.

According to the Acts and Jn xxi, there was a period after the crucifixion during which Jesus showed himself alive to chosen witnesses, though not to any others (Acts i. 1-11, x. 40 f., xiii. 31, Jn xxi); and it was during this period that they actually entertained hopes that at any moment he might manifest himself to the whole world and restore supremacy to Israel: 'Lord, is this the time when you are to establish once again the sovereignty of Israel?' (Acts i. 6).

When this hope proved illusory, and he was finally and decisively withdrawn from sight, they looked forward to a very speedy return. And the vivid manifestation of power and confidence at Pentecost was hailed as an interim gift from the exalted Lord, until the consummation of God's plan, when Jesus would return (Acts ii. 33, iii. 21).

And there is little doubt that this was the prevailing pattern of expectation for a long time—as indeed, *mutatis mutandis* (and *extensis extendendis*), it still is in many Christian hearts to this day: Christ, exalted to God's throne in heaven, destined to descend again at the end, and in the meantime represented on earth by apportionings of his Spirit and power; the Church, meanwhile, being charged with the task of spreading the good news and winning converts.

That, basically, is the pattern of Paul's expectation throughout his extant epistles. However much his inspired understanding deepens the theological and religious meaning of the Spirit, it is still true of Paul's view that to be incorporated in Christ is to possess a citizenship in heaven, whence we expect Christ to come as Saviour (Phil. iii. 20). Christ dwells by his Spirit among us now: to cry 'Abba! Father!' is to be enabled to utter, by God's Spirit, the cry of Christ's filial obedience (Rom. viii. 15, Gal. iv. 6). But this is yet to be consummated at the revealing of God's sons: the Holy Spirit is still only the pledge and first-fruits of something in the future (Rom. viii. 21-23, 2 Cor. i. 22, Eph. i. 14).

Even St John's Gospel, often taken to represent the complete exchange of future expectation for present realization, with the coming of the Paraclete replacing the return of Christ, really goes no further than to stress the importance *on the individual level* of the present indwelling of the Spirit.[1] To each individual who responds there is already a coming of the Holy Spirit; already the disciple is where Christ is. But there is nothing here to replace the corporate consummation of the whole People of God as a future event. And it is becoming clear that it would be a gross oversimplification to arrange New Testament eschatology as an evolutionary tree, with a primitive *parousia*-expectation at its roots, with St Paul as an important transitional stem, and with the Fourth Gospel as the ripe fruit of developed and integrated thinking at the top. The already 'realized' coming of Christ in St John is only on the individual level, and it requires comparatively little lapse of time or development of thought to attain to that conviction. Conversely, a vivid expectation of a future consummation is perfectly compatible with a doctrine of the Spirit on an even deeper level than the Johannine: that is proved by Rom. viii.

Thus the New Testament, taken as a whole, offers us little deviation from this essentially simple pattern: Jesus has been declared the royal Son of God by the resurrection (Rom. i. 4):

[1] See C. F. D. Moule, 'The Individualism of St John's Gospel', *Nov.T.* (*Festheft* for E. Stauffer), forthcoming.

God has made him both Lord and Christ (Acts ii. 36). Already he reigns in the hearts of his own. But he has passed from sight without yet being universally recognized and acclaimed. It is for the Church, empowered by the Holy Spirit, to work for this end (Acts i. 7 f., etc.).

Therefore, if the Christian is asked, or asks himself, 'Where is your King? Why is not his reign evident?' he is bound to reply that the Kingdom, though indeed inaugurated, is not yet consummated. The clearest expression of this is in 1 Cor. xv. 25, 'he is destined to reign until God has put all enemies under his feet' (the allusion is to Ps. cx); and its conclusion (*v.* 28) that when this is achieved, then Christ himself will be subjected to God, is (in the light of later credal formulations) startlingly 'subordinationist' (cf. 1 Cor. xi. 3, where there is a kind of hierarchy, 'God-Christ-man-woman'). But, though more faintly, the same idea seems to make itself just audible in Rev. xi. 15, where the sovereignty of the world is declared to have 'passed to our Lord (God) *and his Christ*'—implying some consciousness of a distinction. So in Matt. xxv. 31 ff., there may be some relics of an awareness of 'the kingdom of Christ' as distinguishable from 'the Kingdom of God'.[1] If so, however, Rev. iii. 21 shows how, side by side with such a notion, the conception of the equal kingship of Christ and of God can occupy the thoughts ('I myself was victorious and sat down with my Father on his throne'); and it is doubtful whether even those Pauline passages indicate more than a recognition that the Church is living in an interim-stage, waiting for the consummation and implementation of Christ's victory which is God's victory. The Pauline formula which describes Christians as 'in Christ' rather than 'in God' is comparable: and, significantly, the sole instance of his using the double formula, 'hidden with Christ in God' (Col. iii. 3) is in a context of eschatological expectation.

Relevant to the same issue is the New Testament attitude to the conquest of the demonic powers by Christ. Cullmann[2] has argued that Christians saw the cross as the conquest of the

---

[1] See C. H. Dodd, 'Matthew and Paul', in his *N.T. Studies* (1953), 53 ff. (originally published in *E.T.* 1947).

[2] O. Cullmann, *The State in the New Testament* (1957).

malign powers, who thenceforth are reduced to obedient servitude—so much so that now it is a positive duty for Christians to obey and be subject to them as servants in Christ's kingdom. C. D. Morrison, on the contrary, argues[1] that, although, on the Christian showing, Christ always had been and is eternally supreme over the 'powers', his death, in itself, made no difference to their temporary ascendancy, but only relieved Christians, as such, from the necessity of submitting to their tyranny. The most problematic verse for Morrison's position is Col. ii. 15 ('on that cross . . . he made a public spectacle of them . . .'), which seems very explicitly to define the cross as the occasion of the triumph over the powers. But in the main his position is convincing. In any case, what matters for the moment is that Christian speculation about these demonic angel-powers bears further witness to the sense of an interim-stage, awaiting the final consummation.

Closely related to the same is the sense that the evangelization of the world must be achieved before the consummation can come. The Acts narrative seems to run along this pattern (Acts i. 11, ii. 33, iii. 19 ff.), although, curiously enough, Lk. xxi. 24 speaks not of the evangelism of the Gentiles but (apparently) simply of a necessary quota of years during which the Gentiles must domineer over Jerusalem: '. . . Jerusalem will be trampled down by foreigners until their day has run its course'. Contrast with this the Matthean parallel: '. . . this gospel of the Kingdom will be proclaimed throughout the earth as a testimony to all nations; and then the end will come' (Matt. xxiv. 14—whether Mk xiii. 10 means the same is another matter).[2] At any rate, Paul clearly saw the evangelization of the Gentiles as the essential step towards the consummation: '. . . this partial blindness has come upon Israel only until the Gentiles have been admitted in full strength; when that has happened, the whole of Israel will be saved . . .' (Rom. xi. 25 f.).[3]

[1] C. D. Morrison, *The Powers that Be* (1960).
[2] See G. D. Kilpatrick, 'The Gentile Mission in Matthew and Mark xiii. 9-11', in *Studies in the Gospels* (ed. D. E. Nineham, *in mem.* R. H. Lightfoot, 1955).
[3] See J. Munck, *Paul and the Salvation of Mankind* (Eng. trans., 1959, of *Paulus und die Heilsgeschichte*, 1954).

Such variety as there is in the New Testament formulations of this interim-idea depends on the variety of situations addressed. There will be more to say about this when we come to consider error and heresy within the Church. But for the time being it is worth while to observe that there were two extremes in misunderstanding which had to be met. First, there were those who said that the resurrection (of Christians) had already taken place (2 Tim. ii. 18; cf. 1 Cor. xv and ? 2 Thess. ii. 2).[1] This was presumably a dualistic and 'gnostic' type of thinking: denying the reality or the importance of the material world and concentrating on the private religious experience of the individual soul, these heretics maintained that by baptism they were already made partakers of the risen life and that there was nothing further to follow. (They could quite easily have misunderstood the outlook represented by Jn in this sense.) In reply, Christians who were loyal to the apostolic witness maintained that the visible, resurrection-body of Jesus was the firstfruits and guarantee not of escape from this world, but of its redemption, and that they looked for a corporate event still in the future—the raising of all God's people together into a new life, 'the emancipation of the body' (not 'from the body', Rom. viii. 23). They affirmed corporate redemption as against individualistic escape.

Secondly, there were the 'scoffers' who said, 'You can wait forever and nothing will happen. Things are going on exactly as they were before. There will never be an end to the world.' The real mistake here is to make time the determining standard at all. The very form of the scoffing bears witness to a misunderstanding of the real issue. For the Christian's hope is not to be measured primarily in terms of lapse of time but in terms of the continuous working out to its completion of a *datum* already given—namely the incarnation.[2] New Testament eschatology at its deepest level concentrates upon entering into, implementing, loyally expressing that which is already given, which is Christ: it does not say, 'How long will it be before the whistle blows

[1] Cf. E. Schweizer, *Lordship and Discipleship* (as on p. 56, n. 3), 112, and see 28, n. 1.
[2] See J. A. T. Robinson, *Jesus and his Coming* (1957), where this point is finely made, even if one does not go all the way with other aspects of the argument.

"no side"?' but, 'Where ought I to be now, to receive the next pass?' In other words, the fact that the kick-off has taken place, that the game is on, and that we have a Captain who can lead us to victory, is all that matters. Yet, once the false question was formulated, it was difficult to avoid an answer in its own terms; and 2 Pet. iii. 8 shows us the application of Ps. xc. 4 as an *ad hominem* reply: God's time-scale is different; to him a thousand years are as a single day; therefore you cannot blame him for delay!

Whenever time-scale considerations come in, we seem to find unprofitable judgments. If the scoffers traded on 'delay' to draw false inferences, the opposite extreme—the oppressive sense that 'the time is short'—seems to have led Paul to some of his least enduring judgments. Both the expectation of a *parousia* the day after tomorrow and its postponement *sine die* seem to have led to unfruitful conclusions. But neither of these is characteristic of New Testament thought, which concentrates far more on the *datum*—on the fact that already the Kingship of Christ has been established, already the Kingdom of God has been inaugurated, and that the responsibility of the children of the Kingdom is to act here and now as those who are charged to bear witness to its reality.[1] And always at moments of Christian worship, time and space are obliterated and the worshipping Church on earth is one in eternity with the Church in the heavenly places:

. . . you stand before Mount Zion and the city of the living God, heavenly Jerusalem, before myriads of angels, the full concourse and assembly of the first-born citizens of heaven, and God the

---

[1] Cf. E. Schweizer, *Lordship and Discipleship* (as on p. 56, n. 3), 22 f.: 'It is possible that for a while the expectation of the approaching *parousia* suppressed any other questions. But we must say that this expectation has not exercised any substantial influence on the earliest summaries of the Church's faith.' E. Käsemann writes: 'The Johannine assertion that the judgment is already taking place was, *in nuce*, already anticipated in the Christian community of the earliest post-resurrection period, even if, in John, it is expressed in a form which is different from the point of view of the history of theological development'. ('Die Anfänge christlicher Theologie', *Z.Th.K.* 57. 2 (1960), 183 (my paraphrase)).

See also O. Cullmann, 'Unzeitgemässe Bemerkungen zum "historischen Jesus" der Bultmannschule' (from the Evangelische Verlagsanstalt, Berlin, 1960), 276, pointing out that in very few New Testament passages is the 'problem' of the delay of the *parousia* discernible as a *motive*.

judge of all, and the spirits of good men made perfect, and Jesus the mediator of a new covenant, whose sprinkled blood has better things to tell than the blood of Abel. (Heb. xii. 22ff.)

Thus, the future (in detail) was never the primary concern; it was the past leading to the present that occupied the attention of Christians when they were really Christian. And consequently, it is a mistake to read the New Testament as though the 'delay of the *parousia*' were a conditioning factor of essential importance—still worse to measure the chronological sequence of the writings by supposed developments depending upon it. There may be—there probably are—developments in *emphasis*:[1] but the general programme of expectation varies little; and even changes in emphasis are an unreliable measure of chronological development.

This is, perhaps, the most natural point at which to mention New Testament apocalyptic. While all Christian doctrine is inescapably eschatological (because of the Christian conviction of the finality and absoluteness of Christ as the eschaton, 'the ultimate'), eschatology is not necessarily nor always apocalyptic. Apocalypse—the anticipatory raising of the curtain to display the final scene—is a way of conveying, pictorially and in symbol, the conviction of the ultimate victory of God. And this particular form of teaching tends to take shape at times of stress or of tense expectancy, when the human resources of believers are more than ordinarily exposed in all their futility and helplessness, and when the human or demonic forces of tyranny seem to be making their last desperate bid for supremacy. Then it is that the seer is given to see, dramatically and in vast images, thrown up in boldest black and white on the screen of his vision, that

> Though the cause of evil prosper,
> Yet 'tis truth alone is strong;
> Though her portion be the scaffold,
> And upon the throne be wrong,
> Yet that scaffold sways the future,
> And, behind the dim unknown,
> Standeth God within the shadow,
> Keeping watch above his own.

[1] See C. H. Dodd, 'The Mind of Paul: Change and Development' in *New Testament Studies* (1953, but originally in *B.J.R.L.* 18. 1 (1934)), 69 ff.

Exactly so the seer of Dan. vii had perhaps seen the frail, defenceless human figure vindicated and invested with glory in the face of the bestial powers who stamped on him and crushed the life out of him:[1]

I saw in the night visions,
and behold, with the clouds of heaven
there came one like a son of man,
and he came to the Ancient of Days
and was presented before him.
And to him was given dominion
and glory and kingdom,
that all peoples, nations and languages
should serve him;
his dominion is an everlasting dominion,
which shall not pass away,
and his kingdom one
that shall not be destroyed. . . .

As I looked, this horn made war with the saints, and prevailed over them, until the Ancient of Days came, and judgment was given for the saints of the Most High, and the time came when the saints received the kingdom.

Such was God's message through apocalyptic to the Maccabaean martyrs and their generation. And in the New Testament, besides many apocalyptic phrases and sections interwoven with the rest, there stand out three main examples: the Revelation— a long, sustained piece of apocalyptic writing—the Gospel apocalypses (Mk xiii and the various parallels), and 2 Thess. ii.

Speculation on the origins of these three or more apocalypses is rife. The attempt of Caligula to introduce his image into the Temple, and the beginning of persecution in connexion with Emperor worship are the obvious crises by which to account for these manifestations; and these, and additional circumstances, call for further consideration in the next chapter.

[1] It is, of course, true that 'the human figure' ('one like unto a son of man') of Dan. vii is not described as crushed: indeed, at his first and only appearance, he is already invested with glory (v. 13). But the fact that, in the interpretation of the vision, he stands for 'the saints' against whom the tyrant makes war and prevails (v. 21), and the extremely probable application of the whole scene to the Maccabaean martyrs, warrants, I believe, the interpretation of the symbol as meaning the triumph, *through suffering and eclipse*, of those who have no armour but their inflexible loyalty. Cf. C. H. Dodd, *According to the Scriptures* (1952), 117, n. 2.

## CHAPTER VII

# THE CHURCH UNDER ATTACK

ACTIVE hostility to the Christian Church is a matter which is clearly relevant to our enquiry into the circumstances which led to the formation of the New Testament; for the attacks of opponents both give rise to certain types of document embodying defence or counter-attack, and also afford, from time to time, clues to chronological order and circumstances. The basic Christian Creed, 'Jesus is Lord' or 'Jesus is Christ' might well find a setting in a persecution context as well as in a baptismal;[1] and elaborations of that confession may be indicative of a particular period.

When we were considering the Church's explanation of itself, we found that it was *vis-à-vis* Judaism that such explanation was, in the main, required. And similarly the thesis of this chapter (which is concerned not so much with question and reply as with active attack and defence) is that Judaism bulks by far the largest among the antagonists of Christianity which have left their stamp upon the New Testament. It is a tragedy that 'the Israel of God' should have found its chief opponents from within Judaism—a tragedy made the more poignant when pre-Christian Judaism itself had had so noble a roll of martyrs to its credit, and indeed non-Christian Judaism was to continue to suffer at least obloquy and ridicule for its faith concurrently with Christianity.[2] But that is the fact. And, as we have already

---

[1] See O. Cullmann, *The Earliest Christian Confessions*, 1949, p. 27, (Eng. trans. of *Les Premières Confessions de foi chrétiennes*, ²1948), in which 1 Cor. xii. 3 is discussed in the light of such persecution as tried to make the Christians renounce their confession κύριος Ἰησοῦς in favour of κύριος Καῖσαρ and to say ἀνάθεμα Ἰησοῦς. I would doubt whether one needed to look as far as Caesar worship. If it is a persecution context, Acts xxvi. 11 is a more plausible one, where, before his conversion, Paul the scourge of the Nazarenes tries to compel them to blaspheme. But it is not easy to place 1 Cor. xii. 3 in a context of persecution at all.

[2] Horace, though slightly earlier, Juvenal, and Philo (*Legatio ad Gaium* and *In Flaccum*) provide evidence; and there is the expulsion of Jews from Rome by Claudius, Suet. *Claud.* 25. 4.

seen, the Christians were quick to realize that the persecution of a minority by the majority of the religious community to which they belonged was a phenomenon already deeply embedded in the Jews' own history: which of the prophets had not their forefathers persecuted (Acts vii. 52)? To make the situation more complicated, it appears to be true that the non-Christian Jews were most prone to persecute the Christians when Judaism was itself under attack by the Roman imperial authorities. The times when there was most tolerance were precisely the times when external pressure was at its least. Relations between Christians and Jews were strained to breaking-point most naturally when it was dangerous for the one to acknowledge any contact with the other.[1]

In the New Testament there are allusions to persecution, whether as forecasts or as narratives of events, in the Gospels and the Acts; and the other documents chiefly concerned are 2 Thess., the Pastoral Epistles, Hebrews, 1 Pet., and the Revelation. It will be well to look at these in turn.

All four Gospels contain allusions to impending antagonism against Christians, both on the private level, within households, and, publicly, on the level of both Jewish and Gentile courts (Mk xiii. 13 pars., Matt. x. 22, Lk. xii. 11, xxi. 12, Jn xvi. 2).[2] It is relatively immaterial, for our purposes, whether or not these allusions are genuine prophecies or whether they sprang, *post eventum*, from the actual occurrences. In either case they stand for the recognition of the elements of conflict at the heart of the Christian situation. The Fourth Gospel actually depicts the excommunication, during the ministry of Jesus, of the blind

---

[1] See the very suggestive essay by Bo Reicke, 'Der geschichtliche Hintergrund des Apostelkonzils und der Antiochia-Episode, Gal. 2: 1-14' in *Studia Paulina* (ed. J. N. Sevenster and W. C. van Unnik *in hon.* J. de Zwaan, 1953), 172 ff. 'He distinguishes three phases: (i) the thirties, when the young church was attacked both by the Jerusalem authorities and by the "Zionist" diaspora; (ii) the forties, when there came, first, Herod Agrippa I's persecution, favouring legalistic Jews, and then, under the Procurator, a corresponding recession of the stricter Judaism; (iii) the fifties, which saw the Zealot terrorism blaze up and the fuse lit which kindled the conflagration culminating in A.D. 70' (from my review in *J.T.S.*, n.s., v. (1954), 93).

[2] Lk. xii. 11, xxi. 12 does not mention *sunedria* although there were Sanhedrins even in the diaspora, because the Gentile Christian was more familiar with *synagogues*—A. Strobel, 'Zum Verständnis vom Rom 13', *Z.N.T.W.* 47 (1956), 73.

man who had received his sight. For refusing to declare Jesus a sinner, he is banished from the synagogue (ix. 34). It is questionable whether there is any inherent reason for declaring this to be unhistorical (xii. 42 mentions excommunications again in passing);[1] but it is certainly described in terms which make a type for all baptizands out of this blind man, who receives his sight through washing, at the behest of Jesus, in water described as (divinely) 'sent', and then is expelled by the Jews; and later in the same Gospel, excommunication and even death are promised to the faithful followers of Jesus (xvi. 2). (See above, pp. 94 f.)

Whether or not these allusions are *post eventum*, it is impossible to deny that Jesus himself was brought to book before both Jewish and Gentile tribunals. E. Stauffer has even made a persuasive case for the view that, long before his trial—indeed, during much of his ministry—the Jerusalem hierarchy and the rabbinic authorities had been systematically spying on him, setting traps for him, and collecting evidence against him as a teacher of error, and that he eventually came under their discipline on these grounds (see note 2, p. 41). In that same Chapter ix of St John, the Jews are said to have agreed (*v.* 22) that anyone who confessed Jesus as Messiah should be banned from the synagogue.

The pattern of Jesus' own life, with its provocation of fierce antagonism and its undeviating courage, was recognized by Christians as the norm for the lives of them all:

> Run the great race of faith and take hold of eternal life. For to this you were called; and you confessed your faith nobly before many witnesses. Now in the presence of God, who gives life to all things, and of Jesus Christ, who himself made the same noble confession and gave his testimony to it before Pontius Pilate, I charge you to obey your orders irreproachably and without fault until our Lord Jesus Christ appears. (1 Tim. vi. 12-14.)

> Remember Jesus Christ, risen from the dead, born of David's line. This is the theme of my gospel, in whose service I am exposed to hardship, even to the point of being shut up like a common criminal; but the word of God is not shut up. And I endure it all for the sake of God's chosen ones, with this end in view, that they

---

[1] Though W. Schrage, *T.W.N.T.*, *s.v.* ἀποσυνάγωγος, taking συναγωγή to mean the whole people, holds that the word can only reflect the ban on heretics, after A.D. 70.

too may attain the glorious and eternal salvation which is in Christ Jesus. Here are words you may trust:

> 'If we died with him, we shall live with him;
> If we endure, we shall reign with him.
> If we deny him, he will deny us.
> If we are faithless, he keeps faith,
>     For he cannot deny himself '.
>
> (2 Tim. ii. 8-13.)

Yes, persecution will come to all who want to live a godly life as Christians, . . .

(2 Tim. iii. 12.)

From the very beginning, therefore, Christians who had their eyes open set out on their way expecting antagonism and persecution. And, indeed, it had already been the lot not only of Jesus himself, but of John the Baptist, and of all the messengers of God before them. The story of the persecution of Christians is continuous with the story of their predecessors under the old dispensation, and they had ready to hand a considerable Jewish literature of martyrdom. In the books of Daniel and Judith, and in the Maccabaean stories, they could read of Jewish witness before the heathen; while in the legends of the Prophets were the patterns of heroes suffering at the hands of their own people. The writer to the Hebrews found solace in both. And simultaneously with the rise of the Christian literature, Philo the Jew was writing his indictment of Flaccus and his account of the deputation to Caligula, monuments of the contemporary Jewish witness in the face of pagan opposition.

So in the Acts the narrative of actual persecution begins: and from start to finish it is instigated by the Jews. When the Gentiles do join in, it is only in the unthinking manner of excited mobs (once, at least, their indiscriminate violence recoils upon the non-Christian Jews who are attacking the Christians, Acts xviii. 17), or because they momentarily imagine that their political peace is threatened. It is the Jews who are really the aggressors. (This is written in full and penitent realization of the terrible reversal of the roles in later history, when Jews suffered indescribably at the hands of Christians, as well as at the hands of atheists or men of other religions.) If one asks what New Testament references to the persecution of Christians are inescapably and demonstrably to be referred to Gentile action, there are extraordinarily few. Even the one reference which at first looks explicit, in 1 Thess. ii. 14, addressed to Christians at Thessalonica suffering at the hands of their own fellow-countrymen (ὑπὸ τῶν ἰδίων συμφυλετῶν) just as the Jewish Christians had suffered at the hands of Jews, tells us little to the contrary. Commentators *in loc.* such as Milligan and Rigaux are not prepared to interpret συμφυλέται rigorously in a racial sense, but think that it need only be a term of locality (so the 'Ambrosiaster' reads *concivibus*), and, if so, might actually include Jews. It would then, presumably, be necessary to interpret 'Ιουδαῖος also locally, as 'a Judaean'. At most, even if we do assume here the persecution of Gentile Christians by Gentile non-Christians, there is no reason to interpret it in a sense contrary to the circumstantial account of this persecution at Thessalonica in Acts xvii. 5, where Jews are expressly named as the instigators of others—as with the martyrdom of Polycarp a century later (see E. Stauffer, *Theology of the New Testament* (Eng. trans., 1955), note 65, citing *Mart. Polyc.* xiii. 1). The reason why, in this same passage in 1 Thess. ii, the final doom is said to be overtaking the Jews has been interestingly discussed by E. Bammel,[1] who conjectures that it was the expulsion of Jews from Rome that led Paul to think that the final dénouement was imminent. If this is correct, it throws a significant side-light on the interrelation between the persecutions of Jews and Christians.

There is no need here to dwell at length on the stories of persecution in Acts. It is enough to recall that, over and above the Thessalonian persecution just mentioned, all the others in Acts, from the persecution conducted by Paul before his conversion to the persecutions suffered by Paul and others, are uniformly traced to Jews or Jewish instigation, except a joint attack by Jews and Gentiles at Iconium (xiv. 5), and the attacks at Philippi (xvi. 19 ff.) and Ephesus (xix. 23 ff.). The one at Philippi starts for purely mercenary reasons and significantly ends with a complete vindication of the apostles and abject apologies from the Roman authorities. So at Ephesus, it is commercial anxiety that precipitates the attack, and it is civic authority that declares it unjustified. When Roman local judicial

---

[1] 'Judenverfolgung und Naherwartung', *Z.Th.K.* 56 (1959), pp. 294 ff.

procedure does come upon the scene, it is (with the special exceptions of Philippi and Ephesus) invariably the result, as with the trial of Jesus himself, of agitation by the Jews; it invariably leads to a verdict of 'not guilty', and if a Roman official, such as a Felix or a Festus, does try to play into the the hands of the Jews, it is confessedly unconstitutional and immoral. The allusion to Roman beatings in 2 Cor. xi. 25 (τρὶς ἐραβδίσθην) need not fall outside such situations as these.

So far, then, as our only New Testament narratives go, there is no predisposition to expect other than Jewish origins for persecution. And if it is objected that the Acts is biassed in this respect, because it is a studied apologia to the Roman government, the burden of proof rests with those who try to discredit its reliability here. What do our other documents reflect?

Within the Pastoral Epistles, 2 Tim. is the only one containing more or less direct allusion to persecution. In 2 Tim. i. 8, ii. 3, iv. 5, Timothy is bidden accept his share of the suffering involved in the preaching of the Gospel; in ii. 9-12, he is reminded of the apostle's own sufferings as typical of confessional Christianity, and again in iii. 11 they are mentioned, with the corollary, 'Yes, persecution will come to all who want to live a godly life as Christians'. But although the apostolic example admittedly includes imprisonment, which, as we know was generally not Jewish but Roman (Acts v. 18, xii. 4 are exceptions), it has to be remembered that in so far as it was Roman it was protective custody rather than penal. The point of the example, therefore, is simply that the apostle is suffering for his Christian witness even to the length of imprisonment: there is no necessary implication that what Timothy is facing is Roman persecution. On the contrary, the apostle's own predicament is traceable entirely to Jewish antagonism; and indeed Gal. v. 11, vi. 12 had already expressly referred to 'persecution' for not 'preaching circumcision'. The same applies to the allusion in 1 Tim. vi. 13 to the example of Jesus himself, who, before Pontius Pilate made his noble confession. The point need lie in no more than the courageous witness before a high authority; it is no necessary deduction that Timothy is himself facing persecution from the imperial authorities. That the threat of such persecution is by this time a real one may, however, be surmised from the Christology of these epistles. It is well known that they use terms and titles for Christ (e.g. 'God our Saviour' and his 'appearing') which, far more explicitly than those of the acknowledgedly Pauline Epistles, seem to have an eye upon the rivalry of an imperial cult. It is not difficult to believe that the menace of this rivalry is here throwing its shadow over the Christian consciousness: but it is impossible to be sure of more.[1] In Tit. iii. 1 Christians are still urged to be obedient to government authorities.

What of the persecutions alluded to in the Epistle to the Hebrews? The most explicit allusion is in x. 32 ff., where the readers are bidden recall the former days when, after their enlightenment (i.e. their conversion and baptism), they endured a great Marathon of sufferings, whether they were actually themselves made a spectacle as they endured insults and afflictions, or whether they took the side of others who were being subjected to such treatment; for indeed—it continues—they had shared the sufferings of the prisoners and had submitted to the seizure of their property. Further, that there were still, at the time of writing, Christians suffering imprisonment and distress is indicated by xiii. 3, where the readers are exhorted to remember such and to enter with them into their distresses; by xiii. 18 f., which hints that the writer himself may be a prisoner, though expecting release; and by xiii. 23 which announces that Timothy 'has been released'. Finally, in xii. 4, in the course of an extended exhortation to the patient endurance of disciplinary suffering, they are reminded that in their conflict and struggle with sin they have not yet reached the point of shedding their blood; and xiii. 7, the allusion to their leaders' faithful departure from life, looks uncommonly like an allusion to the martyrdom of their original leaders.

All this, whatever its obscurities in detail, at least yields a clear picture of Christians suffering violence and put in prison,

[1] See, however, A. D. Nock in *J.T.S.*, n.s., xi (1960), 64 f., questioning whether the Christian *euaggelion*, good news, was meant in conscious rivalry to the 'good news' of the Caesar cult and whether there is not a misunderstanding of the pagan use of *Soter* ('which is very far from having in its ordinary usage the exalted connotation which it had for the early Christians') in the application of 'Erlösungsreligion' to the Caesar cult. See further C. D. Morrison, *The Powers that Be* (1960), *passim*, and especially 92 f.; and, for the meaning of *Soter*, 134 f.

both in the past and present, with the possibility of martyrdom ahead of them, and perhaps its example behind them. So far as can be seen, this would all be satisfied, in every detail, if one postulated, as has been suggested already, that the origins of this Christian group lay in the circle of Hellenistic Christianity in Jerusalem to which Stephen had belonged and of which he had even perhaps been the founder and martyr-hero. If, as the Acts tells us, a severe persecution had ensued, leading to a dispersion—a Christian 'diaspora'—there is every reason to believe that many members would have cause to look back on the seizure of their property, on imprisonments (such as Paul himself inflicted in his role as scourge of the Nazarenes, Acts viii. 3, ix. 2, xxii. 19, xxvi. 22, Gal. i. 13), and on other sufferings; while at the present time they would be still liable, like Paul the Christian apostle and many other contemporaries or near contemporaries, to similar treatment. There is no trace here of any circumstances that need have lain outside the scope of Jewish violence or even Jewish constitutional procedure against heretics within their midst. There is not the slightest hint of anything that requires state persecution to account for it. Even if we assume that the writer was, and Timothy had been, in Roman custody, this still need be in no way different in origin and circumstances from St Paul's Roman imprisonment to which he was driven by Jewish opposition (Acts xxviii. 19).

As for 1 Peter, this is a well-known storm centre of dispute. Here and here only in the New Testament we meet express allusion to potential suffering ὡς Χριστιανός, 'for being a Christian' (1 Pet. iv. 16), and that, in contrast with suffering as a murderer or a thief or a criminal (κακοποιός—or 'a magician'?) or as ἀλλοτριεπίσκοπος. The last term is of uncertain meaning; but it is sufficiently clear at any rate that, whereas the Christians are warned against the scandal of becoming involved in penalties for ethical misconduct, they are told not to be ashamed if the charge is simply that they are (to use the opprobrious or scornful term invented by their opponents) *Christianoi*. Indeed, they are to welcome it as a chance to bring honour to God for the name (ἐν τῷ ὀνόματι τούτῳ). It is not surprising that this has been interpreted as a reference to some situation in which it was actually an indictable offence to be a Christian, and the celebrated correspondence between Pliny and Trajan (c. A.D. 112) has been appealed to as the closest parallel. Pliny (*Ep.* x. 96) actually enquires 'whether punishment attaches to the mere name (*nomen ipsum*) apart from secret crimes, or to the secret crimes connected with the name' (*flagitia cohaerentia nomini*), stating that he had, in fact, condemned some simply for persisting in the claim that they were Christians, because he believed that 'in any case obstinacy and unbending perversity deserve to be punished'. The Emperor replied that, although they were not to be sought out, yet, if properly accused and convicted of being Christians, they must be punished unless they recanted. The distinction here drawn between 'the name itself' and crimes associated with the name seems at first sight to provide a striking parallel to the passage in 1 Pet. And it has been noted further[1] that the exhortation in 1 Pet. iii 15 f. to give one's Christian witness boldly but with meekness and deference (ἀλλὰ μετὰ πραΰτητος καὶ φόβου) is reminiscent of Pliny's objection to the opposite qualities, *pertinacia et inflexibilis obstinatio*, in the Christians whom he condemned. It must be observed in passing that *pertinacia* and *obstinatio*, if they mean inflexible adherence to the Christian confession, are not really incompatible with meekness and deference, and that the Christians condemned by Pliny do not in fact seem to have shown any qualities other than 1 Pet. approves: this particular parallel is, therefore, more apparent than real. But the main question is whether 1 Pet. reflects a situation in which to be a Christian was itself an indictable offence.

That to be a Christian might lead to suffering is clear enough (although in 1 Pet. iii. 13 f. this is declared to be unlikely). The only question is whether the suffering in view is the constitutional sentence of a Roman or a Jewish court, or is the rough justice of unofficial action. It can, of course, be argued that, since in 1 Pet. iv. 15 'as a Christian' is parallel with 'as a murderer', etc., it follows that being a Christian is an indictable offence comparable to being a murderer. But it is extremely questionable whether this is a fair inference. The word 'suffer' can include both the penalties of a sentence in a court and the sufferings (say) of victims of mob violence; and the phrase in

[1] J. Knox in *J.B.L.* lxxii (1953), 187 ff.

I Pet. iv. 15 might mean: 'do not get into the courts for criminal conduct or even suffer unpopularity or violence for anti-social behaviour of any sort; but if you suffer unpopularity or violence for being a Christian, there is nothing to be ashamed of—rather it is an opportunity to bring honour to God for the name'. More probably still, however, even the charge of murder and the rest is not meant to reflect a constitutional indictment in court but is typical of the taunts of popular spite, that Christians are murderers, cannibals, fornicators, and atheists (see, e.g. Tacitus, *Ann.* xv. 44. 25; Tertullian, *Apol.*, *passim*); and that what the writer means is that Christians must give no handle whatever for calumnies of this sort: they must be beyond reproach in conduct; their only offence must be their allegiance to Christ.

Thus, on careful scrutiny, there is nothing even here to warrant the assumption of a setting or a date in which Christianity was an officially indictable crime; and the conditions are satisfied by precisely the circumstances we have already seen in the Acts: Jewish agitation leading to general unpopularity and suspicion, and then to mob violence, if not to Roman intervention. It remains, however, entirely possible that at the time of this writing pagan opposition to Christianity is gaining in intensity, even without official backing, as it becomes more evident that the Christians will not acquiesce in the imperial cult. Long before any official Roman persecution *eo nomine* need be invoked,[1] one may imagine situations in which some Christian communities were threatened, others actually subjected to unofficial persecution, private antagonism, and mob violence: and, as a matter of fact, a case can be made for I Pet. containing two letters of encouragement, one addressed to Christians under the threat of such attack, the other especially designed for Christians in the actual flame.[2]

There remains the Apocalypse. It is widely recognized that Rev. xiii contains allusions to the emperor cult, veiled as thinly as possible—perhaps too thinly for prudence. Moreover, the titles of Christ in this writing seem (like those in the Pastoral Epistles already mentioned, but to an even clearer degree) to

[1] For a discussion of the grounds for Nero's persecution of the Christians, see A. Momigliano in the *Cambridge Ancient History*, x. 725, 887 ff.

[2] J. H. A. Hart, *I Peter* (*Expositor's Greek Testament*, 1910), and C. F. D. Moule in *J.N.T.S.* 3. 1 (Nov. 1956), 1 ff.

reflect a studied rivalry with the Emperor. Yet even here it is a remarkable fact that, as distinct from other parts, the letters to the seven churches (Rev. i-iii), unless it be in the one allusion to a Christian martyr at Pergamum 'where Satan lives' (ii. 13), reflect only Jewish antagonism. From within the Church, they reflect plenty of scandalous concessions to Gentile immorality: the Christian communities are clearly battling against the inroads of terrible antinomian licentiousness; but so far as danger from without goes, it is entirely located in the bitter antagonism of Judaism—those who call themselves Jews but are in reality the synagogue of Satan (ii. 9). Not a scrap of evidence can be extracted from these letters—if we were to confine ourselves to them—that persecution connected with the imperial cult has begun, unless we believe (and why should we?) that Antipas' death can have been for no other cause. From Chapter xiii one does gain a different picture. Rev. xiii. 16 seems to suggest actual civic disability or boycotting of some sort attaching to a refusal to accept pagan ways. But this is not to be found in the seven letters.

Thus, up to the end of the New Testament period (if that is where this part of the Apocalypse belongs chronologically) the Jewish opponent is in the forefront. But it is certainly difficult to escape the impression that Rev. xiii, and allusions elsewhere in the Apocalypse also, indicate that the state has now begun to attack in earnest. Even if Chapter xiii is interpreted as a prescient lampoon on the essential antitheism of the state[1] before ever its attitude began to be expressed in active persecution, there are still all the allusions to martyrdom: vi. 9, vii. 14 (probably), xii. 11, 17 (introducing Chapter xiii), xiv. 1-5 (perhaps), 13 (probably), xvii. 6, xviii. 24, xix. 2, xx. 4. The Revelation is essentially an 'exhortation to martyrdom', and it is difficult to imagine it taking its final shape except in face of the actual experience of persecution, and difficult to account for all martyrdoms alluded to (whatever we may make of ii. 13) merely in terms of Jewish executions or Jewish and Gentile mob violence, especially when such words as 'butchered', $\dot{\epsilon}\sigma\phi\alpha\gamma\mu\dot{\epsilon}\nu o\iota$ (vi. 9) and

[1] Even this phrase needs qualification; cf. (with C. D. Morrison, *The Powers that Be*, 1960, 106, n. 2.) Rev. xvii. 17: 'God has put it into their heads to carry out his purpose, by making common cause and conferring their sovereignty upon the beast until all that God has spoken is fulfilled'.

'beheaded', πεπελεκισμένοι (xx. 4) are used. This is surely not comparable to a situation such as that in which a mere lynching may take place. It seems, thus, as though the reader of the New Testament is allowed to witness the transition from the earlier 'unofficial' persecutions to the beginnings of 'state persecution', in the sense that by the time the Apocalypse took final shape Christians were already being sentenced to death in Roman courts. But it still does not follow that anything like a concerted persecution had yet been seen in Asia Minor, or even anything on the scale of the outburst in Rome under Nero.

Conversely, it needs to be remembered that Emperor worship in some sense had already appeared before the birth of Jesus. Startling though this may seem to the modern mind, the deity of the Emperor might even have been recognized in a sense by Christians. C. D. Morrison makes this point in *The Powers that Be* (1960), p. 99, and summarizes what was generally believed by all, including Christians, in the words: '. . . the ruler was both divine by appointment and human by birth'. So (pp. 131 ff.), among the early Emperors, he clearly distinguishes the fanatics, Gaius and Nero, from others who did not in the same way claim personal divinity. But the question that concerns us at the moment is not when the Emperor was first deified, or what shades of meaning might attach to the idea, but when and where a refusal to join in the cult became a threat to Christians. It was Domitian (A.D. 81–96) who demanded the style 'Master and God';[1] and it is under him that the provincial *concilia* in Asia Minor, which were concerned with the encouragement of the worship of Rome and Augustus and the supervision of richly endowed games accompanying the religious festivals, are likely to have become a menace to religious liberty. Dio (lxvii. 13) tells of a certain Juventius Celsus (cf. Pliny, *Ep.* vi. 5. 4) who was accused of conspiracy and only escaped by worshipping Domitian. But Trajan, who succeeded Domitian, adopted a very different attitude, as we know from the famous correspondence with the younger Pliny, already mentioned (*Ep.* x. 96, 97). Thus Domitian is peculiar within the New Testament period;

[1] Suet. *Dom.* 13. 2; Dio lxvii. 47. See *Cambridge Ancient History* xi, *s.v.* 'Emperor-worship'; Pauly-Wissowa, *Realenc.*, *Suppl. IV* (1924), coll. 837 f.; F. Taeger, *Charisma*, ii. (1960) 337 ff.; E. G. Selwyn, 'The Persecutions in I Peter', *S.N.T.S.* Bulletin I (1950), 47.

and while it is not unlikely that the Fourth Gospel reflects a consciousness of the rivalry between Caesar and Christ (xix. 12 —you cannot favour Jesus and be a friend of Caesar; xx. 28— Domitian's very style, 'my Lord and my God!'), this in itself does not necessarily imply organized persecution.

We shall proceed shortly to consider some of the questions attaching to this subject. But first, the findings thus far may be summarized in the words of J. Munck (*Christus und Israel*, 1956, p. 46, my trans.): 'The earlier postulate of a first period free from persecution, which was terminated under Nero by a repressive persecution on the part of Rome must . . . give place to the postulate that the Church was persecuted from the very beginning; at first by the Jews, partly by their own judicial proceedings or through accusations before Roman tribunals, partly by taking the law into their own hands and committing murder, and then later by the Roman state. In the transition to this later period, it was possibly again the Jews who led the way, in that the case against Paul seems to have had as its purpose to direct the attention of the Roman officials to the fact that Christianity was no sect of Judaism, but a new religion which (like every other new oriental religion) was illegal.'

This brings us to a consideration of this deferred question— the relation of Christianity, quite apart from persecution, to the imperial cult; and with this question goes, as we have seen, that of the relation of Christianity to Judaism. Within the first century of the Christian era, the two most shocking years, in the eyes of world monotheism, both Jewish and Christian, must have been A.D. 40 and 70. In A.D. 40, Caligula made plans for the erection of his statue in the Temple (Josephus, *B.J.* II. x. 1) —an insane act of provocation[1] which was deferred by the courage of Petronius until the danger was mercifully averted by the emperor's death. But the very intention must have inflicted a deep wound on the sensibilities of Jew and Christian alike; and whatever may be the date of the relevant phrase in Mk xiii. 14, it would certainly have been recognized as particularly significant just then. B. W. Bacon made an exceedingly

[1] This would have been tantamount to a claim very different from that formulated by Morrison (see p. 116, above) as acceptable to Christians among others. (See especially Morrison, p. 133, on Gaius and Nero.)

ingenious attempt to arrange Mk xiii and the Matthean and Lucan parallels in their relative order round this crisis;[1] but whatever one makes of the dating of these documents, and of the other most obviously relevant passage, 2 Thess. ii, there is no doubt that the year 40 must have seemed a religious crisis of such magnitude that many Christians may well have thought that the challenge to Christ had reached its climax and the End was imminent.

We must digress for a moment to consider 2 Thess. ii:

> And now, brothers, about the coming of our Lord Jesus Christ and his gathering of us to himself: I beg you, do not suddenly lose your heads or alarm yourselves, whether at some oracular utterance, or pronouncement, or some letter purporting to come from us, alleging that the Day of the Lord is already here. Let no one deceive you in any way whatever. That day cannot come before the final rebellion against God, when wickedness will be revealed in human form, the man doomed to perdition. He is the Enemy. He rises in his pride against every god, so called, every object of men's worship, and even takes his seat in the temple of God claiming to be a god himself.
>
> You cannot but remember that I told you this while I was still with you; you must now be aware of the restraining hand which ensures that he shall be revealed only at the proper time. For already the secret power of wickedness is at work, secret only for the present until the Restrainer disappears from the scene. And then he will be revealed, that wicked man whom the Lord Jesus will destroy with the breath of his mouth, and annihilate by the radiance of his coming. But the coming of that wicked man is the work of Satan. It will be attended by all the powerful signs and miracles of the Lie, and all the deception that sinfulness can impose on those doomed to destruction. Destroyed they shall be, because they did not open their minds to love of the truth, so as to find salvation. Therefore God puts them under a delusion, which works upon them to believe the lie, so that they may all be brought to judgement, all who do not believe the truth but make sinfulness their deliberate choice.

(2 Thess. ii. 1-12.)

Other suggestions apart, there are two rival interpretations of this passage which claim attention. One, recently revived, is that what prevents the arch-antagonist of Christ from openly show-

---

[1] B. W. Bacon, *The Gospel of Mark* (1925), 53 ff.

ing his hand is the fact that the necessary evangelization of the world (Mk xiii. 10-14 (?), Matt. xxiv. 13-15) is not yet complete. 'That which restrains' (*N.E.B.* 'the restraining hand') is, on this interpretation, the missionary situation, the impenitence or non-conversion of areas of the pagan world: God in his long-suffering is waiting for them to be brought to the truth (cf. Lk. xviii. 7 (possibly), Acts xvii. 31, Rom. ii. 4, 1 Tim. ii. 4, 2 Pet. iii. 15). But, even if this might otherwise be plausible, it is extremely difficult to see how the masculine ὁ κατέχων (*N.E.B.* 'the Restrainer') can be fitted into this sense: it will have to mean the apostle and his missionary colleagues, in so far as they have not yet achieved their task! The alternative interpretation (going back to Tertullian and many others after him)[1] is to take the restraining power to be the Roman law and order, which prevents the outbreak of state persecution (or of persecution by Jews—so E. Bammel *loc. cit.* in note 1, p. 109) against Christians; and the masculine, the one who restrains, might then be the Emperor himself (Claudius) or some governor to whom the allusion would be recognizable. It was indeed after the removal of such restraints and in the reign of Claudius' successor, Nero, that the great antagonist did really come out into the open. And this interpretation still seems the more plausible, despite the vigorous opposition of O. Cullmann (e.g. in *Christ and Time*, (Eng. trans., 1951), 164 ff.), who maintains that the other (which in some form goes back, as he there points out, to Theodore of Mopsuestia and Theodoret, and was revived by Calvin) is far more probable. For a criticism of the latter position combined with a cautious reserve about the former, see B. Rigaux's commentary on the Thessalonian Epistles (1956), 276 ff.

At any rate, the future denouement referred to in 2 Thess ii is described in terms which may well have gained significance from the attempt of Caligula, so nearly realized, only some ten years earlier, to do just what is here predicted. And, returning now to this Caligula crisis, we have to admit that, at such a time, instead of drawing together in face of the common threat to their common faith in one God, Jew and Christian are more

---

[1] Tertullian, *Apol.* 32; *De Resurr. Carnis*, 24; Lactantius, *Div. Inst.* vii. 25; Ambrosiaster, *in loc.*; Augustine, *C.D.* xx. 19; Chrysostom *in loc.*; etc.

likely to have been conscious of estrangement. If the Jews were in for persecution, they had no desire to be embroiled with the doubtfully loyal sect of the Nazarenes; and if the Christians' faith was menaced, they, on their part, could not meet the danger in exactly the same terms as their Jewish neighbours, for their allegiance to the one God was couched in terms quite alien to the Jews—the Lordship of Jesus Christ.

But that crisis passed, and even as soon after it as the writing of Romans, Paul was able to declare that the state derives its authority from God and that a mark of a good Christian is that he should be a law-abiding citizen. Indeed, this would not in any case have seemed to be contradicted by Caligula's madness.[1] The famous saying of Jesus, 'Pay Caesar what is due to Caesar' (Mk xii. 17 and pars.) was still as appropriate as when it was first uttered. Even more noteworthy, in view of the discussion above, is the occurrence of similar sentiments in 1 Pet. ii. 13 ff.—

Submit yourselves to every human institution for the sake of the Lord, whether to the Sovereign as supreme, or to the governor as his deputy. . . . For it is the will of God that by your good conduct you should put ignorance and stupidity to silence;

[1] Cf. Morrison, *The Powers that Be*, 105: 'There is no reason to believe that Paul's view of the State would be lightly altered by troubled circumstances; he had suffered and Jesus had been put to death at the hands of the State, but Paul was peculiarly impressed by the hand of God in it all'. Cf. Philo's panegyric of Augustus and Tiberius, side by side with his attack on Caligula in *Leg. ad Gaium*. See also E. Bammel, 'Ein Beitrag zur paulinischen Staatsanschauung', *Theol. Literaturz.* 11 (1960), coll. 837 ff. He observes that Rom. xiii. 1 ff. is practically alone in the Pauline writings and rare in the New Testament altogether (1 Pet. ii. 13 ff., Tit. iii. 1 are the only parallels), and that it carries a Jewish rather than a Christian (let alone Pauline) stamp, though it goes beyond anything in Jewish Wisdom Literature. The explanation of its presence he finds in the situation at the time of writing. The Jewish community in Rome, though themselves demonstratively loyal to the Emperor, were continually being upset by turbulent elements coming in from Palestine. Hence the repressive measures and the expulsion of the Jews from Rome in 49. Not until 54 were Jews and Jewish Christians beginning to be able to return; and then, in their sense of insecurity, the Jews would be anxious to make the Christians scapegoats for anything that went wrong. Hence Paul's particular concern to emphasize the Christian affirmation of the State's rights and responsibilities. Much more characteristic of Paul's own thought, however, is (according to Bammel) 1 Thess. v. 3 where εἰρήνη καὶ ἀσφάλεια (a good *Roman* slogan, *pax et securitas*) is held up to ridicule in the light of apocalyptic. The Rom. xiii attitude, he holds, is far from central in Paul's thought.

and in 1 Clement lxi. 1 f. (despite the references to persecution in i. 1)—

> Thou, Lord and Master, hast given them [our rulers and governors] the power of sovereignty through Thine excellent and unspeakable might, that we knowing the glory and honour which Thou hast given them may submit ourselves unto them, in nothing resisting Thy will![1]

If the Epistle to Titus is late, the exhortation to obedience in Tit. iii. 1—

> Remind them to be submissive to the government and the authorities, to obey them. . . .

is also noteworthy.

But far more striking than the passing of the crisis of A.D. 40 and the maintenance of a Christian ethic of state loyalty is the remarkably small trace left upon the New Testament by the major crisis and disaster of the Jewish war and its culmination in A.D. 70. One reason for this is perhaps to be found in the fact (as B. W. Bacon pointed out) that 'it was the Synagogue, not the temple, which was the real opponent of the Church; and the effect of the disappearance of the worldly-minded Sadducees, with their outworn sacrificial ritual in the temple, largely divorced from the true religious life of the people, was really on the whole to strengthen essential Judaism' (*The Gospel of Mark* (1925), 81).[2]

But another reason may perhaps be that there is extremely little in the New Testament later than A.D. 70.[3] It has yet to be demonstrated beyond doubt that Matthew's Gospel is later;[4]

---

[1] J. B. Lightfoot's translation.

[2] Morton Smith, 'The Dead Sea Sect in Relation to Ancient Judaism', *J.N.T.S.* 7. 4 (July 1961), 347 ff. (see 355 f.), maintains (but is he right?) that G. F. Moore misrepresents the situation when he suggests that Pharisaism was *representative* Judaism. Rather, the Pentateuch, the Temple, and the *'amme ha'aretz* were the real backbone of Judaism. Daniélou (*Théologie du judéo-christianisme*, 1958, 19) contrasts 'le judaïsme contemporain du Christ, celui des Phariséens, des Esséniens et des Zélotes' with 'le judaïsme rabbinique, légaliste, d'après la chute de Jérusalem' which early Christianity was concerned to combat. Is he right in these distinctions?

[3] K. W. Clark, 'Worship in the Jerusalem Temple after A.D. 70', *J.N.T.S.* 6. 4 (July 1960), 276, asserts that Hebrews was written in the reign of Domitian, but this is questionable. 1 Clement, which K. W. Clark takes as evidence that Jewish sacrificial worship continued after 70, is hardly such: its arguments, like those of Hebrews, are *biblical*.

[4] Note that K. H. Rengstorf argues ('Die Stadt der Mörder (Mt 22⁷)' Z.N.T.W. Beiheft 26, 'Judentum-Urchristentum-Kirche', *Festschrift für*

even if it is, there is less scope here for signs of the situation if (as is here maintained) that Gospel was a genuine attempt to reconstruct the story of Christian beginnings. Lk.-Acts may or may not be later. The notorious allusion to the siege of Jerusalem (Lk. xxi. 20) is not proof positive that the words were written after the event.[1] And even if the Acts is concerned, if not primarily yet *inter alia*, to demonstrate that Christianity is true Judaism and should thus be unmolested by the state and had in fact always been acquitted by Roman law, this proves little or nothing as to its date. As a matter of fact, this particular aspect of its apologetic may easily be exaggerated: if Christianity as true Judaism had really been its primary theme, would its author have gone to such pains to underline the abolition of circumcision as a rule? As for the Epistle to the Hebrews, it has already been argued (above, pp. 44, 53) that it fits best in a period before—perhaps shortly before—A.D. 70. The Pastoral Epistles and the Johannine Gospel and Epistles are of uncertain date: probably after 70, but it is difficult to say how long after. All that can be said is that the Fourth Gospel contains much that would be particularly telling in view of the destruction of the Temple, yet does not underline it heavy handedly; while the Johannine and Pastoral Epistles simply do not make significant allusions. Within the New Testament, then, only the Apocalypse, likely on other grounds to be late, is really striking for its reticence about the events of A.D. 70, though outside the New Testament there is 1 Clement, equally striking for its reticence. In Revelation one might have expected not only a refer-

*Joachim Jeremias*, 106 ff.) that Matt. xxii. 7, usually taken to be a *post-eventum* reference to the destruction of Jerusalem, need not be more than the use of a 'topos' already well-established in Rabbinic literature.

The story of the coin in the fish's mouth (Matt. xvii. 24-27) is connected by both Clement of Alexandria (*Paed.* II. i. 14. 1, ed. Stählin i. 163) and Irenaeus (*Adv. Haer.* v. 24, ed. Harvey ii. 388 f.) with the incident of the tribute-money; but they confuse the temple-tax with the imperial poll-tax. 'This could the more easily happen after the destruction of the Temple in A.D. 70, when the Temple-tax was replaced by the *fiscus Iudaicus*'—T. W. Manson in an unpublished paper on 'Render to Caesar . . .' (where he cites Juster, *Les Juifs dans l'Empire Romain*, i. 377 ff., ii. 282; Schürer, *Gesch. Jüd. Volkes*⁴, ii. 314 f.; Dalman, *Arbeit und Sitte in Palästina*, iii. 182 f.). Possibly the correct deduction from the non-juxtaposition of the two incidents in Matt. itself is that it was before A.D. 70?

[1] See C. H. Dodd, 'The Fall of Jerusalem and "the Abomination of Desolation"', *J.R.S.*, xxxvii (1947), 47 ff.

ence to the vindication of God's martyr-prophets in the city
where their Lord was crucified (Rev. xi. 8), but a description
of her destruction on the analogy of the doom-song on Babylon-
Rome in Chapter xvii. One can only assume that Bacon's observation just quoted—that it was Pharisaism and the synagogue
that mattered—is here illustrated most clearly: not the judgment
on Jerusalem, but the vindication of God's Israel over 'the
synagogue of Satan' is what really concerned the Christian. It
might be a different matter if we had any literature from the
Jewish Christians who escaped to Pella—if indeed this is a
historical event.[1] It is hard to believe that a Judaistic type of
Christianity which had itself been closely involved in the cata-
clysm of the years leading up to A.D. 70 would not have shown
the scars—or, alternatively, would not have made capital out of
this signal evidence that they, and not non-Christian Judaism,
were true Israel.[2] But in fact our traditions are silent: either, as
has been said, there is less of the New Testament than is generally imagined that belongs to a date later than 70, or else, when
the disaster fell upon the centre of Judaism, the spiritual core
of its adherents consolidated so rapidly the already familiar
argument that the heart of their religion was not in sacrifices
but in prayer and almsgiving,[3] that the Christians found little
change of front in their essential opposition, and therefore
found little occasion to appeal to the destruction of the Temple
in their apologetic.[4]

[1] See J. Munck, 'Jewish Christianity in Post-Apostolic Times', *J.N.T.S.*
6. 2 (January 1960), 103 ff.

[2] As a matter of fact, even demonstrably later literature is also strangely
reticent on this issue. Even Justin (*Trypho*, 89. 2) just stops short of using
this argument. But we find it in Hippolytus, *Demonstr. c. Jud.* (Migne, *P.G.*
x. 787–794; critical edn. in Schwartz, *Zwei Predigten Hippolyts*, Sitzungs-
berichte d. Bayer. Akad., 1936, 3); and Sulpicius Severus, *Chronicle* ii. 30
(*c.* A.D. 400) says that by destroying the Temple Titus, far from destroying
Christianity, 'furnished a daily demonstration to the world that they (the
Jews) had been punished on no other account than for the impious hands
which they laid on Christ' (information kindly furnished by H. W. Montefiore). The Jews' retort was that, on the contrary, it was the apostasy of the
Christians that had brought down wrath (see A. Lukyn Williams, *Adversus
Judaeos* (1935), 137, n. 7).

[3] E.g. 'To pray in the synagogue is to bring a pure offering' R. Phinehas
(*c.* A.D. 360), in the name of R. Hoshaiah (*c.* A.D. 225) *T.J.Ber.* 8d, 71 (cited
in *T.W.N.T.* vii *s.v.* συναγωγή).

[4] K. W. Clark, *loc. cit.* p. 121, n. 3, argues that Jewish sacrificial worship
continued on the temple site until 135. His strongest evidence is certainly

To conclude. The New Testament as a whole reflects plenty of attack from antagonists, but little that was official or state-organized. What can be identified is mainly Jewish rather than imperial; and the manner and degree of it varies from place to place and from situation to situation. Relations between Christianity and Judaism depend in part on the relations at any given time between Judaism and Rome. These are the main factors to be borne in mind when trying to discern the genesis of 'persecution-documents'.

Josephus, *Ant.* iii. 224-236 (*c.* A.D. 94), *Cont. Apionem* (a few years later), ii. 77 and 193-198, and the unique Hebrew document discovered in Nablus *c.* 1900, based on a fourteenth-century chronicle and describing a pilgrim going to sacrifice in the High-priesthood of Amram (A.D. 120–130). He thinks that 2 Esdras is between 70 and 135, and if so, i. 31 is a Christian addition shortly after 70.

For Jews and Rome, see further C. D. Morrison, *The Powers that Be* (1960), 137.

## CHAPTER VIII

# BUILDING THE SUPERSTRUCTURE
# AND CONSOLIDATING

FOR the study of Christian beginnings there is value in that architectural metaphor which distinguishes the foundation from the superstructure. It is this which has attached the word 'edification' to a certain type of Christian activity; and although that word has unhappily been spoilt (like too many good words) by association with what the rebellious call 'trying to do them good', it stands for an important distinction within Christian procedure—the distinction between foundation and superstructure. 'I am like a skilled master-builder', wrote Paul (1 Cor. iii. 10), 'who by God's grace laid the foundation.' That foundation, he immediately goes on to say, can be nothing other than Jesus Christ. No structure is a Christian structure which is not so founded. The Christian community is not reared on exhortation but on declaration: not on fine ideals, but on witness to a Person. When, at Caesarea Philippi, Peter declared that Jesus was the King of Israel, he was bearing witness to what he had thus far observed in Jesus. It was only a preliminary finding; it was, as directly appeared, a distorted estimate; but it was the start of an estimate which was corrected and deepened by the resurrection, and which constituted the foundation of the Christian faith. It turned out that the apostles' witness to what they had seen and discovered to have been done by God in and through Jesus was the rock upon which the whole edifice was reared.

Evangelism is thus the laying of the foundation. But what follows upon it is of course the rearing of the superstructure— the work of 'edifying', and consolidating, both the individual convert and the community corporately. And this prolonged task was the cause of much that has come to form part of the New Testament—indeed, of far more than was produced by evangelism, which has left less written deposit. Literature was not then a primary propaganda-medium. The initial 'propaganda' was mostly spoken. But much that followed came to be written. It is therefore to the words, the phrases, and the whole sections that reflect the work of upbuilding and (to change the metaphor) 'pastoral care'—shepherding—that we now direct our attention.

If the work of evangelism, in some form, must needs be always the beginning, the mode of that evangelism and the nature, scope, and time-scale of the response vary widely. In Acts ii the response to Peter's preaching at Pentecost is represented as immediate, and we are told that large numbers were baptized forthwith. As for the gaoler at Philippi, so far as the narrative goes it sounds as though he and his household were baptized there and then, in the night, on no more secure a basis than the desire for 'rescue' from peril and the assurance that to be 'rescued' he need only believe on Jesus (Acts xvi. 30 f.). Such sudden conversions, without background, training, or instruction may sound alarmingly precarious. But it would be arbitrary to say that there can never be situations in which it is right to receive into the Church first and give detailed instructions and 'edification' afterwards.[1]

In other words, we are here confronted with the perennial tension between two ideals: on the one hand, there is the ideal of what later came to be called 'the gathered church'—that is, a Church composed only of 'converted' individuals, gathered out of their setting by the election of God and the careful sifting of the evangelist. On the other hand, there is the 'mass-movement' type of ideal, in which whole clans, whole populations, are swept in collectively. The rights and wrongs of these conceptions of evangelism depend very largely upon the social structure and other conditions prevailing in any given instance. The 'gathered church' ideal is primarily applicable in a context where the individual is already accustomed to act independently—that is, in a society where some degree of sophistication obtains, and where some measure of individualism has resulted: still more obviously, in areas which are already nominally Christian. The opposite extreme is presented by societies which are still

[1] For Jewish catechesis for proselytes, see D. Daube, *The New Testament and Rabbinic Judaism* (1956), 106 ff.

essentially tribal in structure. A well-documented study of such conditions some years ago is to be found in J. W. Pickett's *Christian Mass Movements in India* (Abingdon Press, U.S.A., 1933). There he writes (p. 22):

> The distinguishing features of Christian mass movements are a group decision favourable to Christianity and the consequent pre-servation of the converts' social integration. Whenever a group, larger than the family, accustomed to exercise a measure of control over the social and religious life of the individuals that compose it, accepts the Christian religion (or a large proportion accepts it with the encouragement of the group), the essential principle of the mass movements is manifest.

More recently, D. A. McGavran, in *How Churches Grow* (World Dominion Press, 1959), writes (p. 23):

> Except in individualized, urbanized, homogeneous populations, men and women exist in social organisms such as tribes, castes, and kindreds. They have an intense people-consciousness and tribal loyalty. Churchmen holding Gathered Church convictions proclaim a universal Gospel to them and invite them as individuals, regardless of what others do, to choose Christ. To them this sounds like being urged to leave their own and join the Christian 'tribe'. . . .

Now, curiously enough, in the New Testament we hear scarcely anything of prolonged, individual catechumenates; yet, on the other hand, neither is there direct evidence of any collective, corporate units larger than the household. We are confronted, therefore, with a delicately balanced situation. There is no clear evidence within the New Testament that Christianity advanced into any primitive tribal areas, unless it be Galatia; and even 'Galatians'—so far as Paul's converts went—need only mean the town-dwellers of Derbe, Lystra, and Iconium—vernacular-speaking, admittedly, but worshippers of Zeus, not primitive animists (Acts xiv. 11 ff.). Apart from these—even assuming these to be in any way exceptional—Paul's work seems to have lain in the Hellenized cities and to have reached no lower in the scale of education and intelligence than the household slave. There is no evidence for the penetration of Christianity into the labour-slave-gangs of the great estates, or the mines.[1]

[1] See E. A. Judge, *The Social Pattern of Christian Groups in the First Century* (1960), 51 ff. (esp. 60).

1 Cor. i. 26-29, whatever its stress upon the ignorance and obscurity of the majority of converts in Corinth, certainly need not be read so as to imply the completely inarticulate and illiterate.

Thus we are led to conclude that, for the New Testament, the household is generally the largest unit. It is possible, as has been suggested, that the recipients of the epistle to the Hebrews may have been a group (J. Moffatt called them a 'clan') which had originally formed a synagogue or a section of a synagogue. But it seems to have been the household (including, no doubt, slaves and servants as well as blood relations) that formed the largest evangelized group, and the 'house-church' that represented the normal manner of such a unit's growth and expansion.

Not that there is extensive direct evidence even for this assertion. All that can be said is that, while we hear in the New Testament of the conversion of individuals (and that in large numbers, on the day of Pentecost and shortly afterwards), we also hear of the conversion of the households of the 'official' in John iv. 53, of Cornelius (Acts xi. 14; cf. x. 2), of Lydia at Philippi (Acts xvi. 15), of the gaoler (Acts xvi. 31 ff.), of Crispus, the Corinthian synagogue-official (Acts xviii. 8), and of Stephanas (1 Cor. i. 16; cf. xvi. 15); while Onesiphorus' household is alluded to, evidently as a Christian group, in 2 Tim. i. 16, iv. 19, and in Tit. i. 11 false teachers are described as upsetting whole households, and there is evidence for the existence of house-churches (Rom. xvi. 5, 1 Cor. xvi. 19, Col. iv. 15; Philem. 2). As a matter of fact, even in Pickett's study of the Indian mass movements, one of the most arresting conversion-stories is that of Ditt, the Chuhra hide-dealer in the Punjab, who, on being individually converted, returned to his village and converted first his wife, his daughter, and two neighbours, and later four other men. It was only then that the movement in his area gained momentum (see *op. cit.* 43-45. This was in about A.D. 1900).

New Testament evangelism, then, represents neither the typical mass movement type of primitive tribalism nor the purely individual, 'gathered church' ideal. Its background was the family life and synagogue group of Judaism or of a near-Judaic pattern, unless there were cases when, in the relatively atomized, sophisticated life of the Levantine city, it took the form purely of house-churches, 'gathered' from an amorphous society. And it is in such a setting that we have to place the process of edification which is the subject of our enquiry. As has already been remarked, we hear almost nothing of a prolonged catechumenate. Apollos is scarcely an instance. He was already himself an evangelist when he was taken and further instructed by Aquila and Priscilla (Acts xviii. 24-28); it does not appear whether, in the end, he was given specifically Christian baptism, like the 'disciples' (perhaps Apollos' converts) found by Paul at Ephesus (Acts xix. 1-7). Apart from this, there are indications, indeed, that there were recognized courses of 'training for beginners'; but whether, as in the later Church, baptism was the climax to which such courses led; or whether the New Testament practice was first to baptize and then to instruct, is harder to establish. The only direct evidence, as we have already seen, points to the latter. In Gal. vi. 6 the catechumen is bidden share his goods with his catechist, which seems to imply a substantial period of instruction; but we are still not told whether or not baptism had already taken place.

In three passages in the New Testament, the metaphor of 'milk' as the diet of the immature is used. In 1 Cor. iii. 1-3 the metaphor is applied, first to the Corinthians' condition— a natural one—when they were first evangelized, and then, by way of reproof, to their unnatural continuance in a state of spiritually arrested development (evidenced by selfish rivalry and partisanship). This yields no evidence as to the nature and place of catechetical teaching. In Heb. v. 11-14 the milk metaphor is applied, again by way of reproof, to the failure of those who are addressed to grow up, beyond their elementary grounding, into maturity in the Christian faith; and in vi. 1 f. there follows a very interesting definition of what this grounding consisted of: it was 'elementary Christian teaching' ($\delta$ $\tau\hat{\eta}s$ $\dot{\alpha}\rho\chi\hat{\eta}s$ $\tau o\hat{v}$ $X\rho\iota\sigma\tau o\hat{v}$ $\lambda\acute{o}\gamma os$); it was a 'foundation' ($\theta\epsilon\mu\acute{\epsilon}\lambda\iota os$) 'consisting of' (? or, less probably, 'upon which was to be built') 'repentance from dead (i.e. useless or fatal?) deeds; faith in God; teaching about lustrations ($\beta\alpha\pi\tau\iota\sigma\mu o\acute{\iota}$), (? and about) the imposition of hands, the resurrection of the dead, and eternal judgment'. Fairly clearly, this is catechesis. But again, whether it in fact wholly preceded or in part followed baptism (? and the imposition of hands), who can say? Finally, 1 Pet. ii. 2 urges the hearers to long for the unadulterated spiritual milk ($\lambda o \gamma \iota \kappa \grave{o} \nu \ \gamma \acute{a} \lambda a$) that will enable them to grow into salvation. For those who believe that this represents an address to baptizands on the verge of baptism, it will mean, no doubt, the further training which will follow baptism and might also contain an allusion to the ritual administration of literal milk at baptism as a symbol of the milk and honey of the promised land they were now entering (cf. Heb. vi. 4). But if it be interpreted rather as a recall of Christians who are facing persecution to the great basic experience of their baptism in the past, it will be a reminder of and a recall to their essential nourishment, and will imply neither reproof for immaturity nor the actual imminence of baptism itself (see above, pp. 27 f).

So we are left unable to be certain whether or not, before the end of the New Testament period, the later system of a prolonged catechumenate before baptism had developed. It seems entirely possible that an individual was often baptized as a member of an entire household, after a single hearing of the very minimum of 'Gospel', and only subsequently given detailed instruction. But about the content of the instruction, whenever it was given, there is fortunately more evidence. Even without specific evidence, it would go without saying that, sooner or later, after baptism if not before, the initial evangelism must be followed by a process of detailed instruction—of 'edification'. And this rearing of the superstructure, this up-building, would, according to the stage at which it occurred, comprise more or less of the basic proclamation, the foundation Gospel. In other words, if we maintain the familiar distinction between *kerygma* and *didache* too rigidly, we shall not do justice to the real nature of all Christian edification, which builds, sometimes more, sometimes less, but always at least some of the foundation material into the walls and floors.

In the main it is, of course, true that the foundation is laid by the proclamation of what God has done in the life, death, and resurrection of Jesus ('There can be no other foundation beyond that which is already laid; I mean Jesus Christ himself', 1 Cor. iii. 11), and the challenge to acknowledge Jesus as Lord;

and that there then follows detailed instruction about the implications of this, both for doctrine and conduct.

But, to illustrate how subtly foundation and superstructure interlock, it may be observed—however paradoxical it may seem at first sight—that in the New Testament it is in the Epistles that one may hear more echoes of the work of evangelism than in the Gospels—or, at least, than in the Synoptic Gospels. For the Synoptic Gospels, at any rate, contain virtually no post-resurrection, evangelistic 'appeal': they do no more (essentially) than state the facts; they do not embody the 'Believe, repent, and be baptized' of the pentecostal appeal (Acts ii. 36, 38). The epistles, by contrast, although all addressed to the already evangelized, and, to that extent, speaking retrospectively, nevertheless contain a great deal more reference to the meaning and the means of becoming a Christian—hearing, believing, becoming incorporate in the Body of Christ (e.g. Rom. i. 2-4, 1 Cor. xv. 1 ff., Gal. iii. 1-5, Eph. ii. 8, 13, Col. i. 7, 13 f., 21 f., ii. 6 ff., 1 Thess. i. 9 f.). Thus, in a sense, the roles are reversed: it is the epistles which echo the initial challenge (albeit as a recollection of what happened to the Christians originally); whereas the Synoptic Gospels, viewed from this angle, embody rather that filling out of the initial challenge which was bound to follow. Even when the evangelistic appeal had been accepted and the convert baptized, there followed the stage when the catechumen (for he was still such) must be given some conception of the character of the God to whom, in Christ, he had yielded his life: bare *kerygma*, without personal content, would lack the power to stir and move, which the Gospels, by bringing the character of Jesus to life, do possess.[1] The contents of the Gospels are thus necessary, if the convert's faith is to be concrete and his love glowing. The Fourth Gospel to some extent combines both functions, for it alone of the four Gospels both presents a narrative 'portrait' of Jesus and also answers the question 'What must I do to be saved?' But even so, its reply is strangely lacking in corporate and ecclesiastical content. The Johannine Epistles go a little further; but it is Paul who alone provides an adequate answer, though, as has just been said, it needs reinforcing by

[1] See C. H. Dodd as on p. 87, n. 1; also Floyd V. Filson, 'The Christian Teacher in the First Century', *J.B.L.* 60 (1941), 317 ff.

the living portrait of Jesus' character.

Paul speaks in terms of hearing and responding with trust; of divestiture of the old humanity and investiture with the new; of coming to be incorporated in Christ; of receiving the power of the Holy Spirit. And all this is for him clearly 'focussed' in Baptism and Holy Communion (Rom. vi. 1 ff., 1 Cor. x, xi. 17 ff.). Only on such conditions may a Christian look to receive the moral fibre and stamina to become what in reality he now is: it is to the Holy Spirit that he owes his life; it is by the Holy Spirit that he must now let his conduct be shaped (Gal. v. 25). Only on such conditions, perhaps, can the Sermon on the Mount be faced. J. Jeremias has proposed (*The Sermon on the Mount* (1961), Eng. vers. of *Die Bergpredigt*), to see in the Sermon on the Mount in its present form in Matthew a body of teaching intended only for the already baptized.

We have, then, to recognize an interlocking of foundation and superstructure something like this:

(A) Initial proclamation: Jesus, approved by miracles and deeds of goodness, was handed over by the Jews to Pilate and killed; but God raised him from among the dead and made him Lord and Messiah. All this was according to the scriptures.

(B) Initial appeal: therefore repent, be baptized, and you will receive the Holy Spirit.

(a) Extension of proclamation: Jesus' life and miracles and deeds of goodness were such as the following (extended examples). His clash with the Jews, his sentence and execution followed the following pattern (details). The resurrection was manifested like this (narratives). The relevant scriptures are appropriately inserted throughout.

(b) Extension of appeal: repentance, baptism, and the coming of the Spirit *mean* (a new life, a transfiguring of outlook, the wearing of the new humanity, etc., etc.); they involve (details of character and conduct); they are related to Judaism and pagan religions as follows (discussion of the relevant issues).

Thus, into foundation (A) and ground-floor (B) alike are introduced materials of character (a) and (b). In any case, again and again the initial impact must, in actual life, have come neither from the hearing of 'Gospel' material nor from the direct 'appeal', but from the quality of the Christian community, as family or as house-church, into which an outsider would begin to be drawn by friendship, and only then would hear the explanations.[1] In such cases, (Aa) and (Bb) may occur in any or in no order. In 1 Tim. iv. 13, Timothy is bidden to give his attention to (public) reading (? of the Jewish scriptures), to exhortation, and to teaching: all three, side by side. Nevertheless, it is safe to assume that standard instruction for enquirers—newly baptized or preparing for baptism—did, like the proclamation, the *kerygma*, settle into a certain more or less regular pattern. Instruction, *didache*, both as the 'repent-and-be-baptized' appeal and also as instruction in the meaning and morals of the Christian life, found for itself its own sequences and chapters; and it is possible to reconstruct something of its appearance from the material scattered about the New Testament. It is true that the New Testament contains no elementary handbook of instruction (such as the *Didache of the XII Apostles* may be). But it does contain a good deal of instruction addressed to the already Christian communities, and it seems probable that much of this, with only minor differences, represents what had already been given to them at the beginning. At any rate, this instructional and edificatory material often looks like a reminder, a recall to what they already knew: sometimes, indeed, it is explicitly so described—just as, correspondingly, the celebrated little summary *kerygma* in 1 Cor. xv. 1 ff. is, in so many words, a reminder of what they had heard at the beginning:

> And now, my brothers, I must remind you of the gospel that I preached to you; the gospel which you received, on which you have taken your stand, and which is now bringing you salvation. Do you still hold fast the Gospel as I preached it to you? If not, your conversion was in vain.
>
> First and foremost, I handed on to you the facts which had been imparted to me: that Christ died for our sins, in accordance with the scriptures; that he was buried; that he was raised to life on the third day, according to the scriptures; and that he appeared to Cephas, and afterwards to the Twelve. Then he appeared to over five hundred of our brothers at once, most of whom are still alive,

[1] See R. R. Williams, 'Logic *versus* Experience in the Order of Credal Formulae', *J.N.T.S. I.* 1 (September 1954), 42 ff., pointing out that Eph. iv. 4-6, which manifestly contains 'credal' elements, is nevertheless not in the order of credal logic (God-Christ-Spirit-Church) but in the practically reverse order of experience.

though some have died. Then he appeared to James, and afterwards to all the apostles.

In the end, he appeared even to me.

There is sufficient literature on the tables of household ethics —the *Haustafeln*, to use the convenient German term—to make it unnecessary here to go into much detail about these.[1] In Acts xx, in his moving farewell to the Ephesian elders at Miletus, Paul is represented as committing them to the Lord and to the message about his graciousness which can build them up and give them a share in the promised land with all God's people (*v.* 32). That is a striking description of just that merged *kerygma*-and-*didache* which we have been considering; and we may assume that much the same is intended in the allusion in Rom. vi. 17 to the τύπος διδαχῆς, the typical teaching or outline of teaching, to which the Romans had been 'entrusted' by their evangelist, whoever he may have been. And precisely this kind of τύπος seems to be exemplified both by the brief summaries of the Gospel in 1 Cor. xv. 1 ff. and 2 Tim. ii. 8, and by the rules for domestic and family life (the *Haustafeln*) of the epistles, which contain injunctions to each member of the household springing directly from the baptismal fact of incorporation in Christ. That there seems to be a certain uniformity in the 'headings' relating to baptismal divestiture and investiture, and the resulting conduct, not only as between the Pauline Epistles but also when 1 Pet. and Jas are brought in, argues for a widely recognized τύπος. And the fact that parallels to some of the ethical material can be found, not only within Judaism[2] but also in Stoic and other pagan writers, is only natural. Christianity began within Judaism and quickly spread in Graeco-Roman society; and borrowings from both were to be expected.

[1] The most accessible literature in English is probably: P. Carrington, *The Primitive Christian Catechism* (1940); A. M. Hunter, *Paul and his Predecessors* (1940); E. G. Selwyn, *The First Epistle of Peter* (2nd ed., 1958), 194 ff. (where it is pointed out that, as early as 1903, A. Seeberg had written on the subject in German, *Der Katechismus der Urchristenheit*). See also Seeberg's subsequent work, *Die Beiden Wege und das Aposteldekret*, and K. Weidinger, *Die Haustafeln* (1928). Weidinger (p. 1) notes that the term *Haustafel* is at least as early as Luther.

[2] See O. Zöckler, *Die Tugendlehre des Christentums* (1904); A. Vögtle, *Die Tugend- und Lasterkataloge im Neuen Testament* (1936); S. Wibbing, *Die Tugend- und Lasterkataloge im Neuen Testament und ihre Traditionsgeschichte unter besonderer Berücksichtigung der Qumran-Texte* (1959).

What is striking is the degree to which the distinctiveness of the ἐν κυρίῳ, 'in the Lord', permeates and sets its stamp upon the Christian ethical instruction.[1] It is against membership in the Christian community that conduct is tested. The measure of what is right becomes 'that which is fitting' (ὡς ἀνῆκεν) 'for one who is incorporate in the Lord' (ἐν κυρίῳ), Col. iii. 18; cf. 1 Cor. vii. 39 ('provided the marriage is within the Lord's fellowship').

But one feature of far-reaching importance, which is common to all the ethical teaching of the New Testament and to that of the immediately succeeding period also, must here be mentioned —namely, that, with very rare exceptions, none of the Christians had direct civic responsibilities, because few were Roman citizens and few, if any, had any effective voice in public affairs.[2] This means not only that what we call Christian 'sociology' was unknown as a study but also that the thing itself was not there to be studied. This does not mean that the Christian ethic was individualistic. On the contrary, New Testament Christianity is nothing if not social: the Semitic traditions on which it arose are themselves strong in corporate sense; and, still more, it was quickly found to be impossible to describe Christ himself otherwise than as an inclusive, a corporate personality. To become a Christian, therefore, was *ipso facto* to become an organ or limb of that Body, and the Christian Church is essentially the household of God (see Gal. vi. 10, Eph. ii. 19, 1 Tim. iii. 15, Heb. iii. 5 f., x. 21). Indeed, for all its corporeity in the Old Testament, Israel was never so fully organic a concept as in God's Israel, the Church. But, for all this, it remains true that, strong as the corporate sense was within the fellowship of the Church, the kind of activity in society at large which, in our day, is known as Christian socialism, leading to 'Christian action', was simply not a possibility.

The question of slavery is a signal instance. Everyone knows

---

[1] In 2 Thess. iii. 6 περιπατεῖν κατὰ τὴν παράδοσιν ἣν παρελάβετε παρ' ἡμῶν is contrasted with ἀτάκτως περιπατεῖν, which bears witness to the element of instruction on *conduct* in the παράδοσις (or παραδόσεις, plural, 2 Thess. ii. 15).

[2] Not that it is to be assumed that the more privileged moralists necessarily had much more voice. E. Schweizer, as on p. 56, n. 3, 104, says that the pretentious Stoic's phrase about all the world being his *polis* was in fact only 'a retreat from active political life and an admission that he can no longer exercise any practical influence on this "*polis*"'. But see also the next note.

what a battle had to be fought in Parliament by Wilberforce and others in the nineteenth century to secure the abolition of slavery in the British colonies. For Christians in the first century to take any direct action for the abolition of what was part of the very structure of society was plain impossibility: there was no machinery except bloody rebellion—and that was not the Christian way. Besides, this weapon had in fact failed when, periodically, it had been tried by pagan slave-heroes such as Spartacus. Stoicism had influential members; and although it may too often have been content to proclaim ideals in general, it did sometimes practise them on the individual scale, and it did influence the imperial legislation.[1] But for Christians the only way of advance, apart from purchasing the freedom of individual slaves (cf. e.g., Ignatius, *Ad Polyc.* iv. 3), was to change the relations between individuals. This they did, and nowhere is it more remarkably reflected than in the New Testament Epistles (see especially Philemon). And the same principle applies, *mutatis mutandis*, to all New Testament ethics. The Sermon on the Mount is essentially concerned with individual character and action. The sex-ethics of the Epistles and Gospels are related entirely to individual action within the framework of already existing law and custom. Nothing else would have been realistic.

The result is not only that present-day readers look in vain to the New Testament for directions in social ethics, but also —paradoxically enough—that, in the New Testament period itself, Christianity seemed, to outside observers, to be cut off from religion. For paganism, religion was emphatically an integral part of civic life. For Jews, religion was nationalism and was partly expressed in external ways that symbolized a national allegiance. But Christians, refusing to join in the pagan imperial cult and yet possessing no tangible sacrifices, no priesthood, no place of worship of their own, seemed to be atheists. They could show none of the recognizable badges of a religion. Their political community ($\pi o\lambda i\tau\epsilon\upsilon\mu a$), as Paul put it, was in heaven (Phil. iii. 20), and it was not available for demonstration (cf. above, p. 97).

Thus in two directions this deeply corporate way of life

[1] See A. A. T. Ehrhardt, *Politische Metaphysik von Solon bis Augustin* (1959), ii, 18.

appeared to be something individualistic—or, if corporate, then at any rate withdrawn from public life: it took no part in civic action, and it possessed nothing that the ancient world could recognize as a cultic system. Elsewhere there were religious confraternities—Greek ἑταιρεῖαι and Semitic *haburoth*—within a larger cultus; here, although there were fellowship meals, they seemed to lack the visible background of cultus. But the outsider was mistaken. Within its own communities, the Church was not only aware of the organic unity of limb with limb in the Body of Christ, but was extremely active in 'social welfare'; and, for those who had eyes to see, it had both altar and Priest (see, especially, the Epistle to the Hebrews; cf. pp. 75 f. above).

Further, it needs to be strongly emphasized that what has just been said about the Christians' inability to participate actively in politics does not necessarily mean that they showed a lack of concern for them.[1] On the contrary, in many cases they took a very lively interest in all that went on. A Jehovah's Witness today may watch the Gadarene stampede of the nations without dismay, because he believes that they are irretrievably doomed and that their downfall must bring in the new age. An extreme sectarian today may renounce membership in all societies except that of Christ, citing 2 Cor. vi. 14-vii. 1 ('Do not unite your-selves with unbelievers; they are no fit mates for you . . .') and seeming to forget 1 Cor. v. 9-13 which explains that when St Paul said (perhaps in this very passage, 2 Cor. vi. 14 ff., if that is a fragment from an earlier letter) that the Christians were not to mix with the immoral, he meant immoral *professing Christians*, not the immoral among non-Christians: to avoid the latter they would have had to leave the very world! But, in contrast to such attitudes, most New Testament Christians seem to have believed that the Kingdom of God must show itself in connexion with and not independently of the kingdoms of this age. The outlook of Revelation, admittedly, is more detached; but for Paul, the rule of the Emperor was part of the divine system of law and order (Rom. xiii. 1), and the Kingdom of God could not be conceived of in a vacuum, independently of the events of history. But the Church's role was not yet to take overt political or social action. It was still to grow within the body politic as a (usually

[1] See K. L. Schmidt in A. A. T. Ehrhardt, *op. cit.* 20 n. 1.

unrecognized) revolutionary force. It was leaven, like the Kingdom of God of which it was the agent. The only point, within the New Testament period, where it inevitably came out into the open was in relation to idolatry, and so to Emperor worship. Here, 'passive resistance', even, if need be, to the length of martyrdom, was the only course for the loyal. But until the Roman authority demanded something that the Christian could not conscientiously give, because it conflicted with his ultimate loyalty, it was his duty, as an obedient member of society, to promote that law and order which, in principle, belonged to the God of peace whose very act of creation was itself a triumph over anarchy (cf. 1 Cor. xiv. 32 f. and Rom. xvi. 20). God is a God of 'cosmos', orderliness; the principle of authority, and ordered society, is part of the divine structure of things (cf. 1 Cor. xi. 3). Human authority therefore goes wrong only when it assumes the supreme authority which belongs to God alone: 'pay Caesar what is due to Caesar', but also, 'pay God what is due to God'. New Testament Christianity thus proved itself to be revolutionary but not anarchical. Revolutionary, because the recognition of a divine, ultimate authority always, in the last analysis, must overturn the secular lust for absolute power; but not anarchical, because it renounced violence, and, when its ultimate loyalty clashed with the secular demand, it still accepted the principle of authority and submitted to the penalties imposed by the secular authority even when they were irresponsibly imposed. Its weapon, in other words—when it was true to itself—was not the sword but the cross.[1]

Here, then, was the focus of extremely vital instruction for the new convert. Having renounced Satan and made Jesus his Lord, was he not to refuse to pay taxes, was he not to reject all civic authority? Might it not be his positive duty to join revolutionary bodies like the Zealots, and use force to overthrow the secular power—the arm of Satan? No, said the Christian catechist. God's whole creation owes its coherence to the principle of orderly, stratified, authority: God-Christ-Man-Woman; God-the Powers-the Subjects;[2] and if sin and disobedience have

---

[1] On the agonizing tension between these two, see J. A. T. Robinson, *On Being the Church in the World* (1960), 43 ff.

[2] Cf. C. D. Morrison, *The Powers that Be* (1960), *passim*.

introduced dislocation and chaos, it will not be mended by anarchy, but by costly, suffering obedience. This is the very principle of the incarnation. Therefore, although 'the children of the kingdom' are indeed free (in the sense that to them belongs the true citizenship and that they are not a subject people), yet they pay taxes as their contribution to the principle of orderliness (Matt. xvii. 24 ff.); they obey civic authority, not for fear of the sanctions, but as a positive contribution to the same principle (Rom. xiii. 5, 1 Pet. ii. 13-15); and if they should be forced to disobey because of a head-on collision of loyalties, then they will without question accept the cost. Above all, they must never make themselves liable to penalty for immoral conduct: ethically they must be exemplary.[1]

This brings us to the situations reflected more than once in the New Testament—the situations in which pagan standards in sexual conduct conflict with Christian. Was a convert to make a clean break with his past by renouncing his pagan partner? If he did, might he marry again, within the Christian community? Or was sex itself evil, and must the Christian renounce it totally? One can see these questions being dealt with tentatively, sometimes inadequately, by Christian pastors; and there is clear enough evidence of gross moral failure within the Church, necessitating severe disciplinary action. (See especially 1 Cor. v, vi. 12 ff., vii and the Pastoral Epistles.)

Another problem, that of the right attitude for Christians to the participation with pagans in eating meat that had been consecrated to idols, bulks large in 1 Cor. viii-x; but whether instruction along these lines formed a regular part of catechesis it is impossible to say. That it was, according to Acts xv, dealt with in general terms by the Jerusalem council, only adds to the uncertainty: what had become of this decree when Paul wrote 1 Cor.? Why does not the question figure at all in the other Paulines (unless it be in Rom. xiv) and in 1 Pet.? It is difficult to imagine a Gentile-Christian community in which it would not

---

[1] On the consciousness that failure to exhibit Christian conduct and qualities brought discredit on the Name of Christ, see W. C. van Unnik, 'Die Rücksicht auf die Reaktion der Nicht-Christen als Motiv in der altchristlichen Paränese' (*Z.N.T.W.* Beiheft 26, für J. Jeremias, 1960). In the New Testament there are: Rom. xiv. 16, 1 Cor. x. 32 f., Phil. ii. 15, Col. iv. 5, 1 Thess. iv. 11 f., 1 Tim. iii. 7, vi. 1, Tit. ii. 8, 10, 1 Pet. iii. 17, iv. 13.

be a problem; yet Acts xv (generally) and 1 Cor. viii-x (in great detail) are the only clear allusions to it. The parallel food-problem—whether Gentile Christians were to be expected to observe Jewish tabus in their common meals with Jewish Christians—is also dealt with in Acts xv and is perhaps hinted at here and there (Gal. ii. 11 ff., Rom. xiv, Col. ii. 16?), but otherwise it is not mentioned—not even in Rev. ii. 24, which in some other respects recalls the decree of Acts xv. One may readily imagine that, as the Christians became progressively distinct from Judaism and more and more Gentile in membership, this soon ceased to be a live issue: table-fellowship with someone possessing a sensitively Jewish conscience ceased to arise.

In addition to the ethical problems confronting the Christian, about which instruction was offered in the catechetical tradition, there were what may be called the matters concerning quality of character. Strictly speaking, there are no 'cardinal' virtues in Christianity, for Christian character does not 'hinge' round the disciplined practice of virtue: it is a spontaneous growth, it is a crop of qualities springing from the seed of new life divinely sown (see Gal. v. 22, Eph. v. 9, Phil. i. 11, Heb. xii. 11, Jas iii. 18); or—more characteristically described—it is life in the new age, resulting from incorporation in the new humanity which is Christ (see Rom. xiii. 14, 2 Cor. v. 17, Gal. iii. 27, Eph. iv. 20-24, Col. ii. 11 f., iii. 9 ff.). *Agape* is not a virtue among other virtues so much as a totally new impulse, divinely implanted: it is God's love for us in Christ, reflected and responded to. And what in other systems might be called virtues are the shape spontaneously taken by *agape* in the Christian community (1 Cor. xii. 31-xiii. 7).[1] Therefore, although in fact many Christian qualities

---

[1] On *agape* the fullest treatment is to be found in C. Spicq, *Agapè: prolégomènes à une étude de théologie néo-testamentaire* (1955), and *Agapè: dans le Nouveau Testament, analyse des textes,* i (1958), ii, iii (1959). On various aspects of New Testament Ethics, and their Jewish and pagan background, the following may be consulted: J. Bonsirven, *Le Judaïsme palestinien au temps de Jésus-Christ, sa théologie* (2 vols., 1935, abridged edition, 1950); F. B. Clogg, *The Christian Character in the Early Church* (1944); D. Daube, *The New Testament and Rabbinic Judaism* (1956); C. H. Dodd, essay on Pauline ethics in *The Evolution of Ethics* (ed. E. H. Sneath, 1920); C. H. Dodd, *Gospel and Law* (1951); M. S. Enslin, *The Ethics of Paul* (1930); R. N. Flew, *The Idea of Perfection* (1934); T. E. Jessop, *Christian Morality* (1960); J. B. Lightfoot, dissertation on Paul and Seneca in *Philippians* (1868; reprinted 1957); W. F. Lofthouse, essay on biblical ethics in *A Companion to the Bible*

seem to coincide with those on the Stoic list, the difference is a radical one. The Stoic virtues are the proud struggle of the human spirit to conform to nature and to gain the mastery over weakness; the Christian virtues emerge after the recognition of sin and the confession of human helplessness: they are the result of committal to God and dependence upon him. It is not by chance that ἀνδρεία, 'courage', so prominent in pagan ethical systems, is a word never occurring in the New Testament (the verb ἀνδρίζεσθαι occurs once, 1 Cor. xvi. 13). The courage of the Christian martyr is not the result of the steeling of the soul to endure; it is the by-product of self-forgetfulness and abandoned loyalty—sheer dependence upon the Lord. By the same token, the Christian character is notable for just that warmth and graciousness of which the Stoa might actually have felt ashamed.[1] Catechetical teaching about character accordingly consists largely of a recall to baptism, and only derivatively of an enumeration of those qualities of graciousness, forbearance, and sympathy which are the crop springing from the baptismal seed of the Spirit (e.g. 1 Pet. i. 23-ii. 3). It contains, however, plentiful warnings against a relapse into the indiscipline and immorality of pagan days.

One of the most impressive features of the new life, for the recent convert, must have been the deliverance from fear—fear of witchcraft and evil spirits and the forces of evil. The typical exhortation therefore speaks in terms of the realm of darkness from which the Christian has been rescued into glorious light, of the conquest of the powers of darkness and of this age, of the slavery from which Christ releases into the freedom of the new creation (Rom. viii. 35 ff., xii. 2, xiii. 12-14, xvi. 20, 1 Cor. viii, 5 f., xii. 2, Gal. iv. 8 ff., Eph. *passim*, Col. i. 13, 1 Thess. i. 9, 1 Pet. ii. 9, etc.). The hag-ridden world of superstition looms up

(ed. T. W. Manson, 1939); T. W. Manson, *Ethics and the Gospel* (posthumous, 1960); L. H. Marshall, *The Challenge of New Testament Ethics* (1946); C. H. Moore, essay on life in the Roman Empire in *The Beginnings of Christianity* (ed. F. J. Foakes-Jackson and K. Lake, i, 1920); L. B. Radford, Introduction to Philemon in *Colossians and Philemon* (1931); C. A. A. Scott, *New Testament Ethics* (1934); R. H. Snape, excursus II, 'Rabbinical and Early Christian Ethics' in *A Rabbinic Anthology* (ed. C. G. Montefiore and H. Loewe, 1938); A. N. Wilder, *Eschatology and Ethics in the Teaching of Jesus* (1939); 'Kerygma, Eschatology and Social Ethics' in *The Background of the New Testament and its Eschatology* (*in hon.* C. H. Dodd, eds. D. Daube and W. D. Davies, 1956).

[1] See Spicq, *op. cit.* iii, 262 n. 3.

very clearly behind the catechumen. Yet, now that he is released from fear, he finds that among the chief dangers of the new life are rivalry, partizanship, disunity; and much catechesis is concerned with meeting these, as may be seen towards the end of Rom., Gal., Eph., Col., and throughout 1 Cor. and Phil.

Thus the New Testament material reflecting primitive Christian catechisms[1] ranges from the repetition of the Gospel foundations, through specific ethical problems, to the building up of character in the common life in the Body of Christ. And there is no reason to be surprised if similar material was used again and again even in the later stages. Every Christian, however mature, profits from a recall to his baptismal vows and his earliest instruction in the Christian way. And this brings us back to the subject of the Christian homily. This has already been mentioned in the chapter on worship (pp. 30 f.). It need only be repeated here that catechetical instruction on the meaning of baptism and the conduct springing from incorporation in Christ are so integral to the whole Christian life that one is not surprised if it is impossible to be sure whether, for instance, material in 1 Pet. represents a baptismal homily, or epistolary instruction for the already baptized. Both alike have the same content.

Much more specific are the passages relating to false teaching. These are prominent in many of the New Testament writings, and, while some are evidently addressed to a single, given situation, there are others which may well represent recurrent difficulties. The various types of error attacked may be fairly succinctly catalogued. There is the Judaistic tendency to rely upon human action as meritorious, instead of constantly casting oneself on the mercy of God alone—one of the chief dangers attacked by Paul (see especially Rom., Gal., and Phil. iii). At the opposite extreme is antinomianism—the assumption that the mercy of God condones licentious living or a selfish unwillingness to act charitably—also attacked by Paul (e.g. Rom. iii. 5 ff.,

[1] For the next phase in this fascinating study, outside our period, the reader is referred to H. Chadwick's edition of the *Sentences* of Sextus (1959), where he writes (pp. x f.): 'The interest governing the present study has lain in the affinity and difference between Christian morality of the second century and that of the surrounding world. The work is set forth, therefore, as a contribution to the much discussed question of the continuity and discontinuity between the early Church and contemporary society. . . .'

vi. 1 ff.), but taken up with special vigour in James (ii. 14 ff.). Behind both this antinomianism and the opposite extreme of legalism stands a false doctrinal position often combatted in the New Testament—the dualism which regards the material world, as such, as evil; and this, in its turn, naturally fraternizes with a false Christology which does not allow for a real incarnation but either places Jesus in the (Arian) position of a demi-god, or reduces him to the wholly human level, or splits him into two not really united aspects.

With this kind of error goes, indeed, a generally weak grip upon the historical. As G. Stählin points out in his article μῦθος in *T.W.N.T.*, the New Testament uses this word 'myth' in a pejorative sense: it signifies a divorce from the reality which had been historically manifested, and most of all in the incarnation (1 Tim. i. 4, iv. 7, 2 Tim. iv. 4, Tit. i. 14, 2 Pet. i. 16). For the New Testament, 'truth' is not abstract: it is in Jesus. Thus the myth-mongers are vigorously assailed in the Pastoral Epistles and 2 Pet.[1]

Christological error bound up with moral laxity receives its classic refutation in 1 and 2 Jn. Another agitating problem, which assumed larger proportions in the sub-apostolic era, is the question of sin after baptism, and of perfectionism.[2] The Epistle to the Hebrews is the New Testament writing that seems to exhibit the clearest signs of this (see vi. 4 ff., x. 26 ff.; but also 1 Jn v. 16 ff.).

Thus individual instruction for catechumens, homilies addressed to groups of worshippers, and special admonitions in the face of particularly critical situations can all be seen to have contributed content and form to different parts of the New Testament. And whereas in certain communities and in some conditions an outward looking concern for evangelism seems to override the concentration upon internal difficulties, in others (see especially 1 Jn) the struggle for purity of doctrine has driven them in upon themselves as a closed community.

It remains now to enquire into the use made by the New Testament Church of the parables of Jesus, for these present important material for the investigation of 'edificatory' teaching.

---

[1] See G. Miegge, *Gospel and Myth* (Eng. trans., 1960), 103 ff.
[2] See W. Telfer, *The Forgiveness of Sins* (1959).

The work of form criticism in general, and, in particular, the researches of modern scholars, especially C. H. Dodd (*The Parables of the Kingdom* (1935)) and J. Jeremias (*Die Gleichnisse Jesu* ([3]1954), Eng. trans. *The Parables of Jesus* (1954)), into the transmission of the parables, have established beyond reasonable doubt that, by the time the Gospels were written, the parables as originally told by Jesus had undergone considerable alteration in the process of telling and re-telling. In particular, it is clear enough that the early Church had applied and adapted them to their own circumstances. If confirmation of this tendency were needed, the so-called Gospel of Thomas, recently discovered in Coptic,[1] provides an extensive gallery of parables, almost all recognizable as the parables we know, but freely and still further adapted to the doctrinal interests of this writer or group; and although it is outside the canon whereas the four Gospels are inside, there is no reason why the canonical Gospels should have been immune. Yet, although an irresistibly strong case has been made for the existence of moulding and adapting processes in the transmission of the parables, the extent of it in any given instance always needs careful testing, and current criticism sometimes tends to be over mechanical in its techniques.

But before we examine some specimens, it is worth while to observe that material both from the parables and from other parts of the Gospel tradition seems here and there to have left its mark on the epistles. If this is a correct reading of the facts, it suggests that long before the canonical Gospels were universally recognized, teachers and preachers were using the Gospel tradition to illustrate or drive home their lessons. The language of 1 Cor. vii. 35, 'I am thinking . . . of your freedom *to wait upon the Lord without distraction*' (πρὸς τὸ εὐπάρεδρον τῷ κυρίῳ ἀπερισπάστως), is so strongly reminiscent of the Lucan narrative of Martha and Mary (Lk. x. 39 f., 'Mary, who *seated herself at the Lord's feet* . . . Martha *was distracted* . . .', Μαριάμ, ἣ καὶ παρακαθεσθεῖσα πρὸς τοὺς πόδας τοῦ κυρίου . . . ἡ δὲ Μάρθα περιεσπᾶτο . . .) that one cannot help wondering whether Paul was not holding this picture in his mind as he chose his words, knowing that his Corinthian friends also had it in

---

[1] Conveniently accessible, in English translation by W. R. Schoedel, in R. M. Grant and D. N. Freedman, *The Secret Sayings of Jesus* (1960).

theirs. If there is any truth in the idea, it would mean that he may actually have illustrated a desirable attitude by recounting the anecdote. Again, the parables of growth seem to be in mind, not only in the embryo parable of 2 Cor. ix. 10 (God gives growth to grain: he will also make almsgiving produce fruit) but in the phrases in Col. i. 6, 10 (yielding fruit and growing), so naturally fitting a background consisting of the parable of the sower.[1] In Acts xx. 35, Paul is represented as actually appealing to an otherwise unknown saying of Jesus ('Happiness lies more in giving than in receiving'). In 1 Thess. v. 21 occurs a parabolic saying which returns in more explicit form in Clement of Alexandria, *Strom.* i. 28. 177, 'be good bankers, rejecting some things but retaining what is good' (ἡ γραφὴ . . . παραινεῖ· γίνεσθε δὲ δόκιμοι τραπεζῖται, τὰ μὲν (?) ἀποδοκιμάζοντες, τὸ δὲ καλὸν κατέχοντες), which may well be a genuine saying of Jesus; and the identification of the metaphor by Clement as a metallurgic one lends plausibility to the interpretation of what follows in 1 Thess. v. 22 in the same vein: 'have nothing to do with anything counterfeit' (ἀπὸ παντὸς εἴδους πονηροῦ ἀπέχεσθε ? = bad types of coin). It is actually appropriated in this sense by Basil, *Hom.* xii. 6, '. . . and like an approved banker, he will retain what is approved but will keep clear of every bad type' (καὶ ὡς δόκιμος τραπεζίτης, τὸ μὲν δόκιμον καθέξει, ἀπὸ δὲ παντὸς εἴδους πονηροῦ ἀφέξεται, cf. *id. In Isa.* 47).[2] Thus the complete metaphor may be a dominical parable in embryo. Again, in 1 Tim. vi there are not a few echoes of Gospel sayings and settings.[3] It must be emphasized that these are only straws in the wind, impressive only for their individual slenderness and fragility. Thus, to take one example of the great lacunae in the evidence, 2 Tim. i. 12, 'I know who it is in whom I have trusted, and am confident of his power to keep safe what he has put into my charge', which seems to clamour for an allusion to the parable of the money in trust, offers no evidence

---

[1] The *hysteron-proteron*, yielding fruit before growing, might be explained as a reminiscence of the Hebrew of Gen. i. 28 (where, addressed to *persons*, it is not an anomaly: they are to be productive and thus to multiply their race). But the fact remains that the LXX there does not use καρπός or καρποφορεῖν, and the Gospel parable is the closer parallel to Col. i.

[2] A. Resch, *Agrapha* (1889), 116 ff., collects no less than 69 citations of this saying from the Fathers.

[3] See Excursus II: *Luke and the Pastoral Epistles.*

for any awareness of it whatever. Conversely, we are at a loss to know what picture lies behind such a metaphor as 'cutting straight' in 2 Tim. ii. 15 (ὀρθοτομοῦντα—is it ploughing, stone-masonry, or what?). But collectively and cumulatively there is enough, all the same, to leave us in little doubt that evangelists used material, such as eventually came into the Gospels, to illustrate and drive home their points—material both from the sayings of Jesus and from his life and work.[1]

Now, when the parables were used for this purpose, what would be the result? It goes without saying that the morals drawn from them would be contemporary: otherwise, they would have significance only in the setting of Jesus' own life, and would not have been taken out of it in the first place. Correspondingly, the parables themselves would suffer some degree of adjustment and re-touching so as to fit the intended lessons. It is difficult to resist the impression that Lk. xvi. 8 ff. represents a whole series of morals, attached, at one time or another, to the parable of the dishonest bailiff:

> . . . For the worldly are more astute than the other-worldly in dealing with their own kind.
>
> So I say to you, use your worldly wealth to win friends for yourselves, so that when money is a thing of the past you may be received into an eternal home.
>
> The man who can be trusted in little things can be trusted also in great; and the man who is dishonest in little things is dishonest also in great things. If, then, you have not proved trustworthy with the wealth of this world, who will trust you with the wealth that is real? And if you have proved untrustworthy with what belongs to another, who will give you what is your own?
>
> No servant can be the slave of two masters; for either he will

[1] See C. F. D. Moule, 'The Use of Parables and Sayings as Illustrative Material in Early Christian Catechesis', *J.T.S.*, n.s., iii (1952), 75 ff.; and note further the following: Phil. iv. 12 has some of the vocabulary of the parable of the Prodigal Son in Lk. xv (I owe this observation to Dr G. S. Duncan); 2 Pet. i. 13, 15 is reminiscent especially of the Lucan version of the Transfiguration story; Rev. iii. 3, 20 has the thief, and the knocking at the door, and 2 Tim. ii. 19 (ἔγνω κύριος τοὺς ὄντας αὐτοῦ, καὶ ἀποστήτω ἀπὸ ἀδικίας πᾶς ὁ ὀνομάζων τὸ ὄνομα κυρίου) might be regarded as a (reverse) reminiscence of Matt. vii. 21-23; but see further Excursus II. See also M. S. Enslin, *The Ethics of Paul* (1930), 116, n. 18, and J. C. Hawkins, *Horae Synopticae* (²1909), 196, n. there cited; and C. Spicq, *l'Épître aux Hébreux*, i (1952), 100, n. 2; and H. Riesenfeld, 'Le Langage parabolique dans les épîtres de saint Paul', *Recherches bibliques* v (1960), 47 ff.

hate the first and love the second, or he will be devoted to the first and think nothing of the second. You cannot serve God and Money.

It is equally hard to avoid the impression that the two stories of the great feast, in Matt. xxii. 2 ff. and Lk. xiv. 16 ff., have both been adapted, in different ways, to situations obtaining after the beginning of the apostolic Church's mission. Again, the allegorical interpretation of the tares among the wheat (Matt. xiii. 36 ff.) seems better suited to the apostolic age, when 'Church' and 'world', true Christian and spurious Christian, were contrasting but confused elements, than to the ministry of Jesus himself when the antithesis might rather have been disciple over against antagonist, with very little danger of mixture or confusion.

But criticism ceases to be scientific if, on the basis merely of such clear examples as these, it jumps to the conclusion that no allegory can have been dominical, that all the attack and reproof in the original parabolic teaching of Jesus was directed to his opponents, and that Jesus never told parables having reference to the ultimate 'end of the age' or directed to his own disciples' condition. The fact is that a far greater bulk of parabolic teaching, as it stands in the Gospels now, can be fitted quite naturally into a setting within the ministry of Jesus, than modern critical scholarship sometimes allows; and that we must not too lightly assume the marks of 'edificatory adaptation' everywhere. Take a seldom noticed instance from Matt. xxiv. 45, Lk. xii. 42.

In these two parallel passages there is a saying of Jesus beginning, in both cases, with τίς ἄρα; 'Who, then . . . ?' and continuing, with only small divergences of vocabulary and style through a full-length parable. (The ἄρα is not translated in the *N.E.B.* of Matt. xxiv. 45; in Lk. xii. 42 it appears as 'Well . . .') The only substantial difference between the Matthean and Lucan versions is that Matthew's 'Who, then . . . ?' is absolutely unheralded, whereas Luke's is introduced by (*v.* 41) 'Peter said, "Lord, do you intend this parable specially for us or is it for everyone?"'. But this small difference is a most remarkable one. In the first place, one is familiar with the idea that it is Matthew, not Luke, who multiplies allusions to Peter. Yet here it is Luke who mentions Peter. Secondly, the direct question about the intended recipients of the preceding saying—are they the disciples or everyone generally?—is arresting and unparalleled. And thirdly, it is this question alone that lends logic to the ἄρα, 'then', which, in Matt., without this antecedent cause, is practically pointless. It is true that there is one other instance of such an unintroduced ἄρα in Matt., namely Matt. xviii. 1, where the disciples ask 'Who, then, is greatest in the kingdom of Heaven?' But this may at least be explained as meaning something like the English 'after all', and as implying antecedent discussion among the disciples.

These considerations together add up to a case for regarding the Lucan version as the closer to the original; or, to put it otherwise, a case against the assumption that Lk. xii. 41, the Peter-clause, is a mere editorial invention. If this is a 'Q'-passage, then Luke's fuller text has perhaps reproduced it more faithfully. The Matthean hanging ἄρα, 'then', is hanging precisely because it is torn from its context.

If this be conceded, then the very setting of the parable goes back to an early source; and the assumption that the question, or even the whole passage (in either Gospel) is a later (and so post-dominical) accommodation to an ecclesiastical situation and to the delay of the *parousia* is to that extent weakened. And yet, if one adopts the opposite assumption—that it is substantially a dominical dialogue from within the ministry—does it yield a conceivable sense? It appears to say: 'This summons to alert readiness (Matt. xxiv. 44, Lk. xii. 40) is directed not to all and sundry but to you, the specially chosen Twelve. You are to be faithful in dispensing whatever it is that you are commissioned to dispense; otherwise you will be caught off your guard.' Is there any conceivable *Sitz im Leben Jesu*, any setting within the ministry, for such a summons?

Perhaps there is. It is notoriously difficult (see p. 90 above) to 'place' Matt. x. 23 (the famous saying—central in Albert Schweitzer's theory of a disillusionment in Jesus himself—about the Son of Man's coming before the cities of Israel had all been visited); but the very fact that it so ill suits a post-resurrection setting with the beginnings of the Gentile mission gives some plausibility to finding some place within the ministry of Jesus for the prediction of a limited (though only a limited) delay of the Son of Man. And in Lk. xix. 11 ff. the parable of the minas is introduced by the preface: '. . . He went on to tell them a parable, because he was now close to Jerusalem and they thought the reign of God might dawn at any moment'. Why this very circumstantial linking of the parable with the approach to Jerusalem, if in fact the purpose of the evangelist was to detach it from the ministry and apply it to a permanent situation?[1]

Is it possible, then, after all, that the parable of the unfaithful servant has been too hastily assumed to have been shaped to the needs of ecclesiastical office-holders? Is the hanging ἄρα, 'then', pointing to the genuineness of the Petrine exordium (preserved by Luke, not by Matthew with his Petrine interests!), a possible clue to the historicity of injunctions given by Jesus during his ministry to the Twelve to be faithful in their dispensing of the message of the Kingdom? It is far from a demonstration of the case, but it is perhaps enough to demonstrate the insecurity of the opposite assumption if it be based only on such arguments as are here called in question.

Another example of the questionable wisdom of assuming the adaptation principle too readily is the parable of the sower in Mk iv.[2] It is often said that the parable proper (vv. 3-9) is, more or less, original and authentic, but that the allegorizing interpretation (vv. 14-20) represents an addition and adaptation by early Christian teachers and preachers—not to mention the further reflections in vv. 21-25. Furthermore, it is either held that the difficult vv. 10-13 ᵃᵉe not dominical, but reflect a rather later predestinarian attitude regarding unbelieving Jews (and appeal is made to the vocabulary of these sections to support the hypothesis of their alien character); or else that the verses, though dominical, are misplaced, and belong in a different context.

But there are weaknesses in such assumptions. First of all, what did the original parable mean, if not what it is made to mean in vv. 14-20? The answer offered by C. H. Dodd is that it meant: 'Can you not see that the long history of God's dealings

---

[1] Cf. O. Cullmann, 'Unzeitgemässe Bemerkungen zum "historischen Jesus" der Bultmannschule' (from the Evangelische Verlagsanstalt, Berlin, 1960), 279.

[2] The five paragraphs which follow are borrowed (by kind permission of the S.C.M. Press) from what I wrote in *Religion in Education*, spring 1961, 61 f.

with His people has reached its climax? After the work of the Baptist only one thing remains: "Put ye in the sickle, for the harvest is ripe"' (*Parables*, p. 180). J. Jeremias' answer is similar: 'In spite of every failure the Kingdom of God comes at last' (*Parables*, p. 92). But this brief message is better conveyed by such parables as that of the leaven and the mustard seed. Why all this circumstantial detail—path, rock, thorns, good ground (all, moreover, perfectly natural, unforced features)—if that is all that was intended? Surely it is actually more scientific to recognize the simple fact that this realistic picture of a sower at work presents, without the slightest forcing or squeezing (how different from the frigid, laboured allegory of, e.g., Hermas, *Similitudes*, ix. 17 ff.!), a vivid analogy to the varied response with which the teaching of Jesus was met. In other words, here is a parable about the reception of Jesus' own parabolic teaching —a parable so circumstantial that it happens also to be a ready-made allegory.

'Parable', as it is commonly distinguished from 'allegory' by writers on this subject, presents a genuine, straight analogy— say, from the realm of physical life to that of human character. But this particular parable chances to be also an unforced allegory: there are good, natural analogies in its details as well as in its broad effect. Is that unthinkable for the original teaching of Jesus?

Then, next, even the difficulty of the bridge-passage, *vv.* 10-13, has been exaggerated. First, it is quite gratuitous to assume that the categories of 'those outside' and 'those inside'[1] are meant to be rigid and 'predestined'. What about Mk viii. 18, where the disciples themselves are clearly being classed as deaf and unseeing? Surely the simplest view is that men are 'outside' or 'inside' according to their response. It is impossible to convert or persuade by mere dogmatizing or ranting. No amount of mere statement, no 'spoon-feeding' (as every teacher knows) will achieve this end. There is nothing for it but to sow 'seed-thoughts'—to set something germinating in the hearers. If they respond, they begin to be 'inside', they 'come for more'; if they

---

[1] On 'those without' see also W. C. van Unnik, 'Die Rücksicht auf die Reaktion der Nicht-Christen als Motiv in der altchristlichen Paränese', *Z.N.T.W.* Beiheft 26 (*Festschrift für J. Jeremias*, 1960), 223, n. 6.

pay no heed—or for as long as they pay no heed—they are self-excluded. Hence the use of parables. We are being perversely literalistic if we imagine that the free quotation from Isa. vi ('that they may look and look without seeing . . . lest they turn . . .') is really intended to mean that parables are used *in order* to exclude, deliberately to make the message difficult for all except the favoured few. As in its original setting in the Book of Isaiah, so here, it is most naturally taken as an arresting, hyperbolical, oriental way of saying 'Alas! many will be obdurate'. (Even the most rugged of prophets might justly lose his faith, were he really summoned to preach *in order to* fail!) And secondly, the linguistic difficulties of this bridge-passage almost disappear if *vv.* 10-12 are recognized as a generalization (like *vv.* 33 f., and, like them, using the imperfect tense): to those who did ask for explanation, Jesus used always to say, 'To you is granted the secret, which is hidden from the rest as long as they stay outside'. This is a grammatically sound interpretation, and it accounts for the generalizing plural, 'parables' (*v.* 10), as contrasted with the particularizing singular which follows (*v.* 13) when 'this parable' is considered.

This leads straight into the 'allegory' (*vv.* 14-20), where it is, after all, not really surprising to find several words which are seldom or never used elsewhere in the Gospels and which remind us more of Paul's vocabulary. This phenomenon need only mean that the themes in question happen not to recur. The words are perfectly suitable to the theme; the theme fits the parable naturally; and neither seems to be incompatible with the actual ministry of Jesus.

This is perhaps enough to warn us that the recovery of the precise use made of the parables of Jesus by Christian evangelists and teachers of the apostolic age is no easy task, and that the critical scalpel, invaluable and indispensable though it is, cannot by itself ever decide for us when the authentic 'lowest layer' has been reached. What we can reiterate, with conviction, is that the parables were undoubtedly used and adapted freely, and that the Christian Church was much too confident of the living presence of the Spirit of prophecy to attempt to abide by a rigid authoritarianism in its attitude to the traditions. The very reshaping and adaptation of a parable might be the work of the

Spirit of Jesus in them: the test of authenticity was adherence
not to the original words, but to the truth of the message as a
whole. It is possible that the Gospel of Thomas, for all its
manifestly doctrinaire adaptations, may also preserve traces of an
ancient stream of tradition (possibly from the Gospel according
to the Hebrews)[1] which had run parallel to those which flowed
into the canonical Gospels; and H. Köster's re-examination
of evangelic matter in the Apostolic Fathers[2] points (even if
one does not accept the extremes of his position) to independent channels of tradition. Evangelists and teachers were using
and adapting freely and uncritically, with an eye chiefly upon
their main task of edification.

Thus, the parables and parabolic material in the New Testament, as well as passages containing direct admonition about
character and conduct, reflect the edificatory work of evangelists, catechists, and pastors, and help us to draw for ourselves
a mental picture of the setting in which such material was preserved. Among other things, this investigation will serve as a
reminder that such clearly distinguishable types of New Testament literature as Gospels and Epistles both alike drew upon a
common fund of tradition, and equally that they both contributed their own modes of adaptation and application to the
contemporary situations.

[1] On the affinities of the *Gospel of Thomas*, see H. W. Montefiore, 'A
Comparison of the Gospel According to Thomas and of the Synoptic Gospels',
*J.N.T.S.* 7 (1961), 220 ff.; H. E. W. Turner and H. W. Montefiore, *Thomas
and the Evangelists* (1962).
[2] H. Köster, *Synoptische Überlieferung bei der apostolischen Vätern* (1957).
Earlier, the well-known study, *The New Testament in the Apostolic Fathers*
(Oxford, 1905), had been rather more ready to allow for direct dependence.
See further A. D. Nock in *J.T.S.*, n.s., xi (1960), 68.

## CHAPTER IX

# VARIETY AND UNIFORMITY
# IN THE CHURCH

IN the Church of England at the time of writing, the variety obtaining is such that a travelling worshipper, going from Church to Church, will never know what he is in for, but only that it will be most unlikely to be exactly the service as prescribed in the Book of Common Prayer. Among the Protestant Episcopalians of Ireland, by contrast, uniformity prevails: the visitor can be tolerably certain that the book will be adhered to. In the New Testament Church, before ever there was even a written liturgy—let alone an authorized one—and before there were any generally accepted formularies of doctrine, the Christian on his journeys might expect to meet the very widest varieties. Indeed, one of the problems would be to decide what was the minimum requirement for a community to be a Christian one at all.

A traveller soon after the middle of the first century—say about A.D. 60—going from Jerusalem to Ephesus, would encounter a wide range of doctrine and practice among communities who all, nevertheless, claimed some attachment to Jesus of Nazareth. Somewhere in Judaea he might have found the circle of James the Lord's brother still worshipping in a Christian synagogue consisting of practising Jews who also believed in Jesus as God's Messiah, but who may have gone only a very little way towards formulating a doctrine of Jesus as divine: the Ebionite type, entertaining a diminished Christology.[1] In Samaria, who knows what kind of a Christian colony there might be? One, possibly, which highly honoured the name of John the Baptist (whose mission had been vigorous in those

---

[1] For the extra-biblical evidence about James, see Euseb. *H.E.* ii. 23. 4 ff., iii. 5. 2; and, in addition to standard discussions of this in Dictionaries etc., note a recent one by N. Hyldahl, 'Hegesipps Hypomnemata', *Studia Theologica*, xiv (1960), 70 ff.

parts and whose tomb, perhaps, they boasted), and which treasured traditions many of which are now embodied in the Fourth Gospel. They would see in Jesus the one who had been destined to come—the prophet like Moses.[1] Cosmopolitan Antioch (even to judge from no more than the references to it in the New Testament, let alone its later history) would present within itself a considerable range of different types of community—Gentile, Jewish, Judaizing, Hellenizing—with different shades of Christology; while the Lycus valley, if our traveller followed that route, would present a strange amalgam of oriental astrology, Jewish legalism, and Christian beliefs (see Colossians and commentaries thereon). By journey's end, he would be prepared for the seething diversity of Ephesus where the Pauline churches were to be quickly invaded by antinomianism, Judaizing Christianity, and influences of a Johannine type (see Acts xx. 29 f., ? Eph., Rev. ii. 1 ff., and the Gospel and Epistles of John). If he then took ship from Miletus to Alexandria, he might there find himself confronted with yet other types of Christian colony —or, if he had already met them at Ephesus or elsewhere, they would here be even more concentrated and more clearly defined (see, perhaps, Heb., and Acts xviii. 24 ff.). Finally, in Rome, all sorts and kinds would jostle one another—Judaizing Christian synagogues, the most liberal of liberal 'gnosticizing' sorts, looking more like a mystery cult than the Israel of God, Petrine congregations, Pauline congregations, and all the rest (cf. Phil. i. 12-17, and the implications of Rom. xv. 20).

[1] For John the Baptist's connexion with Samaria, note the tradition of his burial there (for which see Jerome's Latin version of Eusebius' *Onomasticon s.v.* 'Someron' (p. 155, ed. Klostermann): 'dicunt autem nunc pro ea Sebasten vocari oppidum Palaestinae, *ubi sancti Ioannis baptistae reliquiae conditae sunt*' (the italicized words correspond to nothing in Eusebius' text), and Theodoret *H.E.* iii. 3, where, under Julian the Apostate, they opened ἡ θήκη of John the Baptist, burned his bones, and scattered the ashes). For his connexion with the Fourth Gospel, see *inter alios*, J. A. T. Robinson, 'The "Others" of John 4, 38', *Studia Evangelica* (*T. und U.* 73), 1959, 510 ff.; and for an exposure of the thinness of the evidence for rival 'Baptist sects', see *id.* 'Elijah, John and Jesus: an Essay in Detection' *J.N.T.S.* 4. 4 (July 1958), 279, n. 2.

For Samaritan eschatology, and the interpretation of Deut. xviii. 15 ff. in terms of *Ta'eb* (the 'returning' or 'restoring' one), see J. A. Montgomery, *The Samaritans* (1907), 245 ff., F. J. Foakes-Jackson and K. Lake, *The Beginnings of Christianity*, i (1920), 406, A. Merx, *Der Messias oder* Ta'eb *der Samaritaner* (1909), O. Cullmann, *Christology of the New Testament* (Eng. trans., 1959, of *Die Christologie des Neuen Testaments*, 1957), 19.

What was the minimum constituent of a Christian community? How far away from the apostolic *kerygma* must one stray to be altogether outside the fold?[1] What are we to make of the 'disciples' at Ephesus who knew only John's Baptism (Acts xix. 1 ff.)?[2] Or, what should we say (to take an instance from much later and from a remote field) of the account given by the seventeenth-century Jesuit missionary Matteo Ricci of what a Chinese Jew told him when asked if he had any knowledge of the Christians in the towns from which he came? He did not even recognize them by that name, but when explanations were made by signs he acknowledged that there were certain foreigners who had come to China with their ancestors and worshipped the cross. Why they worshipped the cross neither he, nor, so he believed, they themselves could say; and their only name was 'men who do not eat animals with uncloven hoofs', because 'while the Moors and Jews and the whole of China eat the flesh of horses, mules and other such beasts of burden, they follow the custom of their native land and do not eat it . . .' (A. C. Moule, *Christians in China* . . ., 1930, 1 ff.). To have gone so far from a consciously accepted Christian confession is obviously to have left the essentials far behind; but what is the limit? Is the test nothing more than baptism in the name of Christ?

The answer to which the early Church was feeling its way is reflected in the canon of the New Testament. As will be seen (see Chapter X), the writings ultimately excluded from the canon were mainly those which, even when claiming some apostolic connexion, presented an estimate of Jesus out of accord with the apostolic estimate now reflected in the New Testament collectively. This means that there must have been a commonly recognized norm of Christian confession forming itself on the basis of the apostolic *kerygma*. Judged by this standard, any estimate of Jesus which did not acknowledge his historical existence and his real death would be out; so would any which did not acknowledge the resurrection and the decisiveness of his fulfilment of God's plan of salvation outlined

[1] See W. Bauer, *Rechtgläubigkeit und Ketzerei im ältesten Christentum* (1934).
[2] See E. Käsemann, 'Die Johannesjünger in Ephesus', *Z.Th.K.* 49 (1952), 144 ff., reprinted in *Exegetische Versuche und Besinnungen*, i (1960), 158 ff.

in the Old Testament. In other words, a gnostic dualism which denied either the historical humanity or the absolute 'transcendence' of Jesus would be disqualified. This test finds explicit expression in 1 and 2 Jn.

But within these limits there is a wide range of emphasis; and the writings of the New Testament help to make it articulate for us. As mountain-tops stand up from the ocean bed to form islands and to be, for the voyager, the only visible expression of the submerged continent beneath, so the writings of the New Testament give us some idea of the range and variety of the less articulate Christianity within the ambit of the apostolic confession. Outside that ambit, the apocryphal New Testament[1] articulates the vagaries of belief and speculation standing up in the alien seas into which so many voyaged. But the two submerged continents are more nearly continuous than the distinctions above water might suggest. If apocryphal writings are fairly clearly separated from orthodox, that only indicates the difference between the leaders on either side: the masses beneath them were quite likely found merging.

If we ask what factors helped to shape the variations and to give different and distinctive characters to different colonies of Christians, it may be well to begin from a consideration of social and economic conditions. Not that the New Testament writings can be divided into those for the poor and those for the rich, or even, very satisfactorily, into those for the simple and those for the learned. But such a picture of social structure as can be reconstructed, certainly contributes to our understanding of the range of thought and feeling in our documents.

When one is asking about the social and intellectual standing of New Testament Christians, one passage inevitably springs to mind—1 Cor. i. 26 ff.; 'My brothers, think what sort of people you are, whom God has called. Few of you are men of wisdom, by any human standard; few are powerful or highly born. Yet, to shame the wise, God has chosen what the world counts folly, and to shame what is strong, God has chosen what the world counts weakness. He has chosen things low and contemptible,

---

[1] For the New Testament apocrypha, see E. Hennecke, *Neutestamentliche Apocryphen*[3] (ed. Schneemelcher); and M. R. James, *The Apocryphal New Testament*.

mere nothings, to overthrow the existing order. . . .' If one adds to this the fact that, in the Pauline Epistles, there are several allusions to slaves as members of the Church, one is tempted at first sight to conclude that, at this stage, there were few Christians drawn from the more educated or more influential and wealthy levels of society.

But such a conclusion requires considerable qualification (cf. W. L. Knox, *St. Paul and the Church of the Gentiles*, 1939, 125). In the first place, the passage in 1 Cor. i would probably never have been written had there not been educated Christians in that congregation who were contemptuous about the crudities of others. To some extent, then, it bears witness to the very reverse of the conditions it is often used to illustrate. Next, as for slaves, though many may indeed have been uneducated, we are told that they were by no means generally illiterate (see, e.g., A. C. Bouquet, *Everyday Life in New Testament Times*, 1953, 161). Then again, the Jewish element is a complicating factor. It seems fair to assume that, broadly speaking, the average Jew was better educated than the average Gentile, if only because Jewish family life was the soundest in the empire, and also the education which Jewish children received in the synagogue school was, within its limits, probably more conscientious and thorough than the teaching given by Gentile schoolmasters who had not necessarily the intensity of vocation belonging to a devout teacher of the Torah.[1] It is far from impossible that, on the whole, the Jewish members also included a high proportion of the reasonably prosperous—such is the notorious diligence, efficiency, and astuteness of their race. On the other hand, they are not likely to have had specially influential connexions, considering how few Jews held office in the Empire. Not 'influence', then, but intelligence, literacy, and familiarity with the ways of fair prosperity, even when they were not themselves enjoying it— these qualities might be represented by such as Paul, Apollos, Aquila, and Priscilla, and, indeed, even the original disciples like Peter and John. The latter are, it is true, called 'unlettered',

---

[1] See *T. J. Kethuboth*, 32c, 4; W. Barclay, *Educational Ideals in the Ancient World* (1959), ch. 1; G. Bertram, 'Der Begriff der Erziehung in der griechischen Bibel', *Imago Dei (Festschrift für G. Krüger* (1932)), 41 ff., and article παιδεύω in *T.W.N.T.*

ἀγράμματοι, in Acts iv. 13, but that need only mean that they were not up to rabbinical standards in their knowledge of the exegetical niceties, not that they could not read or write (see p. 183, n. 2 below).

Still considering the Jewish Christian element in the New Testament period, we note that the Epistle of James would be important evidence if only we knew anything about its provenance and purpose. If it really is addressed to Christians, then in their 'synagogue' there were extremes of wealth and poverty (see ii. 1-13, iv. 1-v. 6); and, doctrinally, the writer and his readers were 'Ebionite'. But we simply do not know enough to say whether such conditions were representative or exceptional —if, indeed, the Epistle is not basically an address to Jews who were not yet even Christians.

For the rest, it is difficult to find positive evidence of Christianity having, by this period, won any lasting allegiance from the influential or wealthy: Clemens is too common a name for it to be even likely that the one named in Phil. iv. 3 might be otherwise identifiable. That he was 'Clement of Rome' is unlikely enough; as for the attempt to make him into the Flavius Clemens who was a relation of the Emperor Domitian, this labours under vast difficulties, one of the least being the necessity of making Philippians post-Pauline. (See J. B. Lightfoot's demolition of the theory *in loc.*) The Erastus of Rom. xvi. 23 was 'the *oikonomos*' (i.e., perhaps Treasurer) 'of the city' (i.e., probably Corinth); but there is no need for such an officer of a provincial city council to have been a man of more than local eminence, if of eminence at all.[1] It is true there are one or two Christians named in the New Testament who seem at least before their conversion to have had some connexion with the

[1] See H. J. Cadbury, 'Erastus of Corinth', *J.B.L.* 50 (1931), 42 ff. (an examination of the possibility of identifying with a New Testament Erastus the Erastus of a Corinthian inscription discovered in 1929, and concluding against identification). He argues (47 ff.) that in the Roman period οἰκονόμος in such a context may well have corresponded with *arcarius* (as it is translated in the Vulgate), and adds (p. 51) 'The *arcarius* was invariably a slave or of servile origin, though he may often have been wealthy'; (p. 57) '. . . the associations of *arcarius* or οἰκονόμος do not imply social preeminence such as wealth and station bring, and those commentators are probably wrong who cite Erastus as an exception to Paul's description of the first Corinthian Christians. . . .' See also E. A. Judge, *The Social Pattern of Christian Groups in the First Century* (1960), esp. ch. v.

Jewish or semi-Jewish aristocracy of Palestine. Such are Manaen, who had belonged to the court circle of Herod Antipas (Acts xiii. 1), and Joanna whose husband Chuza held responsible office in the household of some Herod, probably, again, Antipas (Lk. viii. 3).

But otherwise, it appears that the most influential Christians were only locally influential while the majority were, in the eyes of the world, nonentities, nobodies, often slaves. On the other hand, it is only fair to add that there is equally no evidence of Christianity having reached the lowest of the low, namely the pathetically degraded land-slaves or condemned criminals who worked in the forced labour gangs on the great estates or in the mines and factories—except, that is, when Christians were themselves condemned to the mines.[1] The New Testament allusions to slaves, where they are sufficiently explicit, imply the household slaves, whose lot, equally intolerable in principle, was generally in fact mitigated by at least some sense of 'belonging' to a small and intimate community and did not necessarily reduce them to a completely mechanical, sub-human condition. At least some of these may have been educated persons.

All this adds up to the conclusion that, if one were compelled to generalize, one would say that the social level of most Christian communities was probably towards the lower end of the scale without touching 'rock bottom'. If the Christian Gospel had never reached down to the bottom it is because the labour-gang type were incapable of being reached: who was there to preach to them, and how could he preach?—unless, indeed, there were one or two who had been converted to the faith before being taken prisoner and forced to join such a labour-gang. But even so, their chances of reaching their fellow slaves would be slender in the extreme.

But, within the social limits just defined, there was, in fact, almost certainly a considerable range of variety, as between one local group and another. The geographical situation and

[1] The only actual instance for this in the New Testament period, however, is that of John on Patmos, if this is how his situation is to be interpreted. But this cannot be demonstrated to be penal exile, still less condemnation to work in the mines. See again E. A. Judge, *op. cit.* 60. The evidence for the later persecutions is collected by J. G. Davies in *University of Birmingham Historical Journal*, 6 (1958), 99-107.

condition of the towns and villages in question no doubt had its effect. Corinth and Athens, Alexandria, Ephesus and Antioch, and, above all, Rome, were commercial centres of great importance. Philippi and Laodicea, on main roads, must have been cosmopolitan towns. On the other hand, little Palestinian communities were on a much more primitive level of culture. The level of intelligence and quickness in Church meetings at a place like Corinth must have differed from that at, say, Samaria in its early Christian days much as a London youth organization might differ in speed of uptake and smartness from a club for village youths in some tiny rural community. And there would be differences in material prosperity also. But the wealth of a particular locality only implies the possibility of wealthy members being enlisted to a community: it of course does not guarantee it. And in fact the Philippian Christians were desperately poor—and (as so often happens in such circumstances) wonderfully generous (2 Cor. viii. 2). At Corinth there may have been some relatively rich Christians (1 Cor. iv. 8?). The Jewish Christian communities in Palestine were poor enough to be in need of alms from the Gentile Churches. In the community addressed by James there were poor being ground down by the wealthy. As for the levels of intellect represented, it would be too much to expect that the more profound parts of the Pauline Epistles were properly understood by all or even many in the communities addressed. If one could be sure that Paul always wrote so as to be generally understood, the conclusion would be that there was a very high level of intellect in, say, Corinth and Colossae: for to catch the full meaning of such a passage as 1 Cor. xv or Col. i at first hearing would imply considerable mental agility, even given an intimacy with the circumstances to which the letters were expressly addressed. But there is no guarantee that great minds always rightly estimate the capacity of others (often the reverse is the case), and the slaves, shopkeepers, and smallholders in Paul's congregations probably admired but at certain points gaped at the apostle's storm of words.

There were, nevertheless, at Corinth certainly, and perhaps elsewhere also, a certain number who prided themselves on their intellect and on their superiority to superstition: so much so that

Paul, while understanding and accepting their own position, had to admonish them to consider the conscience of others. And presumably in the Lycus valley churches there were at least a few subtle exponents of the complex doctrines which Paul attacks in Col., while the Johannine Epistles imply some degree of perverse subtlety in the heretics and their converts. Again the recipients of the Epistle to the Hebrews must have been steeped in the Greek Old Testament and in certain techniques of exposition, if the writer's arguments were to be in any way effective—so much so that commentators rightly observe that they must surely have constituted a smallish group of particularly highly educated persons—a little 'clan' of rabbinically trained thinkers. The suggestion has already been made (see p. 75 above) that they may have all at one time belonged to a single synagogue. And if it is right to trace, behind St Matthew's Gospel, a school of Christian exegesis (see p. 74 above), that, too, points to what might be called a kind of Christian higher education, privately developed within the Christian communities: a 'scribal' Christianity.

As for the writers of the New Testament themselves, much could be said about the varieties of style among them.[1] If one were to summarize the facts very briefly, it might be said that Hebrews and James, though in different ways, both show a command of idiomatic Greek; that Luke is versatile—capable now of imitating the self-conscious and rather ornate style of contemporary historians, now of writing biblical (Septuagintal) Greek, and now of accepting distinctly un-Greek, Semitic sources into his scheme; that Matthew seems nearly always to use careful and correct Greek, though he does not indulge in the literary flourishes occasionally displayed by Luke nor attempt to conceal Semitic idioms in his sources; that Mark writes in the idiom of one more familiar with a Semitic tongue than with

---

[1] One specific instance (to name a phenomenon at random) is provided by the examination of the preposition σύν in Kittel's *T.W.N.T.* (*s.v.*) where it is observed that σύν is totally absent from Hebrews and the Johannine Epistles. Vagaries of style in respect of small words often provide important pointers to individuality. For Paul's vocabulary, see T. Nägeli, *Der Wortschatz des Apostels Paulus* (1905); for Matt., Excursus I below. R. Morgenthaler, *Statistik des neutestamentlichen Wortschatzes* (1958) is a most useful guide.

Greek; that Paul, or his amanuenses, wrote in a variety of styles, sometimes very strongly Semitic, sometimes rather less so, but nearly always tense and brilliant and lively; while the Gospel and Epistles of John are in a peculiar style, mainly correct, superficially simple and unadorned, but in fact complicatedly charged with meaning and more Semitic than Greek in essential character. The Apocalypse stands alone as the only New Testament writing containing considerable sections of quite barbarously ungrammatical writing, which, nevertheless, achieve a profoundly moving effect.

But to return to the main theme: given such intellectual activity (even among a minority) as seems evidenced by Hebrews and Matthew and the Pauline Epistles, it is not surprising that rivalry and faction showed themselves also. The *locus classicus* for this is, of course, i Cor. i-iv. J. Munck (*Paul and the Salvation of Mankind*, Eng. trans., 1959, of *Paulus und die Heilsgeschichte*, 1954) has argued that what is indicated by i Corinthians is not necessarily a radical partisanship running right up from the foundation apostles, and that it is possible grossly to exaggerate the cleavage implied. What Paul is castigating, he thinks, is rather the Corinthians' tendency to treat their leaders like Greek sophists and side with one of them against the rest. Whatever one thinks about this in detail, it is true that there is nothing here to prove a conflict between Peter and Paul. But Phil. i. 15 ff, certainly compels us to recognize deliberate partisanship in some quarters. And the *a priori* likelihood is certainly that there would be a variety of emphases, tendencies, outlook, and approach in different groups of Christians, which would ultimately harden into distinguishable schools of thought.

This consideration of the social and intellectual stratification of the Christian communities has thus led to two conclusions: that the average level was low though not as low as it would have been if the slave gangs had been included; and that correspondingly high must have been the respect accorded to the giants of intellect and of spirituality—the Pauls and the Johns—and the temptation to follow the exciting vagaries of sectarians who exaggerated the respective tendencies of these giants. It is not surprising, therefore, if we find marked differences in emphasis and tone as between the representative writings of different localities and various traditions. The marvel is—and this is the main 'moral' of this chapter—that the basic Christian convictions persist with such remarkable consistency through such diversity.

When Christian thought is traced out beyond the New Testament period, it is well known that certain broad distinctions are found setting in as between such centres as Antioch and Alexandria: Antioch, with its tendency to stress the literal and the historical, and with them the humanity of Jesus; Alexandria, with its tradition of allegory and symbol and its greater stress on the transcendent. It is all too easy to contrast these two emphases in a mechanical manner, without allowing for subtle interchanges and variations. For instance, one of the elementary qualifications that would need to be made, were we attempting to describe this period, would be the recognition that even the Antiochene thinkers did not rest content with the plain, historical sense of scripture. If they differed from the Alexandrines, it was not so much in rejecting other senses as in preferring 'typology', which recognizes the importance of historical events as such, to allegory, which would reduce everything to timeless truths.

But if we look back to the roots of this broad divergence in New Testament times, we can already discern its beginnings. Here, too, however, definition is made difficult by the number of different factors already contributing to the thinking of the New Testament Christians. Suppose we start by a too extreme simplification. Abandoning cautious qualifications for the moment, and attempting a kind of caricature, we might say that Jewish Christianity, with its strongly monotheistic presuppositions and its readiness to welcome earthly rulers and prophets in the name of God, might be expected to hold on to the 'fleshly'—τὸ κατὰ σάρκα—in Jesus and to ignore or belittle his divinity. These were, in fact, the tendencies of what soon came to be called Ebionism (from the Hebrew word for 'poor', used proudly for a Franciscan poverty and simplicity or used derogatorily for a poverty of doctrine, a *psilosis* or attenuation in Christology). The Ebionites were among the Judaizing types of sub-apostolic Christianity, and their tendency was towards 'adoptionism'— the theory that Jesus, the human prophet, came to be 'adopted' as God's Son in a supernal sense—won his way up, as it were, by outstanding goodness.[1] Caricaturing the opposite wing, one might call it typically pagan, and say that it started from polytheistic presuppositions and was familiar with the ideas of the demi-god and of the pre-existent saviour who descends into the material world to rescue those who respond or who are predestined. When converted to faith in Jesus, such a type will stress Christ's pre-existence and his descent from heaven, and, by concentrating on his supramundane origin, may lose grip upon his real humanity. If the 'Jewish' error leads to adoptionism, the latter is the road to monophysitism—the obliteration of the human in the transcendent.

But in fact neither of these types ever existed in an unadulterated form. To draw them thus as clearly contrasting shapes is to caricature. We know, more decisively even than previous generations of New Testament students, that already by the time of Christ monotheistic Judaism had been deeply penetrated by an oriental dualism: witness the Qumran sect. Possibly even a measure of western rationalism had also crept into the recesses of Hebrew thought (Ecclesiastes has been accused of Epicurean tendencies!). And thus even the strongholds of Jerusalem rabbinism had already been penetrated by many extraneous ideas. Indeed, it might be nearer the truth to say that the antecedents of Israel, in Egypt and Mesopotamia, had long before sown seeds of this type. Hellenistic ideas are thus not *a priori* unthinkable in James the Lord's brother; nor 'gnostic' ideas in Paul (though in fact they are hard to find); nor even the idea of a divine hero-king in such comparatively early Hebrew writers as Isaiah or a Psalmist.

We shall not, therefore, expect to find anywhere—least of all in the New Testament—the reflection of 'pure' Ebionism or 'pure' transcendentalism. But tendencies in one direction or another may be looked for and are worth tracing; and it is of real importance to ask to what extent the writings ultimately held within the New Testament canon show a consistent controlling conviction which both includes complementary tenden-

[1] But see E. Schweizer, *Lordship and Discipleship* (as on p. 56, n. 3), 37, for warnings against tracing a direct connexion between New Testament phrases and adoptionism.

cies and excludes really incompatible elements in such a way as to produce coherence.

The answer to the latter question is that the criterion of 'apostolicity'—faithfulness to the apostolic *kerygma*—did in fact admit within the canon only those writings which kept sufficiently close to the Christ-event to achieve this coherence. Once begin to speculate and to dogmatize about what must be or may have been, and any extremes may set in; but to keep close to the apostolic witness is necessarily to affirm that the Gospel 'is about [God's] Son: on the human level he was born of David's stock, but on the level of spirit—the Holy Spirit—he was declared God's Son by a mighty act in that he rose from the dead: it is about Jesus Christ our Lord' (Rom. i. 3 f.). The real humanity, and, with it, the inclusive, representative person, such that (as Paul saw) his resurrection *is* the general resurrection on the Last Day—these are the two elements in the apostolic *kerygma* which give coherence to all the diversity within the New Testament.

But at the margins it sails dangerously near to the excluded area: the Epistle of James might, for all the signs it shows of Christology, be near-Ebionite; 2 Pet. makes startling concessions to Greek ideas of divine nature: '. . . you may escape the corruption with which lust has infected the world, and come to share in the very being of God' (i. 4); and the Fourth Gospel, if it were the only Gospel, might leave us with an almost monophysite Christ, and a markedly individualistic religion (see pp. 94, 98 above). It is the central conviction which holds together these diversities and which also draws the circumference where it does.

How much better our understanding of the New Testament would be if we possessed more information about Judaistic Christianity![1] James the Lord's brother remains a too little known character. In Acts xv we find him, at the head of Jerusalem Christianity, deciding for the non-circumcision of Gentile converts, and clinching his argument by what seems to be a Greek mistranslation of the Hebrew of Amos (Acts xv. 17). In Acts xxi he is counselling Paul to demonstrate his own allegiance

[1] See J. Daniélou, *Théologie du judéo-christianisme* (1958); F. C. Grant, *Ancient Judaism and the New Testament* (²1960).

to the ritual law. According to Hegesippus (*ap*. Euseb. *H.E.* ii. 23) he is so Jewish as to be expected by the Jews to denounce the Nazarene faith, and is martyred for refusing to do so.[1] In apocryphal legend he is visited by the risen Lord himself (Jerome, *De vir. ill.* 2). Whatever we make of the Epistle of James, it is not out of character with many of these hints. It betrays a considerable acquaintance with the Greek moralists and sophists; it is so Jewish as to stress the Law and almost obscure the Gospel. And although it scarcely mentions Jesus, yet, try as one will, one cannot eliminate from its texture a certain number of phrases which seem to be stubbornly Christian in form. Is it, then, perhaps, an attempt by a Jewish Christian to conciliate non-Christian Jews? But if so, it is by one who still actually belongs within their synagogue, and is that conceivable? Is it not, then, rather the extremest example within the New Testament of Judaistic Christianity, reflecting a community whose members still worshipped in synagogue style, and threw a characteristically Jewish stress on character and conduct, but confessed Jesus as God's 'glory' (ii. 1) and believed themselves re-born by the Christian Gospel (i. 18)? Yet, if so, we have to date it, nonetheless, at a period when an antinomian interpretation of Christian liberty had already set in (Jas ii. 14 ff.)—whether through Paul's disciples or not is not clear. Whichever way we turn, the interpretation of the Epistle is beset by problems. But at any rate it reflects a type of Christianity as different as can well be imagined from the Pauline or Johannine, yet one that confesses Jesus as Lord (i. 1, ii. 1), believes in rebirth by God through the Gospel (i. 18), and looks forward to a denouement (v. 7).[2]

At the opposite extreme to the tendencies exhibited in James, there must have been a temptation so to identify Jesus with the

[1] See p. 153, n. 1.

[2] In a discussion of Jewish diaspora homilies H. Thyen takes James to be a synagogue homily worked over very slightly by a Christian (*Der Stil der jüdisch-hellenistischen Homilie*, 1955, 14-17). But on such a hypothesis it is difficult to explain why the working over was both so slight and so subtle. Paul Feine's study (see p. 30, n. 2 above) contains much that is still of value. He argued for the possibility that all the allegedly non-Jewish allusions in James could have reached a Palestinian Jew such as the Lord's brother through Jewish apocalyptic sources. On the whole, more recent discoveries (especially the Qumran literature, etc.) go to support this view.

Spirit or the Wisdom of God as to minimize his historical particularity. As a matter of fact, however, it is remarkable how difficult it is to illustrate this end of the spectrum from the New Testament itself. The *Logos* in St John is notoriously (and no doubt to the pagan reader shockingly) portrayed as having become flesh, σάρξ (i. 14); and although the Fourth Gospel does lean sometimes in a docetist direction (Jesus' questions are artificial ones, framed for the sake of the disciples, vi. 6), yet nothing is clearer than the evangelist's determination to stress the reality of the incarnation: the 'scandal of particularity' and of materiality is never avoided but positively embraced (vi. 52). The Epistles to the Colossians (i. 15 ff.) and to the Hebrews (i. 1 ff.) both contain what is a 'logos-doctrine' in all but the actual term; yet they too are as clear as can be about the reality of the earthly life. And although later writers like Justin confuse Word and Spirit, the New Testament very strikingly confines 'Spirit' almost entirely to its account of God's dealings with his People in the 'new creation', using the Logos and Christ, not Spirit, in its allusions to the universe and cosmogony. Christ and Spirit are sometimes interchangeable—or nearly so—within the Church, but never outside it. And all this probably bears witness to the successful avoidance, in the New Testament, of that dualism, so common in the pagan world and in heretical Christianity, which treated matter as evil—essential Manichaeism. The doctrine of matter and of creation is the real touchstone: and, for all its range of diversity, the New Testament does not founder on the Manichaean rock.

Part of the New Testament's diversity is due precisely to the variety of alien positions which are combated: it debates from a single platform, but from different corners of it; and so far as it does lean over towards any extremes, it is because the writers, at those points, recognize particularly clearly what are the positions that are being occupied by error and recoil violently from them. Paul sees especially vividly what principle is involved in the superficially good or harmless stress on Jewish legal rectitude, and therefore goes so far as to say that if Christians get themselves circumcised Christ will be useless to them (Gal. v. 2). James sees the selfish laziness which claims that correct belief is sufficient without corresponding conduct (ii. 14 ff.), and 1 Jn throughout attacks the dangerous position which holds that once baptized the Christian is secure, whatever his morals: and both James and John are led to extreme statements—faith without conduct is dead (Jas ii. 26); a Christian cannot sin (1 Jn iii. 9).

It is not unlikely that Christian congregations originally founded by one or other of these great protagonists would tend (rather like denominations today) to retain and exaggerate or stylize the particular emphases with which the Gospel had originally been presented to them. There may well have been distinctive stamps upon, respectively, Pauline, Petrine, Johannine, and Jacobaean churches. According to the Acts, Philip the evangelist and probably Barnabas (with John Mark) also engaged in independent evangelism (Acts viii. 26 ff.; cf. xxi. 8, xv. 39), and, for all we know, their churches too may have stood for something distinctive. It would be particularly interesting to know more about the Gospel in Samaritan territory: is it not likely that here, too, there were particular characteristics (see p. 154 above, and note 1)? But everywhere there hangs a curtain of obscurity; and all that we can say is that the traditions that accumulated in any given centre must have to some extent been selected, moulded, and applied in accordance with the local tendencies, and that this explains the diversity of emphases in the Gospels—both internally and in relation to one another.

Turning, then, to look more closely at the diversity of emphases within the New Testament, we shall do best to offer a crude, rough-and-ready classification of types, leaving it for further study to break them down and qualify them more precisely. And it will be well to recall frequently how much wider is the gulf that separates the New Testament as a whole from non-canonical writings than the distances between different parts within the New Testament itself. Even the so-called Apostolic Fathers are (with the partial exception of the letters of Ignatius) separated from most of the New Testament by a considerable gap in outlook and approach.[1]

First, then, there is the broad distinction between the Epistle to the Hebrews and, one might almost say, the rest of the New

[1] See T. F. Torrance, *The Doctrine of Grace in the Apostolic Fathers* (1948), though it is a question whether, on his showing, James ought not to join the ranks of the Apostolic Fathers.

Testament. Hebrews, more than any other part, presses into service the Platonic conception (adopted also by Philo) of a supra-sensible world of absolute reality over against a sensible world which is only its reflection or copy (though even in Paul there is 2 Cor. iv. 18, v. 7, Col. ii. 17); and entertains a conception of Christ as the Hero and Leader—the Pioneer whom Christians are to follow to the heights. Neither idea is consistently carried through: the Christian tradition is too strong to allow it. This shadow-world which is but a copy of the transcendent is not so Platonic but that in it the decisive act of history takes place—the purgation of sins; and Jesus is not really only a Hercules toiling upwards to the stars, for he is already the pre-existent utterance of God. The writer to the Hebrews makes bigger concessions to Greek ways of expression than Paul or John; but there is never a doubt but that, in common with all apostolic Christianity, he takes time seriously and thinks of history as significant and of this world as an important arena of divine action, and that he sees Jesus as infinitely more than a hero winning immortality. Perhaps Paul, and even John, are more firmly on the Hebrew side of the line; but Hebrews, for all its concessions, never surrenders 'the scandal of particularity'. Indeed, it is clear enough that throughout the treatise, it is non-Christian Judaism that is being combated by being claimed, absorbed, and transcended; and even if it is a Philonian, Alexandrian Judaism, it is nothing like a genuinely Greek philosophy or a rootless gnosticism.[1]

Then, secondly, there is the broad distinction between, on the one hand, the Pauline emphasis on the essential powerlessness of man—his complete helplessness to save himself[2]—and, on the other hand, the tendency of the Epistle of James to see

---

[1] On the Epistle to the Hebrews, besides the Commentaries, note C. Spicq, 'Le Philonisme de l'Épître aux Hébreux', *R.B.* lvii. 2 (April 1950), 212 ff.; C. K. Barrett, 'The Eschatology of the Epistle to the Hebrews', and J. Héring, 'Eschatologie biblique et idéalisme platonicien' in *The Background of the New Testament and its Eschatology* (eds. D. Daube and W. D. Davies, *in hon.* C. H. Dodd, 1956), 363 ff., 444 ff.; H. Kosmala, *Hebräer-Essener-Christen* (1959).

[2] For this motif also in the Dead Sea Scrolls, see S. Schulz, 'Zur Rechtfertigung aus Gnaden in Qumran und bei Paulus', *Z.Th.K.* 56 (1959), 155 ff., suggesting that Paul himself inherited the idea of justification by faith from an anti-Pharisaic Qumran-stream of tradition which might have come early into the primitive Church.

religion as duty and kindness and to credit man with the ability to resist temptation—a stress by no means alien to the Christ of the Synoptic Gospels, especially Matthew's. Corresponding to this contrast is the Pauline and Johannine conception of Christianity as incorporation or 'abiding' in Christ over against the conception of discipleship, imitating, following, which runs (not unnaturally) through the Synoptic accounts of the ministry of Jesus, but finds a place also in Hebrews. In the New Testament as a whole, Christ is both pattern and power (for this useful terminology, see A. B. D. Alexander, *The Ethics of Paul*, 1910, 105 ff.); but there is more of pattern and less of power in some of the writings than in others. The Pastoral Epistles (as a whole, though they are probably composite of Pauline and deutero-pauline material) seem to represent a confluence of the two streams—a second-generation Christianity which repeats the Gospel of the free grace of God ('not by works . . .', Tit. iii. 5) but which, in a more widely Christianized setting, finds it not unnatural to think of man's ability to keep the law (? 1 Tim. i. 8 ff.).

Thirdly, one may distinguish the apocalyptic tendency—to despair of the present and to look forward breathlessly and count the days to the day of rescue—from the tendency to concentrate on the here and now and to estimate human history positively. At opposite extremes in this respect are the Apocalypse and the Gospel of St Luke. It is not that Luke does not expect a Day of Judgment and a coming of the Lord: about these he is as explicit as anybody. But he is concerned primarily with a positive estimate of the intervening period—and that, a comparatively prolonged one—as a vital part of the working out of the Kingdom of God, and his attention is on that (e.g. Lk. xix. 11 ff.). The Apocalypse, by contrast, is concerned to convey, by symbol and picture, the conviction that it is the end that is decisive and that that end spells victory for the cause of God.

There is an eschatological contrast also, but in a quite different sense, between Luke and the Fourth Gospel. It is Luke, not John, who most definitively represents the non-apocalyptic end of the scale: the Fourth Gospel is not strictly speaking much concerned with either end, for its real focal point is the relation of the individual to God—Jesus Christ (see above, p. 94). For the individual who loves God and does his will, who believes in Jesus as the Son of God and abides in the real Vine, eternal life is already realized; and the Gospel scarcely concerns itself with the corporate gathering up of God's purposes or the course of the Church's perfecting: that is the theme, far more, of the Epistle to the Ephesians, which has a very strong forward-looking, futurist hope, although its goal is in terms of maturity and fulness of growth, not in terms of judgment and apocalypse (Eph. iv. 11-16; cf. Rom. viii.). A fourth pair of contrasting tendencies, thus, might be the individualist over against the corporate. In the Johannine Epistles there is a mediating position: they are more corporate, and therefore also more apocalyptic, than the Gospel; but the corporate ideas in 1 Jn are less comprehensive and universal than in Eph. and its apocalyptic ideas are more individual.[1]

A fifth contrast might be found in the intuitive genius of St John (well summed up in the famous story of the dying John simply saying over and over again, 'Little children, love one another'—Jerome, *In ep. ad Gal.* vi. 10), and the vigorously intellectual genius of Paul. Paul argues, where John affirms; and John simply utters resonant, suggestive, poetic words, where Paul labours to explain.

Sixthly, there are varieties in the interpretation of authority and Church-order. As has already been said, Christians of the New Testament period recognized the revival of the Spirit of prophecy; and their ultimate authority was always God in Jesus through his Spirit in the Church. But there were varieties of mediation. In Paul almost everything is represented, from the rabbinic interpretation of scripture to the authority of vision and audition in prophetic ecstasy. But in the Pastoral Epistles inspired scripture and sound Christian traditions seem to be the main oracles.

Similarly, it is possible to trace, behind the New Testament, the form both of 'charismatic' communities, and constitutional ministries. Some depended upon no clearly defined order of ministry but upon the spontaneous leadership of inspiration;

[1] See C. F. D. Moule, 'The Individualism of the Fourth Gosple', *Nov.T.* (*Festheft* for E. Stauffer), forthcoming.

others were organized round an articulated ministry of elder-overseers and assistants (presbyter-episcopi and deacons)—perhaps even a triple ministry of 'apostolic men', overseer-presbyters, and deacons; and there may sometimes have been other constitutionally recognized officers corresponding to Jewish types such as scribes and sages.

It is a familiar fact that the Christian scribe appears in Matt. (xiii. 52; cf. xxiii. 34), and it is possible that this Gospel, in its miscellaneous traditions, also reflects a variety of community ideals, some charismatic, some constitutional, some acceptable to the Evangelist himself, others alien to his outlook. E. Käsemann has pointed out[1] that Christian theology, in some of its early phases, represents a conflict between opposing schools, all alike appealing to the authority of the Spirit, but in very different ways—'enthusiasm' (in the technical sense of that word) with miracle-working (reflected perhaps derogatorily in Matt. vii. 22-25), a Jewish and rabbinical type of organization (note Matt. xxiii. 8-10), legalistic Judaism (for which some might quote Matt. v. 17-20, though it can be otherwise interpreted), and, at the opposite extreme, the kind of liberalism and universalism for which perhaps Stephen stood. Different outlooks, embodying different structures of society, criss-cross confusingly in the dim background of the New Testament, within Jewish Christianity as well as in Gentile Churches. In the last analysis, a good deal of it can be expressed in terms of varying eschatologies. Some groups perhaps saw the conversion of the Jews as the first necessity before any further spread of the Gospel; others, led by St Paul, looked for the reverse process: only when the full complement of the Gentiles had come in would all Israel be saved (Rom. xi. 25). Some looked to human labour, others expected a supernatural intervention. To postulate this diversity of organization and of expectation goes some way towards accounting for the diverse traditions that seem to be reflected in such a writing as St Matthew's Gospel.[2]

It would be easy to go on multiplying these rough-and-ready antitheses; but they all need modifying and refining, and these are only mentioned as examples of the type of phenomenon that

---

[1] 'Die Anfänge christlicher Theologie', *Z.Th.K.* 57. 2 (1960), 162 ff.
[2] See p. 87, n. 2; p. 90.

may be watched for—not as the 'antitheses of what is falsely called knowledge'! If we return, for a moment, to the types of error that are attacked in the New Testament, they will serve as a foil to, and in part, an explanation of, these varying tendencies. But again, they can be treated only in a broad way, as a mere preliminary to proper investigation.

An obvious one, already touched on, is the Judaistic effort after merit, attacked by Paul. It is not true that Paul thought of faith as saving from sin. He is sometimes represented as replacing 'works' by 'faith'—as though, whereas a man cannot save himself by his deeds, his faith (if only he can summon up enough of it) will save him. But what in fact Paul is saying is that nothing at all that comes from man's side can make fellowship with God possible: nothing of man's 'own', that he 'possesses', can qualify him to enter the Presence. It is only when he flings away all attempts to qualify, and accepts what God offers as a free gift (as an act of 'grace' or gracious generosity) that he can be brought into fellowship with God. But fellowship is a personal relationship; and the offer of restored fellowship therefore requires the entire person's trust—his whole-hearted response—if it is to be entered into. Faith is, for Paul, this commitment to God's goodness and faithfulness which is not the ground of, but simply the response to, God's gift. Paul thus radically opposes—rules out altogether—human merit and deserving. In contrast, Judaism (though only at its crudest) did hold that man could make himself deserving of God's favour by performing acceptable deeds such as almsgiving. And it is this conception of deserving and of self-reliance in all its forms that Paul attacks (Rom. ix. 31, x. 3)—whether in the form of reliance upon good conduct, or of reliance upon ritual correctness (such as circumcision), or upon Jewish descent, or upon correct belief. This conflict helps to explain much of Galatians and Romans. Paul, himself a circumcised and well-born Jew, was quite ready to observe Jewish ritual and custom (1 Cor. ix. 20; cf. Acts xxi. 20 ff.); but he is out like a flash against anyone who claims that anything of the sort can be a basis for salvation (Gal. ii. 17 ff., v. 4).

On the other hand, there is another error, which at first sight looks like the opposite of this legalism or reliance on human merit and correctness—the error that came to be called anti-nomianism. If nothing that man can do is of avail, then why trouble about conduct? Why not sin recklessly and offer the more scope to God's generosity? Such blasphemy Paul had actually encountered (Rom. vi. 1)—indeed, he had even himself been accused of holding such a position (Rom. iii. 8). He says tersely that its condemnation is well deserved. It constitutes, of course, a complete failure to recognize the meaning of fellow-ship with God as involving the whole personality and total response: it is a fatal departmentalizing of human nature. But it took various forms, some of them at least more sophisticated than the formulation derided by Paul, as may be seen from what is attacked in the Epistle of James and the Johannine Epistles. James is attacking people who claim that they are saved because their beliefs about God are orthodox: they are good monotheists. So, replies the writer, are the demons (Jas ii. 19)! What matters is that the belief should issue in a good life: 'the kind of religion that is without stain . . . is . . . to go to the help of orphans and widows . . .' (Jas i. 27). In the Johannine Epistles we wit-ness an attack upon another form of antinomianism. It is fairly clear that it was sharply 'dualistic', regarding matter as evil and spirit as distinct and separable; and from this its exponents seem to have made two deductions. First, they evidently could not accept that 'the Word became flesh'—that was, for them, too crassly material; and secondly they refused to regard conduct as relevant to initiation. They believed themselves, evidently, to have become initiates with the true, saving knowledge. What did it matter that they took no trouble to show practical kindness to others or were loose in their morals? It will be recognized that these antinomians were really as far from the Pauline (indeed the Christian) position as the legalistically minded. The latter tried to win merit by good deeds; the antinomians regarded their knowledge and their initiation as securing them. Both alike were relying on something other than the free and undeserved graciousness of God. And although from time to time Paul had been and has been tarred with the antinomian brush, nothing is in fact less fair to his position.

By now it has become evident that Christians, holding to central, distinctively Christian emphases, were being compelled to walk a tightrope. Beneath were chasms—the disconnecting of Christ from God, the disconnecting of creation from the Creator, the disconnecting of belief from conduct, the disconnecting of the gracious approach of God from the human response. Did they waver or falter? Paul has often been called one-sided and charged with failure to recognize the value of good deeds; but nothing is clearer, in fact, than that he strenuously called for good deeds, but as part of man's response of trust to God's initiative, not as a *means* of acquiring God's favour. The Pastorals, whatever their origin, look like a compromise, a crystallization of Pauline doctrine in a setting of organized Church life. (Perhaps St Luke compiled them.)[1] 1 Pet. does not stress the grace of God over against human effort, but its exhortation to good deeds is no stronger than Paul's. 2 Pet. is much nearer to the recognition of the attainability of salvation by human effort (i. 5 ff.) and the Greek idea of attaining to deification (i. 4), but even so there is the phrase 'to grow in the grace . . . of our Lord' (iii. 18). The Apocalypse is simply a call to Christians to hold on and remain loyal. Jude is chiefly occupied with attacking antinomians, but there is his noble and unforgettable doxology:

Now to the One who can keep you from falling and set you in the presence of his glory, jubilant and above reproach, to the only God our Saviour, be glory and majesty, might and authority, through Jesus Christ our Lord, before all time, now, and for evermore. Amen. (Jude 24-25).

Only James is nearly without allusion to the grace of God in Jesus, and concentrates on the attainment of such a character as will lead to salvation.

All this, if the New Testament were representative of the generality of Christians at that time, would indicate that, if one travelled from centre to centre, one might find varieties of emphasis, but seldom any abandonment of the unique, distinctive Christian Gospel of the undeserved graciousness of God actually effected in history in Jesus Christ. But in fact one suspects that the *communis sensus fidelium*, expressed in the 'summit' pronouncements, which became the New Testament, was more tenacious of the central verities than were the uninstructed and

[1] See Excursus II: *Luke and the Pastoral Epistles.*

obscure local members. One suspects that in some communities Jesus was looked back to as an example rather than looked up to as Lord—followed as Rabbi rather than dwelt in as limbs dwell in a body,[1] that what we should call purely 'humanistic' ideas of him were cherished; while elsewhere he was thought of as the Saviour of a mystery religion, scarcely historical at all; that in some places sermons on the atonement were seldom heard; that sometimes Baptism and the Eucharist were treated as little more than charms to safeguard the members of the Church, while in others little doctrine was ever heard, only exhortations to good living.[2]

If so, it is the more remarkable that the differentia of the faith did survive and come through; and it is to the Church's pastors and teachers that we must look for part of the explanation. It is their leaders' writings that stand out from the undifferentiated masses, and that help to preserve the faith. For although in respect of organization and of ministry also, there was almost certainly, as we have seen, a considerable variation from congregation to congregation, the leadership of each congregation must usually have included some responsible person called and commissioned and entrusted with the Gospel. It is noteworthy that the Acts more than once alludes to this care: in xiv. 23 and xx. 32 the verb *paratithenai* is used of 'committing' a Christian group to the Lord or to the Gospel; and correlatively in 2 Tim. ii. 2 the same verb is used of entrusting reliable men with the well-authenticated facts of the Gospel—that which, correspondingly, is called *paratheke*, 'a deposit', 'a trust' in 2 Tim. i. 14. The sense of responsibility for receiving, preserving, and handing on the authentic Christian Gospel is strikingly strong throughout the epistles (1 Cor. xi. 23, xv. 1, Gal. ii. 2, Col. i. 5 f., 1 Thess. ii. 2-4, 1 Tim. ii. 7, 2 Tim. ii. 8, Heb. ii. 3, Jas i. 18, 21, 1 Pet. i. 23-25, 1 Jn ii. 20, 27, Rev. ii. 25). That is presumably why the Pauline lists of functions within the Christian ministry begin with apostles. It is the ministry of witness to the facts which stands first. Without the *datum*, no

---

[1] Cf. E. Schweizer, *Lordship and Discipleship* (as on p. 56, n. 3), 77 ff.; but I believe that he allows too little for the possibility that the Synoptists are consciously reconstructing a 'pre-resurrection' scene.

[2] Campbell N. Moody, *The Mind of the Early Converts* (n.d., preface 1920), has much to say on this.

deduction. Then come the prophets and teachers—those who, within the community which is built upon the rock of the confession of Christ, are able to discern and expound God's will, and inculcate the facts and conduct attaching to the faith. Once again, although there may have been considerable variation in the manner of worship as between different congregations, the worship (it seems probable) revolved round one and the same narrative of the Last Supper with the breaking of the loaf and the sharing of wine or its equivalent.

Thus, wherever one went throughout the ancient world, the Christian community would be distinguishable as at least having at its head men who preserved a single Gospel, and led the worship of God in the name of the same Lord Jesus. And one further factor in the maintenance of the unity and purity of the faith must have been the inter-communication between one centre and another. A little later we get a picture of the elaborate care taken by Ignatius of Antioch to write to and then meet the Christians at the chief centres on his triumphal progress to martyrdom. But even in Paul's day messengers travelled rapidly between the towns, and it is astonishing to see, from his letters, what close contact was maintained.

Thus, despite all their individuality and distinctiveness, despite the probably alarming vagaries of the 'underworld' of Christian communities from which they sprang, despite the considerable range of variation between the levels of language and style represented in the New Testament, its various writings speak with a remarkably unanimous voice of a single Gospel and of one Lord. One only needs to compare an extra-canonical writing such as 'the Gospel of Thomas' with the New Testament to recognize this. H. E. W. Turner well sums up the contrast when he points out[1] that, in 'the Gospel of Thomas' we miss completely 'the tang of historical reality', the Cross, the doctrine of grace, and 'the robust personalism of New Testament religion' (as contrasted with the unitive mysticism of 'Thomas'). Such were some of the distinctive aspects of the Christian good news which the struggling Churches preserved. Is this not a miracle of the Spirit?

[1] H. W. Montefiore and H. E. W. Turner, *Thomas and the Evangelists* (1962), forthcoming.

## CHAPTER X

# COLLECTING AND SIFTING
# THE DOCUMENTS[1]

THE story of the formation of what is known as the New
Testament 'canon' is a story of the demand for authority. The
Christian Church set out with a preposterously unlikely tale:
that a person who had recently been executed by the Romans at
the instigation of the Jewish religious authorities had been
restored to life and was the very corner-stone of the entire
building called 'Israel'. Where was their evidence for this, and
what was their authority? Probably the most immediately cogent
evidence was the very existence of this group of 'Nazarenes', so
confident and convinced in their witness to the events, bound
together in such transparently sincere brotherhood, attended by
such unmistakable signs of God's power and presence. The early
chapters of the Acts strikingly suggest (in a narrative of which
there is no reason to doubt the substantial veracity) the impact
of such a community suddenly making itself felt in Jerusalem.
The whole population was shaken: a large number were convinced. It was difficult to believe that such results sprang from
hallucination or a huge mistake.

But, more particularly defined, the authority for the Christian
statements about Jesus was the eye-witness of twelve men.

---

[1] B. F. Westcott, *A General Survey of the History of the Canon of the New
Testament* (1855, ⁴1875); T. Zahn, *Geschichte des neutestamentlichen Kanons*
(2 vols., 1888–92); *id. Forschungen zur Geschichte des neutestamentlichen
Kanons* (10 parts, 1881–1929); A. Jülicher, *Einleitung in das Neue Testament*
(1894; 7th ed. by E. Fascher, 1931), Eng. trans., *An Introduction to the New
Testament* (1904); C. R. Gregory, *Einleitung in das Neue Testament* (1909);
*id. Canon and Text of the New Testament* (Eng. trans., 1924); A. von Harnack,
*Die Entstehung des Neuen Testaments* (1914), Eng. trans. *The Origin of the
New Testament* (1925); *id. Die Briefsammlung des Apostels Paulus* (1926); M.
Albertz, *Die Botschaft des Neuen Testaments* (4 vols., 1947–57); A. Souter,
*The Text and Canon of the New Testament* (1912, ³1930, revised by C. S. C.
Williams, 1954); C. L. Mitton, *The Formation of the Pauline Corpus* (1955);
F. L. Cross, *The Early Christian Fathers* (1960), chs. iv, v; D. Guthrie, *New
Testament Introduction: the Pauline Epistles* (1961), ch. xii.

According to the Gospels, Jesus himself had in his lifetime chosen and commissioned them to be with him and to be sent out as heralds of the Kingdom of God (Mk iii. 13 ff. and pars.). One of them, Judas Iscariot, had turned traitor; but the remaining eleven are claimed, in the Acts, to have received a further express commission from the risen Master to be his witnesses, and a new twelfth, Matthias, was afterwards selected by lot as between two chosen from among the other eye-witness disciples. It was agreed (Acts i. 21 f., and cf. John xv. 26) that a condition for election should be that a new member must have been with the Twelve all the time from John the Baptist's mission until the ascension—that is to say, he must have been an intimate participant in the whole ministry of Jesus and a witness of the resurrection and its sequel. His evidence must cover the scope of the *kerygma*—the Christian proclamation. The use of lots (Acts i. 23 ff.), representing divine guidance, was evidently intended to be the equivalent of the express commissioning of Jesus. Thus was repaired the body of the Twelve, all intimate participants in the ministry of Jesus and witnesses of the resurrection, and all authoritatively commissioned to give such witness. 1 John i. 1 again alludes to the eye-witness evidence (cf. 2 Pet. i. 16). It is natural to see in the number twelve a deliberate allusion to the tribes of Israel: it was as much as to say 'Here *in nuce* is the real Israel's witness to the world'. It is possible also to see in the Acts narrative of the solemn restoration of the eleven to twelve a hint of the intention to underline the true, inner Israel's appeal to the wider, less loyal Israel in the Church's mission: here is a concentrated, twelvefold appeal to the twelve tribes themselves.[1] In this respect it is comparable to the mission of Yahweh's Servant to the rest of Israel in Isaiah.

However that may be, the Twelve evidently constituted the earliest Christian 'canon' or measuring-rod—the standard by which the authenticity of the Church's message was to be gauged, for the duration of their lifetime. They are the pillars of the whole structure (cf., though with wider reference, Gal. ii. 9, 1 Tim. iii. 15), and to such one must refer one's preaching (Gal. ii. 2). But there is no sign that the Twelve were intended

[1] See further K. H. Rengstorf, 'The Election of Matthias (Acts i. 15 ff.)', in *Festschrift for O. Piper*, edd. W. Klassen and G. F. Snyder (1961).

to be perpetuated by succession. Here was no calipnate: if there was a caliphate anywhere in the Christian Church, it was in the line of James the Lord's brother, not of the Twelve.[1] They were regarded as essentially a dominically chosen and commissioned foundation body, expressly authorized to give eye-witness evidence of the decisive events. As such they were, by definition, irreplaceable in any subsequent generation. Whereas the removal of Judas by apostasy was met by the special lot-casting for Matthias, none of the subsequent depletions, by martyrdom or natural death, were made up. The Twelve were no self-perpetuating body: they were simply the initial authority for the Christian claims about Jesus.[2]

Alongside this authority, and indeed as an integral part of it, there ran also the authority of the Jewish scriptures. The 'argument from Scripture', that is, the demonstration that what the apostles bore witness to was no isolated phenomenon, but could be shown to be the culmination and fulfilment of God's design for his People already sketched in scripture, has already been discussed in some detail (Chapter IV). It is enough here to recall that what the apostles had seen was claimed to be 'according to the Scriptures', and that the very form in which they framed their evidence was itself sometimes influenced by scripture. The witness of the Twelve was at once a confirmation of scripture and was confirmed by scripture. The way was already being paved for the recognition of the apostolic witness as itself material for inspired writing.

St Paul's efforts to establish his own claim to apostolic status seem to imply the same criteria as those defined in Acts i. 23 ff., in however abnormal a form. In 1 Cor. xv. 8 he reckons the appearance of the Lord to him on the Damascus road among all the other post-resurrection appearances, though at a different time; in 1 Cor. ix. 1 again he appeals to the fact that, in this

[1] See A. A. T. Ehrhardt, *The Apostolic Succession* (1953), and E. Stauffer, 'Zum Kalifat des Jakobus', *Zeitschrift für Religions- und Geistesgeschichte* 4 (1952), 210 ff.

[2] W. L. Knox's speculations (*St. Paul and the Church of Jerusalem*, 1925, 169) about James the Lord's brother in some sense taking the place of his namesake the martyred apostle are thus misleading. 'The mere death of an apostle need not have created a vacancy . . . but apostasy is a different matter.'—C. H. Dodd, *According to the Scriptures* (1952), 58, n. 1 (on p. 59). The whole note is very instructive.

sense, he is an eye-witness of the resurrection; and in Gal. i. 1, 11 f. he makes it clear that his commission as an evangelist came directly from the Lord. The peculiarity of his commission is that it is expressly to the Gentiles (Gal. i. 16, ii. 2; cf. Acts xxii. 21, xxvi. 17), and that he is outside the body of the Twelve—a thirteenth[1]—and never knew Jesus intimately during his earthly life. But his claim remains that he is an eye-witness of the risen Lord and personally commissioned by him to bear that witness.

Thus, to challenge the Christian message was to doubt a body of living eye-witnesses authorized by the Lord himself; and, so long as they or even their close followers still lived, one can readily understand the preference expressed by Papias (about A.D. 150) for the living voice rather than for writings. 'For I did not suppose', said he, 'that information from books would help me so much as the word of a living and surviving voice' (ζώσης φωνῆς καὶ μενούσης), Euseb. H.E. iii. 39. 4 (Loeb translation). Admittedly, Papias himself nevertheless valued at least three of the written Gospels (for Matthew and Mark, Euseb. H.E. iii. 39. 15 f.; for John, an argument prefixed to a ninth-century Latin MS. of the Gospels in the Vatican library[2]); but it remains true that the Christian community was in essence not 'bookish': it had been called into existence by a series of events well remembered; it lived under the continued personal guidance, as it believed, of the central figure of those events; and the time would not be long, so it imagined, before he would return to sight. Its authority was 'the Lord and the Apostles'.[3] The only

[1] See A. Richardson, An Introduction to the Theology of the New Testament (1958), 314, n. 1.
[2] See F. V. Filson, Which Books Belong in the Bible? (c. 1956), 152, for further reservations on Papias' evidence for the valuation of oral tradition. For the MS. in question, see J. B. Lightfoot in Contemporary Review, October 1875 (=Essays on Supernatural Religion (1889), 210 ff.); also Harnack, Geschichte der altchristlichen Litteratur (1893), 68. For Papias' knowledge of the Gospels, see R. M. Grant, 'Papias and the Gospels', Ang. Theol. Rev. xxv (1943), 218 ff.
[3] Whatever may be intended by the controversial phrase τὰ βιβλία καὶ οἱ ἀπόστολοι (if indeed this is the right reading) in 2 Clement xiv. 2 (see the discussion in H. Köster, Synoptischer Überlieferung bei den apostolischen Vätern (1957), 67 ff.), this homily certainly uses λέγει (εἶπεν) ὁ κύριος elsewhere (iv. 5, v. 2, etc.): so that ὁ κύριος and οἱ ἀπόστολοι may justly be said to be its two sources of authority. For the date of 2 Clement (first half of second century?), see B. Altaner, Patrologie (⁵1958), 82 f. (Eng. trans. (1960), 103).

book it needed was the collection of scriptures already recognized by the Jews, in which the Christians now found explanation and confirmation of their own convictions, while, conversely, they found the scriptures explained and confirmed in an entirely new way by the recent events.

But the last of the Twelve died before 'the consummation of all things', and it began to become evident that the Church must continue for an indefinite time in an imperfect world. Where were the guarantees to be found for the authenticity of its claims, after the accredited eye-witnesses had ceased to be available, and when even their immediate followers were growing scarce? The answer lay inevitably in written records. With the appeal to 'the Lord and the Apostles' begins an inevitable process of development leading to accredited writings.[1]

What did books look like at this period, and how general was literacy? The answer to the first question seems to be that important, and especially sacred, books had usually been in roll form, until the Christians adopted the codex form (essentially the form of a modern book) for their own sacred writings. Codex (*caudex*) is Latin for a tree-stump, and then a slab of wood; and hence a slab or tablet for writing—the wax-coated board for note-taking; and then, eventually, the term was transferred to the flat, rectangular piles of folded paper, or, in some cases, parchment, constituting what we now call a book. By association and derivation, therefore, the codex tends to be used for the more incidental, transitory jottings, as contrasted with the *biblion* (or Latin *volumen*), the roll, containing the treasured, sacred writings. And although the word *biblion* is merely derived from the word for the papyrus reed, from the pith of which paper was made, in fact it came to denote the form (roll) rather than the material. And although rolls were sometimes written not on papyrus but on animal skin—parchment or vellum—while many a codex was made of paper (that is, papyrus) leaves, yet, while *biblion* tended to mean a roll, *membranae* (skins) tended to mean a codex. Hence it is plausibly suggested[2] that when, in 2 Tim. iv. 13, Timothy is instructed to

---

[1] Cf. W. Schneemelcher in E. Hennecke, *Neutestamentliche Apokryphen*[3], i (1959), 9.

[2] See C. H. Roberts, 'The Codex', *Proc. Brit. Acad.*, xl (1954), 169 ff.

bring the *biblia*, but particularly the *membranae*, what is meant by the *biblia* is the Jewish scriptures (in roll form), while the *membranae* meant the apostle's own notes (in codex form, whether in loose sheets or stitched together)—perhaps his sermons and disquisitions, perhaps copies of letters, perhaps simply notes. If this is correct, the *biblia* and the *membranae* stand (in this particular context) for Jewish and Christian writings respectively (though the latter would not at this stage have attained to 'canonical' standing or been regarded as among ἱερὰ γράμματα, sacred writings, 2 Tim. iii. 15); and it appears that it was in the Christian communities that the codex came into its own, so that eventually it superseded the roll as the recognized form for permanent—even sacred—writings.[1] That this took place earlier than used to be thought is important for New Testament criticism. The displacement of leaves in a codex is a possibility, as it is not in a roll; and the date of the use of the codex is relevant, therefore, to the discussion, for instance, of the possibility of displacement in St John's Gospel. On the other hand, as we shall see (below, pp. 201 f.), certain theories about the order of books in the New Testament canon depend upon the assumption of roll form.

As for literacy, Paul, the possessor of those 'books and parchments', was of course well educated, and so were his assistants who acted as his amanuenses; and indeed most religious Jews would be at least literate, for they would at least have had the training of the local synagogue school, and would be used to reading the scriptures in translation if not in Hebrew (see above, p. 157). Jesus, it is true, is contemptuously described in Jn vii. 15 as never having learnt letters, but that would only mean that he had never been through the full course of training for a rabbi.[2] Gentiles within the Christian Church would probably include among their numbers a good many (especially among the slaves) with little or no education; but a high proportion, of St Paul's converts at least, had already come into contact with the synagogue and had presumably begun to be familiar with the sound, if not the sight, of the Old Testament writings.

---

[1] See P. Katz, 'The Early Christian Use of Codices instead of Rolls', *J.T.S.* xlvi (1945), 63 ff.

[2] J. Jeremias, *Jerusalem zur Zeit Jesu* (²1958), 104.

Although it is impossible to go far beyond guess-work, for lack of data, one may guess, then, that most Christians of the New Testament period could read. That, however, is not the same as being wealthy enough to possess books; and presumably the average synagogue congregation would depend largely on remembering the scriptures and hearing them read Sabbath by Sabbath, while Christians, if they did not attend synagogue, might largely have to learn by listening to what was read at assemblies for Christian worship. In discussions and disputes, in the defence and confirmation of the Gospel, they would have to quote what they could remember of the Old Testament scriptures and of the sayings and writings of apostolic men. Comparatively few would be able to refer to writings in their own possession.

Scarce and precious, then, were Christian books and writings, and very long would Christian memories need to be. And it is against this mainly unliterary (though not illiterate) background that we have had to picture the rise of a Christian literature and must now consider the ultimate selection from it of authoritative writings. One of the obvious consequences of such a situation is the natural leadership that would be acquired in a given community by anyone sufficiently well equipped both with good character and learning to hold what few books might be available and to communicate their contents. (In 1 Tim. iv. 13, when Timothy is bidden to attend to reading this means, no doubt, reading aloud to his congregations.) Another consequence is, of course, that Christian assemblies for worship and religious instruction would be the most natural seminaries for such communications. Thus we may confidently assume that the messages of Christian writings took root largely through the ears of the faithful and of enquirers and catechumens, and in the context of worship and religious instruction.

But what were the factors that controlled the writing, and then the selection or rejection, of the various Christian books? Such evidence as we possess suggests that before the last of the apostles had died, there were already in existence various written documents containing sayings of Jesus and perhaps certain anecdotes in his life, and at least one full-length Gospel—St Mark's. It is difficult to establish more than this. The earliest (and most plausible) tradition about Mark places the writing even of his Gospel after Peter's death (though that would not mean after the last surviving apostle's death): the traditions which put it within Peter's life-time look suspiciously like 'improvements'. The direct apostolic authorship of St John's Gospel, maintained by tradition, has been very widely disputed. And Matt., in its present form, can hardly have been written by an apostle.[1] So far as full Gospels go, therefore, we cannot be certain of more than that Mark's Gospel was written well within the natural life span of the apostolic generation—though in fact the most plausible dating of Matthew, Luke, and John places them also within this era. But it is not unlikely that Mark used already existing written sources besides spoken traditions. Of the existence of widely current traditions, whether written or spoken, at a very early stage there can be no doubt. One may already detect in the Pauline or near-Pauline Epistles echoes of just such traditions about Jesus as later find their way into the Gospels (see pp. 144 ff. above). Thus a missionary like Paul already had access to traditions, oral or written, such as the evangelists ultimately drew upon. Even much later, in the sub-apostolic writers known as the Apostolic Fathers, there are traces of similar traditions still running free, and possibly running parallel to the Gospels we know rather than through them.[2] Thus is built up a picture of a great reservoir of traditions, some spoken, some already written down, on which the early preachers are already drawing and from which ultimately the full-length Gospels are going to crystallize. Once again, it is the assemblies for worship and religious instruction that are the most likely reservoirs. The use of a writing in worship is the antecedent stage to its recognition as canonical.

Once the first full-length Gospel appears, a new genre of writing is in being. As we have seen, it is in essence only a fuller, more circumstantial, more pictorial form of the basic *kerygma*,

---

[1] See the evidence for the traditions about Mk and Matt. in Huck-Lietzmann, *Synopse*[9] (or Eng. ed. by F. L. Cross), or in any good N. T. Introduction (e.g. A. Wikenhauser, Eng. trans. (1958), 160 f., 179 ff.); and see B. H. Streeter, *The Four Gospels* ([4]1930) *passim*. See also pp. 89 ff., above.

[2] See H. Köster, *Synoptische Überlieferung bei den apostolischen Vätern* (1957).

the Christian proclamation. If we accept the priority of Mark over the other canonical Gospels—and despite the challenges to this view from some of the Roman Catholic scholars, it is soundly based[1]—we do not know positively of any full-length Gospel earlier than Mark's, though it is possible that he had precedessors, perhaps in Aramaic, or even Hebrew.[2] After him, in due course, there came to be a great spate of Gospels. But it is noteworthy that of these the now canonical Gospels of Matthew, Luke, and John are still plausibly dated earlier than almost any others we know of (whatever may be implied by Luke i. 1 with its reference to 'many' predecessors); and many of the others,[3] whether still extant or known through references

[1] J. Chapman, *Matthew, Mark and Luke* (1937) and B. C. Butler, *The Originality of St Matthew* (1951) are comparatively recent Roman Catholic representatives of the arguments for the priority of 'Matthew' (in some form or other). But it has to be added that this position is not by any means maintained by all R.C. scholars, and an instance of a Roman scholar abandoning it is W. Trilling, *Das wahre Israel* (1959). For some discussion of the Chapman-Butler position, see B. T. D. Smith (reviewing Chapman), *J.T.S.* xxxix (1938), 170 ff., A. M. Farrer (reviewing Butler), *J.T.S.*, n.s., iii (1952), 102 ff. See further Excursus IV: *The Priority of Mark*, kindly contributed by G. M. Styler.

[2] For Hebrew, not Aramaic, as a medium for early Christian writing, see M. H. Segal, *A Grammar of Mishnaic Hebrew* (1927), H. Grimme, 'Studien zum hebräischen Urmatthäus', *Bibl. Zeitschr.* 23 (1935–36), 244-265, 347-357, *apud* P. Nepper-Christensen, *Das Matthäusevangelium* etc. (as in next note); and for the possibility of some form or forms of *spoken* Hebrew side by side with Aramaic, see the interesting discussion (concluding in favour of the possibility), *id.* 101 ff., with special reference to H. Birkeland, *Språk og religion hos jøder og arabere* (1949), whose view is criticized by J. A. Emerton, 'Did Jesus speak Hebrew?', *J.T.S.*, n.s., xii (1961), 189-202. Further, C. C. Torrey, 'The Aramaic Period of the Nascent Christian Church', *Z.N.T.W.* 44 (1952), 205 ff. (cf. *id. The Apocalypse of John* (1958)), suggests that the list of canonical scriptures discussed by J.-P. Audet in *J.T.S.* n.s. i (1950), 135 ff., lying as it does in the manuscript between 2 Clement and *Didache*, is probably of Christian origin, and therefore that Aramaic was the religious language even of Greek-speaking Christians before A.D. 70; he alludes (as does Audet, *loc. cit.*) to the lists in Epiphanius, *De mens. et pond.* 23, and Origen, *In Ps. i*, cf. Euseb. *H.E.* vi. 25, 1 f.

[3] Jerome alludes to an *evangelium juxta* (or *secundum*) *Hebraeos* (*Adv. Pelag.* iii. 2 and *De vir. illust.* ii.), and in the former passage says that many affirm that it is *juxta Matthaeum*. But it is notoriously doubtful how far (if at all) there really was a Semitic antecedent to Matt.: and in any case P. Nepper-Christensen, *Das Matthäusevangelium: ein judenchristliches Evangelium?* (1958), 64 ff. has cast grave doubts on almost every sentence of these two *testimonia* from Jerome. There is but slender evidence, then, that even this Gospel (if it ever existed) was prior to the canonical ones. When Luke refers (i. 1) to 'many' predecessors, does he mean more than Mk and whatever other component parts he employed?

and quotations, are not Gospels in the same sense at all, but are either anecdotes about Jesus or mythological romances, or sayings-collections.[1] Perhaps in the end it was really not so much a matter of selecting as of recognizing that only four full-length Gospels were available from within the apostolic period. And if it be asked why these maintained their independence, instead of suffering fusion (as in Tatian's *Diatessaron*) or instead of one alone coming out as sole survivor, the answer may be found in the authority of local churches or in some other prestige. The one of the four that most nearly went under was Mark, because of its brevity and because of the fact that its substance was so largely included in Matthew; but, perhaps because it was connected with Peter or because it was connected with Rome or because of both, it held its own. And each of the other three evidently represented an influential centre of Christianity. Not that they all immediately gained universal recognition. Towards the end of the second century, Luke was still only hesitantly recognized, and John was to meet much opposition until as late as about A.D. 220.[2] But the point is that what ultimately emerged was not a single Gospel but four—neither more nor less. Marcion and Tatian both tried, in their different ways, to establish a single Gospel, but did not carry the whole Church with them.[3] The

[1] It is striking that comparison of the Coptic Gospel of Thomas with the Greek Oxyrhynchus sayings suggests that the Greek sayings may represent earlier sayings-collections used by the writer of the Gospel of Thomas. If so, we are presented with an instance of non-canonical sayings-collections circulating and being absorbed into a subsequent writing, rather as we may assume happened earlier in the compilation of the canonical Gospels. See H.-W. Bartsch, 'Das Thomas-Evangelium und die synoptischen Evangelien', *J.N.T.S.*, 6 (1960), 249 ff. But there is the important difference (noted by Bartsch) that the Synoptic antecedents are *not* mere collections of sayings detached from their narrative settings. The sayings-collections behind *Ev. Thom.* are not therefore closely comparable. G. Miegge, *Gospel and Myth* (Eng. trans. by S. C. Neill, 1960, from the Italian of 1956), 121 f. points out that, whereas orthodox Christian writing moved in the direction of 'theological meditation', the apocryphal writings with Gnostic leanings moved in the direction of 'mythological imagination'.

[2] See Schneemelcher, after Bauer, in Hennecke[3] (as on p. 182, n. 1), i. 11.

[3] According to W. Bauer's thesis (in *Rechtgläubigkeit u. Ketzerei im ältesten Christentum*, 1934) the Roman Church and other Churches in its sphere of influence, for long recognized only Matt. and Mk, accepting only with hesitation Lk. (discredited by heretical use) and abandoning direct opposition to Jn only *c.* 200. He thinks Papias recognized only Mk and Matt.; Justin did not regard Jn as authoritative; Ignatius used not Jn but Matt. This differs from Harnack (see, e.g., *The Origin of the New Testament*,

process of selection was well under way before ever it began to be consciously reasoned about or rationalized: owing to a variety of causes, some of which have just been mentioned, the four-Gospel canon slid into existence almost furtively. It was certainly not the arbitrary decision of a single Christian body, still less of an individual. Its formal declaration, when it was made,[1] was only the recognition, by the Church collectively, of a conviction that had long been silently growing on their consciousness. Perhaps at least one or two of these writings had been regularly used in assemblies for worship long before they were officially described as authoritative.

As it happens, much the same could be said of the recognition of the Jewish scriptures also. We have to remember that there is no known official pronouncement embodying a Jewish 'canon' of scripture until near the end of the New Testament period (although there is evidence of long debate before this). The Synod of Jamnia (Jabne) in A.D. 90 is usually claimed as the occasion of this pronouncement; and a very interesting discussion of it by P. Katz[2] attributes to this synod also the present arrangement and division of the Hebrew Bible, arguing that this was not an ancient order at all, but that (contrary to generally held opinion) it is the arrangement of the books in the Septuagint that represents the earlier Hebrew order. However that may be, the Synod of Jamnia seems to represent the first official Jewish canon—and even that was only official for a section of Judaism: there was no such thing as an ecumenical organ of Jewish opinion, and doubtless the Jews of the Alexandrine and other dispersions continued to be without a defined 'canon' of scripture.[3] The 'Sanhedrin' of Jamnia (and thus of the Mishnah

Eng. trans., 1925), despite many points in common. Harnack too saw the fixing of a four-Gospel canon as a compromise, and saw Jn as playing a decisive role in the process. But he thought that the opposition to the 'Alogi' led to the championing of the Fourth Gospel in the East at a time when the other Gospels were so well established that they could not be ousted.

[1] For the ultimate determination of the Canon of the New Testament, see the bibliography for this chapter. The date usually given is that of Athanasius' 39th Paschal letter, A.D. 367.

[2] P. Katz, 'The Old Testament Canon in Palestine and Alexandria', Z.N.T.W. 47 (1956), 191 ff.

[3] One wonders what relation, if any, to Jamnia may be assumed for the use by a Christian of the phrase 'every inspired scripture' in 2 Tim. iii. 16. Was it known by this time precisely what 'scripture' comprised?

Tractate *Sanhedrin*) is not the lineal descendant of the Jerusalem Sanhedrin of the pre-70 period; it consisted not of priests and elders but of rabbis. Tractate *Sanhedrin* is not to be incautiously used as evidence for the Jerusalem Sanhedrin.[1] Jamnia may well, however, have added some momentum to the corresponding Christian process.

If we ask what criteria the Church consciously applied to test the authenticity of its writings, we shall find that they are criteria dictated by controversy with heretics or disbelievers. The most obvious one is 'apostolicity'. If not actually written by one of the Twelve, a Gospel (to confine our enquiry for the moment to this category) must at least have some kind of apostolic *imprimatur*: it must be shown to come from some close associate of an apostle and, if possible, with the apostle's express commission. Consequently, it must necessarily belong to an early period, and would be expected (one may suppose) to show signs of at least derivation from the primitive Aramaic-speaking Church. A corollary of this, itself constituting another criterion, was that no genuinely apostolic Gospel could contain an interpretation of the incarnation contrary to that orthodoxy which (however difficult to define exactly) undeniably belonged to the *communis sensus fidelium* of these early decades, despite the great range of differences already described. For by the time the last of the Twelve had died, there was a sufficiently powerful uniformity, so far as the basic convictions of the Church's leaders go, running throughout the Christian centres all over the empire, to detect and extrude 'heresy'—that is, any opinion incompatible with the apostolic witness. Finally, no doubt a Gospel needed to be a Gospel. There were evidently a number of fragmentary documents in circulation then, as there continued to be later—sayings-collections, collections of miracle stories, perhaps, and of other anecdotes; but these could not stand on their own feet as Gospels proper, comprising the *kerygma*.

Now, when the Church came consciously to apply these tests, it was sometimes one of them, and sometimes another which was uppermost. The original apostolic contact was clearly a primary demand; but it was not always possible to test this as rigorously as might have been desired; and alongside came the

[1] Lohse in *T.W.N.T.*, s.v. συνέδριον.

additional test of usage: had the book proved its worth? had it survived the critical sense of the Christian tradition?—for it is possible that certain writings had already asserted themselves as eminently useful and sound before evidence for apostolic contact was discovered. In some few instances it may even be that the latter was a *post-hoc* rationalization. But in such cases the *communis sensus fidelium* had already been so soundly informed by authentic tradition that its own *imprimatur* was in fact sufficient.

It must be added, in all fairness, that we have, in Christian antiquity, at least one instance of an author being very severely penalized for a work which, though perfectly orthodox (at any rate by the standards of his period), turned out to be a fiction. This is the story told by Tertullian in *De Baptismo* 17 of the priest of Asia who admitted to having written the *Acts of Paul* (which includes the *Acts of Paul and Thecla*) and was deprived of office (presumably on the charge of passing off fiction as though it had been history). This gives the lie to the idea that the early Church never exercised any historical criticism, but relied entirely on its sense of what was orthodox and edifying. The unsuspecting priest had done it in all good faith, meaning to enhance the honour of the apostle; and he had written anonymously, not attempting to assume the authority of another. How much severer (it might have been supposed) would the Church have been towards one who was caught impersonating (say) an apostle! On the other hand, it is one thing to write fiction as though it were history and quite another to communicate teaching in someone else's name. This latter was a time-honoured technique and scandalized nobody unless the teaching was either maliciously intended (cf. 2 Thess. ii. 2, iii. 17)[1] or heretical (cf. the case of the Gospel of Peter, below, p. 193). Yet even in the realm of teaching, if they did indulge in what has just been called a *post-hoc* rationalization, one may assume that it was not consciously thought to be a rationalization. The acceptance of Hebrews as Pauline is an instance. There were at first some doubters in the East and many in the West. But it was indispensable; it was compatible with Pauline doctrine; and the prevailing

[1] But 2 Thess. iii. 17 represents the stress of dangerous circumstances: by the time of the Pastorals, things may have been different.

opinion of the Eastern Churches was eventually accepted—that it was Pauline (Moffatt, *I.L.N.T.*, 431). And it must be remembered that Hebrews was not accepted without challenge. As late a writer (in our time scale) as Tertullian, *De Pud.* 20, attributes Hebrews to Barnabas, and, though preferring it to Hermas, does not treat the work as *scripture* (Gregory, *Canon and Text*, 222 ff.; see further Moffatt, *I.L.N.T.*, 437).

Moreover, it must be remembered that Hermas, the writer of the popular *Shepherd*, did not, even as a teacher, try to write under another name; and it is noteworthy, further, that in the ante-Nicene era, forgeries were relatively rare and often detected. 'No one in this period made much use of most of the forgeries we later encounter in such quantities.' (R. M. Grant, 'The Appeal to the Early Fathers', *J.T.S.* n.s. xi (1960), 23.)

Nevertheless, even though the early Church was much more alert against 'forgery' than is sometimes supposed, we have to recognize a two-way traffic: the living community was indeed constantly subject to check and correction by the authentic evidence—by the basic witness, first of accredited eye-witness apostles and later of the written deposit of that witness; yet also the documents which soon began to circulate in considerable numbers were themselves in some measure subject to check and correction, whatever their origin, by the living community— simply because it by that time contained within it, or among its leaders, a sufficiently firm and uniform tradition to constitute it corporately a preserver of tradition. One may see the living community's control operating in the Johannine Epistles, where appeal is made to authentic, early, eye-witness tradition against the opinionated interpretations and assertions of men who were running contrary to these. Something similar, though without the allusion to eye-witness, is to be seen in the Pastoral Epistles. The further one goes in time from the original sources of evidence ('that which was from the beginning', 1 Jn i. 1, etc.) the more precarious becomes the claim of the Church, in its own right, to test the evidence. But until there is a recognized body of authentic documents to appeal to, there is no other way; and this is how we see the Church proceeding before the establishment of the canon of Christian scriptures. It is certainly a fact that the claims of documents were, until this stage, checked by that tradition of orthodoxy which was generally diffused through the living, worshipping communities.[1] That tradition, in its turn, however, was subject to the check of apostolic eye-witness as long as the apostles were available; and before the death of the last apostle, as we have seen, there had already begun to exist at least some soundly attested apostolic documents.

At this point it is worth while to observe that a distinction has been drawn, by K. Aland[2] between an earlier period (to about A.D. 150) and a later. In the earlier period, the prophetic afflatus was recognized, and a teacher could stand up and speak in a Christian assembly in the name of the Spirit and in the name of some great apostolic leader, and be accepted. This (Aland suggests) is how some writings that we should be tempted to call pseudonymous came to be openly accepted: they were *bona fide* utterances of formerly known (though now anonymous) speakers in the name of apostolic men. But when the afflatus waned, and the Church became conscious of living in an era separated from that of the apostles, the more literary tests of authority began to come in, as did also deliberate forgeries.[3]

Such extra-canonical documents styling themselves 'Gospels' as we actually possess are all of a suspect character. The two most recently recovered—the probably Valentinian *Gospel of Truth* and the *Gospel of Thomas*—must certainly have been rejected for their contents, even if on other grounds they had seemed to carry impressive claims. As a matter of fact, neither of them is a Gospel in the sense of comprising the *kerygma*, and the *Gospel of Truth* has not even the semblance of apostolic authority either. There is no known extra-canonical Gospel material which is not (when it can be tested at all) in some way subject to suspicion for its genuineness or its orthodoxy: many

[1] Very important here is the fact that Gnostic writings, such as *The Gospel of Truth*, are now available to demonstrate what sort of doctrinal criteria the Church must have used in excluding them. See W. C. van Unnik, *Newly discovered Gnostic Writings* (Eng. trans., 1960, of *Openbaringen uit Egyptisch Zand*, 1958), 68, 90, 91. Note, further, that the inclusion of the Paulines and the exclusion of (e.g.) Clement shows that the Church had not lost its appreciation of what Paul stood for.

[2] K. Aland, 'The Problem of Anonymity and Pseudonymity in Christian Literature of the First Two Centuries', *J.T.S.*, n.s., xii (1961), 1 ff.

[3] There is a well-documented essay on 'epistolary pseudepigraphy' in D. Guthrie, *New Testament Introduction: the Pauline Epistles* (1961), 282 ff.

of the recovered fragments are in some sense 'gnostic' in tendency.[1]

The stock example of the application of the test of orthodoxy, as against that of apostolic attribution, is the story of Serapion, bishop of Antioch in about A.D. 200, quoted by Eusebius (*H.E.* vi. 12). The Greek of the passage is by no means lucid; but this much is clear, that Serapion had, without reading it himself, sanctioned the use, in the Christian community of Rhossus (a small town in Cilicia), of a writing calling itself the *Gospel of Peter*. Subsequently, however, he discovered (still possibly not at first-hand—the Greek is very odd) that, while the greater part of this Gospel was 'in accordance with the true teaching of the Saviour', there were heretical additions which had apparently been used by heretical teachers to lead the Christians of Rhossus astray. Against these he warns them, since, whereas 'we receive both Peter and the other apostles as Christ' (cf. Matt. x. 40, Gal.iv.14, 1 Clement xii. 1), 'the writings which falsely bear their names we reject, as men of experience, knowing that such were not handed down to us'. Serapion's treatise from which Eusebius quotes was called περὶ τοῦ λεγομένου κατὰ Πέτρον εὐαγγελίου ('concerning the so-called Gospel according to Peter'), and it seems to be clear that the grounds for this stricture, 'so-called', were entirely its heretical character, not any research into its origin. The fragment of this very Gospel which was discovered at Akhmim in the winter of 1886–87 confirms Serapion's judgment: or, if it is impossible to prove that it is strictly docetic or otherwise heretical, at least its extravagances mark it as spurious and well on the way to heretical fancies. It breathes an entirely different atmosphere from that of the canonical Gospels.[2]

Thus, while the earliest Church was shaped and controlled by the evidence of all the eye-witnesses, and especially the authenticated Twelve, there came a brief period when this evidence had become so entirely a part of the life and thinking of the leaders of the Church that they automatically refused to assimilate into their system what was contrary in doctrinal

---

[1] See, e.g., J. Jeremias, *Unknown Sayings of Jesus* (Eng. trans. (1957) of *Unbekannte Jesusworte* (1948)); B. Gärtner, *The Theology of the Gospel of Thomas* (Eng. trans. (1961) from Swedish); E. Haenchen, *Die Botschaft des Thomasevangeliums* (1961).

[2] See Chr. Maurer in Hennecke[3] (as on p. 182, n. 1), 119 f.

tendency to the now indigenous standards. This brief transitional period, between the earliest stage, when presumably the eye-witness test was constantly applied, and the later stage of confidence when even what claimed to be apostolic witness was itself subjected to the doctrinal test, may perhaps be illustrated by parts of the Pastoral Epistles. These betray an awareness of 'orthodoxy'; and although the 'faithful sayings' cited in the Pastorals are not sayings of Jesus and do not in any sense represent a 'canon', yet the very phrase shows an instinct for classification into true and false.[1] Moreoever, a good deal of prominence is given in these Epistles to the need for careful transmission of the apostolic teaching: it is a precious deposit, entrusted by God to the apostle, and by the apostle to his chosen disciple, to be handed on by him to carefully chosen men. The 'pattern of teaching' ($\tau\acute{\upsilon}\pi o s$ $\delta\iota\delta\alpha\chi\hat{\eta}s$) of Rom. vi. 17, and the 'traditions' ($\pi\alpha\rho\alpha\delta\acute{o}\sigma\epsilon\iota s$) of 2 Thess. ii. 15, iii. 6 (cf. 1 Thess. iv. 1 f.), are on their way, via the 'sketch' or 'outline' ($\acute{\upsilon}\pi o\tau\acute{\upsilon}\pi\omega\sigma\iota s$) of sound teaching (2 Tim. i. 13) and the $\pi\alpha\rho\alpha\theta\acute{\eta}\kappa\eta$ or 'deposit' (1 Tim. vi. 20, 2 Tim. i. 12, 14; cf. ii. 2), into the 'canon' of approved writings.

The recognition in the whole Church of the four Gospels as alone authentic is difficult to date. There are scraps of evidence that they circulated independently for a considerable period after their first appearance. Thus, to judge by the textual history of the manuscripts of Mark, this Gospel was by far the most heavily corrected by scribes; which probably means that it had a longer independent history than the others.[2] Indeed, there are signs that it was early recognized as the First Gospel, despite the later traditions which placed Matthew on the pedestal of primacy,[3] and, if so, it may well have circulated independently. But as soon as Matthew did rise to the highest place in popularity, then, for the same reason, it may be presumed to have been often copied by itself (though, as has just been implied, less often than Mark had been separately copied). Thus, 'for the Syrian

---

[1] See Excursus III: ΠΙΣΤΟΣ Ο ΛΟΓΟΣ.

[2] See G. D. Kilpatrick, *The Transmission of the New Testament and its Reliability* (Victoria Institute Lecture, 1957), 96; and note (with S. E. Johnson, *Mark* (1960), 30) the interesting case of the solitary Mark in the University of Chicago Library (Chicago MS. 972 = Gregory-Eltester catalogue Codex 2427), described by H. R. Willoughby in *Munera Studiosa* (ed. M. H. Shepherd Jr., and S. E. Johnson, 1946), 127 ff. and R. P. Casey in *Journal of Religion* xxvii (1947), 148 f.      [3] F. C. Grant, *The Gospels* (1957), 64 ff.

Church *the* (written) Gospel long continued to be that of Matthew, as it had been elsewhere'.[1]

As for Luke and John, there is much *a priori* likelihood that they both circulated for some time among the particular persons or groups for whom, respectively, they were first intended. Many of the Gospel echoes in the Epistles seem to be exclusively Lucan, suggesting, perhaps, that Luke alone was the Gospel for the Pauline circle; and R. G. Heard, in a posthumously published article,[2] points out the evidence afforded by a comparison among themselves of the 'old Gospel Prologues' for the independent circulation of the Prologue to Luke even in the fourth century. With regard to John, it is a well-known matter for discussion whether even Justin Martyr (*circa* A.D. 150) knew it.[3] There is an echo of what we know as a Johannine saying ('unless you are born again, you will certainly not enter the Kingdom of the heavens') in *Apol.* i. 61, but if Justin did know the Gospel, it has not influenced his theology. On the other hand he cites a 'Q' saying ('All things are committed to me . . .', Matt. xi. 27, Lk. x. 22) with the formula ἐν τῷ εὐαγγελίῳ γέγραπται, 'it is written in the Gospel' (*Dial.* 100).

Rather earlier (? *circa* A.D. 130) the *Epistle of Barnabas* (iv. 14) uses γέγραπται, 'it is written', to introduce a phrase known to us as Matthean ('many are called, but few chosen'). But it must be admitted that γέγραπται need not imply the concept of authoritative scripture; and Köster (*op. cit.*, p. 185, n. 2, 126) questions whether even this saying can be pinned down to an exclusively Matthean origin. However, the main point is that

[1] B. W. Bacon, *Introduction to the New Testament* (1900), 38.
[2] R. G. Heard, *J.T.S.*, n.s., vi (1955), 3.
[3] On Justin's sources, see W. Bousset, *Die Evangeliencitate Justins* (1891); J. M. Heer, *Römische Quartalschrift* 28 (1914), 97 ff.; E. R. Buckley, *J.T.S.* (1935), 173 ff.; A. Baumstark, *Biblica* 16 (1935), 292 ff. B. F. Westcott, *A General Survey of the History of the Canon of the New Testament* (⁴1875), 166, n. 1, cites as the chief passages: Jn iii. 5-8, *Apol.* i. 61; Jn i. 13, *Trypho* lxiii; Jn i. 12, *Trypho* cxxiii; Jn xii. 49, *Trypho* lvi; Jn vii. 12, *Trypho* lxix. Of these, Jn i. 12, 13, vii. 12 are very faintly echoed, if at all; and xii. 49 seems to be cited by Westcott in error (? v. 19). J. N. Sanders, *The Fourth Gospel in the Early Church* (1943), examines a wider range of passages, concluding (31): 'The most reasonable conclusion from this examination of the passages . . . which appear to show traces of the influence of the Fourth Gospel seems to be that certain passages are most naturally explained as reminiscences of the Fourth Gospel, while there are few, if any, which can be certainly said to be dependent upon it'.

here are sufficient hints to suggest a period during which the four Gospels were in existence separately and were used, perhaps, only locally.

But if there was a period when each group or area recognized only one or two Gospels in writing, there came a time when the four emerged into equal recognition. Cullmann[1] argues that there were two conflicting motives for the fourfold canon: (i) the conviction that no one Gospel presented the fullest possible witness to the Incarnate; (ii) the desire of each Evangelist to make a single Gospel which should include his predecessors' witness. The result was reduction—though not reduction to only one. In briefest summary, Cullmann's argument may be outlined as continuing thus: in view of the spate of manifestly gnostic and false writings, it was natural to treasure *all* of the few really apostolic ones. Then (unlike the attitude of the earlier period) came the desire to champion *one* versus the rest. Marcion's is the best known attempt. But it is a docetic tendency to conflate into one, or to choose one against the rest: it is a genuinely historical insight to recognize a plurality in human witness. Irenaeus himself, claiming that four is a divinely rather than a humanly chosen number, really looks in the same (mistaken) direction as docetism. He ought to have seen that the *scandalon* of human diversity should be accepted as such! The earlier Church was right—to accept all that was thought to be truly apostolic, and to see it as mediating through human diversity, the one divine event. (The Muratorian Canon itself is not far from such a recognition when it says '... though various ideas are taught in the several books of the Gospels, yet it makes no difference to the faith of believers, since by one sovereign Spirit all things are declared in all of them ...'[2]; yet, in the preceding section the concept of a single, supreme Gospel has already appeared in the legend of John, of whom it was revealed to Andrew that John was to write all things in his own name.) It was probably from the middle of the second century that it became usual to speak of 'the Gospel *according to* Matthew' etc. (reflecting what have recently become form-critical findings

[1] 'Die Pluralität der Evangelien als theologisches Problem im Altertum', *Th. Zeitschr.* i (1945), 21 ff., = *The Early Church* (1956), 39 ff.
[2] Translation from Stevenson.

about a single *kerygma*, repeated in various ways).

Our earliest extant manuscripts—the Chester Beatty papyri and the Sinaitic Syriac—take us back to A.D. 250 or earlier for the four together; but the Gospel of Peter, the fragment of which, already mentioned, shows signs of the use of all four, cannot be much later than 150, since it was well established at Rhossus when Serapion found it; and Tatian's famous *Diatessaron*—his conflation of the four into a single Gospel— gives us a similar date for the joint recognition of at least the four (even if there are obscure traces of a fifth or of an independent tradition in his conflation—unless these be due simply to the use of a different text).[1] By about A.D. 185, Irenaeus is proclaiming that it is as inevitable that there should be four Gospels as that there should be four winds and four corners of the earth. If this is polemic, as it well may be, the target of his attack is probably heretical opinion: there is nothing to suggest that any considerable section of the orthodox Church would have wished to deny his assertions. After Irenaeus follows Clement of Alexandria and thereafter plenty of evidence to confirm the recognition of the four alone. But it is to be noted that until this mid-second century date there is remarkably little sign of this. Hermas, *Visions*, iii. 13, misses a golden opportunity of mentioning the four (unless one can indeed believe that the four legs of the bench are meant to symbolize the Gospels[2]), and it is a matter of considerable uncertainty whether the recognition of the canonical Gospels can be detected in the Apostolic Fathers generally. But at least it can be said with

[1] See B. M. Metzger, art. *Evangelienharmonie* in *R.G.G.* Tatian was a pupil of Justin's. Hitherto, only one tiny fragment in Greek of his *Diatessaron* has been found (publ. by C. H. Kraeling, 1935). Otherwise, our sources are (for the East) Ephraem's commentary on the *Diatessaron* (*c.* 360) in Armenian translation; Arabic translations from Syriac; some later versions; and scattered quotations in the Syriac and Armenian Church Fathers; (for the West) the harmony, with Vulgate text, in *codex Fuldensis* (before 546); later versions; scattered quotations. There are apocryphal additions and the canonical material is occasionally coloured with ascetical touches. It is these phenomena that G. Messina, S.J., *Diatessaron Persiano* (1951), and others are trying to account for. See an interesting discussion in H. W. Montefiore and H. E. W. Turner, *Thomas and the Evangelists* (1962), forthcoming. Jerome (*Epist.* cxxi. 6. 15) alludes to Theophilus of Antioch's similar work, but of this we have no other trace.

[2] Strongly denied by H. Köster, *Synoptische Überlieferung bei den apostolischen Vätern* (1957), 254.

confidence that the four-fold canon is well established before our earliest official lists of accredited books. Also (to judge by Justin's attitude) Gospels generally (no matter how many) tended to carry more weight, as the apostles' 'reminiscences', ἀπομνη-μονεύματα,[1] than other writings. Before Justin, Ignatius had said that he took refuge in the Gospel as in the flesh of Jesus and in the apostles as in the presbytery of the Church (*Philad.* v. 1). But the margin of time between such vaguely defined independent or partially independent circulation of Gospel material and the solid unity-in-quaternity[2] of the fourfold Gospel canon appears to be slender. It looks uncommonly as though something which we do not know about acted as a rather sudden incentive to the collection.

This brings us to Marcion. Did that extremely interesting heretic find four Gospels already recognized together by about A.D. 140, and did he deliberately drop off Matthew, Mark, and John (as well as the unacceptable parts of Luke)? Or was it rather that the catholic Church, after seeing what havoc Marcion wrought by his one-sided use of documents, brought the four Gospels together to restore the balance and make a fourfold harmony? This is the same problem as confronts us for the whole New Testament canon: was Marcion's the first canon, and is the orthodox canon the catholic Church's subsequent reply? Or did Marcion play fast and loose with an already existing canon? There is at present no absolutely conclusive evidence for the existence of a pre-Marcionite catholic canon. Marcion may have been the catalyst we have already hinted at. We cannot be certain.

Even the evidence of the famous Gospel prologues[3] is incon-

---

[1] See R. G. Heard, 'The ἀπομνημονεύματα in Papias, Justin, and Irenaeus', *J.N.T.S.* 1. 2 (Nov., 1954), 122 ff., with some discussion of the meaning of the word and of Heard's article by N. Hyldahl, 'Hegesipps Hypomnemata', *Studia Theologica*, xiv (1960), 70 ff. Of earlier writers, note E. Lippelt, *Quae fuerint Justini M. ἀπομνημονεύματα* (1901).

[2] There may be something to be learnt from the parallel and contrast offered by the convergence and conflation of various accounts of *Israel's* 'Gospel'—the story of the exodus and the covenant—within the Pentateuch.

[3] See D. de Bruyne, 'Prologues bibliques d'origine marcionite', *Revue Bénédictine*, xxiv (1907), 1 ff.; 'Les Plus Anciens Prologues latins des évangiles', *ibid.* xl (1928), 193 ff.; also Huck-Lietzmann, *Synopse*[9] (or Eng. ed. by F. L. Cross), viii; W. F. Howard, *E.T.* xlvii (1936), 535 f.; R. M. Grant, 'The Oldest Gospel Prologues', *Ang. Theol. Rev.* xxiii (1941), 231 ff.

clusive. These are to be distinguished from the brief descriptive prologues to the *Epistles* which, since de Bruyne's brilliant observations, are believed to have originated with Marcion himself. The oldest *Gospel* prologues, by contrast, were believed by de Bruyne to be anti-Marcionite. The late Mr R. G. Heard,[1] however, questioned this conclusion, at any rate for the prologue to Luke, which, he argued, is independent of the prologues to Mark and John (that to Matthew is not extant),[2] and is free from anti-Marcionite material. Once again, then, little if any light can be shed on the relation of the canon to the heretic.

But meanwhile, how had the epistles and other writings fared? One of the most elusive problems in the history of the New Testament canon concerns the origin of the collected letters of Paul, the Pauline *corpus*. Even when it did first emerge, it was not complete: some Pauline writings had already been lost (or at any rate were omitted). I Cor. v. 10 appears to refer to a previous letter of which, at most, a fragment may be detected in 2 Cor. vi. 14-vii. 1. In 2 Cor. vii. 8 allusions are made to a severe letter which, though it may conceivably be I Cor. itself, is more likely identified either with 2 Cor. x ff. or with a completely lost letter. In Col. iv. 16 a letter 'from Laodicea' is mentioned, which evidently means a letter from Paul which is to be passed on to Colossae from Laodicea in exchange for the letter to the Colossians. This 'Laodiceans' is also either totally lost, or is to be identified with what we now know as 'Ephesians' (or else, as has been conjectured by E. J. Goodspeed, with 'Philemon').[3] Conversely, that some of the letters ultimately included in the canon as Pauline are not by Paul falls only just short of demonstration. The Epistle to the Hebrews, though eventually included in the Pauline canon, was regarded

---

[1] R. G. Heard, 'The Old Gospel Prologues', *J.T.S.*, n.s., vi (1955), 1 ff., and further literature there cited.

[2] The 'Monarchian Prologues' (for description and references, see F. J. Foakes-Jackson and K. Lake, *The Beginnings of Christianity*, ii (1922), 242 ff.), which do include Matt., are not to be confused with the ancient, anti-Marcionite ones.

[3] E. J. Goodspeed, *New Solutions to New Testament Problems* (1927), *The Meaning of Ephesians* (1933), *The Key to Ephesians* (1956).

For theories finding a plurality of letters in Phil., see F. W. Beare, *Philippians* (1959); B. D. Rahtjen, 'The Three Letters of Paul to the Philippians', *J.N.T.S.* 6. 2 (January 1960), 167 ff., replied to by B. S. Mackay, 'Further thoughts on Philippians', *J.N.T.S.* 7. 2 (January 1961), 161 ff.

as not of Paul's workmanship by several writers of antiquity (cf. p. 191 above), and now is widely acknowledged to be un-Pauline; and a large number of scholars regard the Pastoral Epistles as at least in part post-Pauline; while varying degrees of suspicion are cast on other Epistles, especially on 2 Thess. and Ephesians. Thus, some were irretrievably lost, some may have eventually been added from the Pauline circle rather than from Paul himself. It was a deeply ingrained tradition in Jewish circles that certain genres of writing should, as a matter of course, be written under the name of their representative authors: Law was by Moses, Wisdom by Solomon, Psalms mostly by David;[1] and at least during K. Aland's 'earlier period' (see above, p. 192) this may have held good for Christians also. But the question still remains: Who or what prompted a collection of Pauline Epistles in the first instance?

As with the four Gospels, so with the Pauline Epistles, we know that they existed before ever they were presented in a single collection. Not only so, but there is some evidence in the manuscript tradition, comparable to that mentioned above for the Gospels, suggesting that they actually circulated for a time separately (and this, it is to be noted, applies to Eph. i).[2] And the appearance of the collection can be plausibly placed within a fairly short period. Admittedly, we have insufficient data for certainty: hence the word 'plausibly'. But the point is that Acts shows no trace of a knowledge of the Pauline Epistles, whereas 1 Clement (generally dated about A.D. 95) does, and thereafter there are enough echoes to show that they were at least beginning to be known. Yet, even so, evidence for the knowledge of one or two Pauline Epistles is not evidence for the existence of a collection, a *corpus*; and as with the Gospels, so with the Pauline corpus, Marcion is the really important land-mark. He, we know on the evidence of Tertullian, used a collection of Pauline Epistles. Was it then he, in fact, who created it?

Two particularly interesting things we learn from Tertullian about Marcion's *Apostolicon* or collection of the apostle's writ-

[1] See L. H. Brockington, 'The Problem of Pseudonymity', *J.T.S.*, n.s., iv (1953), 15 ff.

[2] See a suggestive footnote in F. W. Beare's commentary on Ephesians in *The Interpreter's Bible* x (1953), 601.

ings: that he knew our Ephesians as 'Laodiceans', and that his collection contained the following letters (probably in this order): Gal., 1, 2 Cor., Rom. 1, 2 Thess., Laodiceans, Col., Philem., Phil. That is, Marcion used the nine great Paulines (and Philem.).

What may be learnt by comparing the order in other known lists? The best-known of these is the Muratorian Canon (Stevenson, No. 124), towards the end of the second century, whose catalogue is: Cor., Eph., Phil., Col., Gal., Thess., Rom. (in that order), and also (though not necessarily in this order) Philem., Titus, 1, 2 Tim. The Muratorian Canon goes out of its way here to mention also the Epistles to the Laodiceans and Alexandrines, falsely, it says, attributed to Paul 'in connexion with' (ad) the heresy of Marcion. A brilliant conjecture by J. Knox[1] relates Marcion's and the Muratorian orders as follows, in two steps: (a) Marcion, using an already established list with Ephesians at its head, transposed Eph. (Laodiceans) and Gal., bringing Gal. to the head because it was specially important for his own doctrinal purposes. (b) Assuming that the letters of the already established list were contained in two rolls of roughly equal length,[2] the two most substantial components, 1, 2 Cor. and Rom., will probably have been placed one in each roll. This might make one roll contain Eph. and Cor.; the other all the rest. And if one divides the Muratorian canon into two sections on this principle and reverses the orders of the two sections, one gets exactly Marcion's order (with the one alteration already

---

[1] J. Knox, *Marcion and the New Testament* (1942).

[2] W. H. Brownlee, in a paper read to the Orientalists' congress (1960, cf. his *The Meaning of the Qumran Scrolls for Bible and Religion*, 1962), wrote: 'The gap between Chapters thirty-three and thirty-four in the complete Isaiah scroll (1Q Isa[a]), together with orthographic peculiarities of each half, points to the practice of bisecting the Book of Isaiah into two scrolls: (1) Chapters i-xxxiii and (2) Chapters xxxiv-lxvi. . . . The ancient practice of bisecting books is well discussed by H. St John Thackeray in his Schweich Lectures of 1920, *The Septuagint and Jewish Worship*, Appendix IV, pp. 130-136. This was done, at times, for the convenience of handling by a purely mechanical division of large works into two scrolls; some of the better constructed books of antiquity, however, were so composed as to yield a natural literary division at about the mid-point of the work. . . . In the scroll, each [half] consists of twenty-seven columns, and the point of division lies between two sheets of skin, so if it were not that they happen to be sewed together they could easily circulate as two separate scrolls. An unprecedented gap of three lines occurs at the bottom of Col. XXVII, separating the two volumes.'

noted in (a)). Is it possible, then, that these two lists are the result of rolling up the two rolls in opposite directions? This, though an exceedingly ingenious guess, is only a guess as the author himself is the first to admit. And, as has already been remarked (p. 183 above), it is by no means clear that the writings catalogued in the Muratorian canon would have been on rolls and not in a codex—in which case the theory would fall to the ground. If we deny ourselves the luxury of Knox's theory, we seem to be left without a clue as to the relation between the heretical and the (presumably) orthodox list: and in that case we still do not know which came first—whether Marcion first collected his *apostolicon* and later the orthodox Church decided to make theirs, or whether Marcion tampered with an already existing list.[1] The situation here is the same as with the Gospels.

One other exceedingly ingenious attempt has been made to find an individual to whom to attribute the formation of the Pauline collection. This is E. J. Goodspeed's theory (see p. 199, n. 3 above) about Ephesians. Noting, as all serious enquirers must, the close relation between Eph. and Col., and, at the same time, the very remarkable differences, and convinced that Eph. was not Pauline, Goodspeed reached the conclusion that it must be the work of a student and admirer of the Pauline Epistles, who was particularly familiar with Col., but knew and echoed all the others also. Who might such an individual be, and what led him to know the whole Pauline *corpus*? Might it not have been the reading of the Acts that led this person to go round the Pauline centres looking for the letters? It is well known that the Acts shows practically no trace of a knowledge of the Pauline Epistles; whereas Eph. (assuming its non-Pauline authorship) is the first writing to reflect them all, and thereafter they are often echoed. Moreover, a fashion for issuing collections of Epistles seems to have set in—witness the seven letters of the Apocalypse and the seven letters of Ignatius (note that the Pauline corpus can itself be seen as seven-fold *plus* one—Rom., Cor., Gal., Phil., Col., Thess., [Philemon] (six) *plus* Eph.). Of Goodspeed's theory that Philemon was 'Laodiceans' we need not here speak. What concerns us at the moment is that, on his showing, Eph. is, as it

---

[1] See a discussion of this problem in E. C. Blackman, *Marcion and his Influence* (1948), ch. 2.

were, the covering letter to the collection. Instead of writing an introduction in his own name, as a modern editor would, this disciple and admirer writes a glowing recapitulation of the apostle's message, modestly concealing his own identity by the then familiar technique of writing as from the apostle himself. And who was he? If an identification were to be hazarded, Goodspeed (supported here by Knox)[1] would suggest Onesimus. Who would be more intimate with Col. (and Philemon) than the slave whose future depended so completely on the success of these letters? And who is so naturally associated with Ephesus as Onesimus who (according to Ignatius' letter to Ephesus) was in later years Bishop of that Church? There are many minor difficulties in the way of this extremely skilful solution of the Ephesians problem (for which the reader must be referred to works of introduction and exegesis); but one major problem is the position of Eph. in lists of the Epistles. In no known list does it occur either first or last (the only positions which seem to be appropriate to it on Goodspeed's theory of its origin and function). Only if we accept Knox's brilliant conjecture about the original order both of Marcion's and of the Muratorian list can Eph. be brought to the head of the list.

If we abandon the idea that the collecting of the Pauline letters was the work of an individual, such as Onesimus or Marcion, we are left with the time-honoured alternative—the slow, anonymous process of accretion, the snowball theory. We have to suppose, that is, that the intercourse between one Pauline centre and another gradually led to the exchange of copies of letters, until, at any given centre, there came to be not only the letter or letters originally sent to it, but also copies of certain others, collected from other Pauline Churches. Thus in each centre there would come to be little nests of letters, and gradually these would move into wider circulation and would be augmented, until the full number, as we know it, was reached. Then all that remained to be done was the making of a careful 'edition' of the whole *corpus*.

Such a theory ignores Acts as a precipitant; it also depends a good deal on the assumption of a live interest in Paul between his death and the decisive acceptance of his letters; and there is

[1] J. Knox, *Philemon among the Letters of Paul* ([2]1959), especially ch. 5.

no evidence that Paul dominated the Christian world of those days as he has (for the most part) dominated it since the inclusion of his letters in scripture. Papias (to cite a famous example), although the friend of Polycarp, shows no evidence of the use of the Pauline writings.[1] Yet, even so, it is hard to believe that the Churches of Paul's own founding did not treasure his memory (cf. 1 Clement xlvii. 1 with its 'Take up the epistle of the blessed Paul the Apostle', implying that the Corinthians had treasured one letter at any rate), and that would be enough to start the process of gradual accretion. Communications were good between different centres, and a process of exchanging and transcribing is not difficult to imagine. Moreover, as against Goodspeed's theory, it must be remembered that Acts makes no mention whatsoever of Paul's letter-writing activities, in spite of its mention of other Epistles (see Acts xv. 23-29, xviii. 27, xxiii. 25-30, xxviii. 21). At best, then, Acts can only have provided the incentive in the sense that it recounted Paul's activity as a founder of various local Churches. But the Churches in question did not need Acts to tell them that.

Thus, although one-man theories are exceedingly attractive, they are highly speculative, and the anonymous, gradual evolution is not by any means ruled out. If one other individual name were to be suggested, however, might it not be that of Luke himself? It has just been pointed out that the Acts would provide no reader with any knowledge of the Pauline Epistles; but what if it was after the writing of the Acts, and after Paul's death, that Luke himself—who must have known about the letters although he had not written about them—began to revisit the Pauline centres which he had described, and to look for the letters there? No one knew better than he the fact that they were written. It is entirely in keeping with his historian's temperament to collect them.[2] And the considerable link, in respect of vocabulary, contents, and outlook, between the Pas-

---

[1] See, e.g., B. F. Westcott, *A General Survey of the History of the Canon of the New Testament* ([4]1875), 77 f. (attributing the silence to Papias' Judaistic sympathies). It must be remembered, however, that Papias' work only survives in scattered fragments, and the silence is not therefore specially significant.

[2] H. Chadwick reminds me that Eusebius collected the letters of Origen, *H.E.* vi. 36. 2.

toral Epistles and Lk.-Acts lends some plausibility to the suggestion that Luke was the collector, editor, and augmenter of the Pauline corpus.[1] Whether the Pastorals were in existence by the time of Marcion or not is still a matter of dispute.

On the nature of the archetype of the Pauline *corpus* there is a valuable discussion in G. Zuntz's Schweich Lectures for 1946.[2] A careful criticism of Goodspeed's hypothesis leads him to the conclusion (276 f.) that 'Whoever wrote Ephesians, it was not the editor of the *corpus*. . . .' He then points out that 'faithfulness, completeness, and non-interference with the available material' are the characteristics of 'the traditions of editorship in antiquity generally'. As instances, he adduced the editing of Thucydides, Lucretius, and the *Aeneid*; of the private diaries of the Emperor Marcus; of Plotinus' essays, with special reference to interesting information about methods in the 'life' of Porphyry, Plotinus' editor. He thinks, therefore, of many faults arising in the Pauline Epistles, individually and (perhaps) in earlier collections, in the fifty years between the autographs and the formation of the *corpus*—a period during which he believes there was some use and circulation—*ergo* copying—of the Epistles; and then he thinks of a *corpus* produced about A.D. 100, which, in the scholarly Alexandrine tradition (and perhaps at Alexandria) aimed at the qualities already mentioned, and thus (e.g.) produced an *Ephesians* with a blank in i. 1 and with ἐν Ἐφέσῳ in the margin. Thus there came to be a splendid *variorum* archetype, from which we may derive many of the later variants.

However and whenever the Pauline *corpus* emerged, at any rate we have Marcion's date as one landmark; and not many decades later, in about A.D. 180, we can listen to the martyrs of Scilli or Scillium (in Numidia, in *Africa proconsularis*) being interrogated by the proconsul about the books in their possession: 'what is there in your *capsa* [book box]'? and replying *Libri et epistulae Pauli viri iusti*[3] (i.e. probably the Gospels, and the Epistles of Paul . . .). 'The books, but especially the parchments' (2 Tim. iv. 13 discussed above, pp. 182 f.) has now taken

---

[1] See Excursus II: *Luke and the Pastoral Epistles*.

[2] G. Zuntz, *The Text of the Epistles: a Disquisition upon the Corpus Paulinum* (1953).

[3] '*Viri iusti*' (as H. Chadwick comments) is meant to show that the books in question were not, as the proconsul might have expected, pornographic.

on a new and wholly Christian significance! If we could date
2 Pet. with any certainty, it might prove (iii. 16) to contain the
earliest reference to Paul as scripture. But who can say when it
was written?

What, now, may be said of a Johannine *corpus*? Extremely
little, it must be confessed. One clear fact, however, is that there
is a close connexion between the Fourth Gospel and the Johannine Epistles (whether or not they are actually by the same
hand).[1] Both these groups, though anonymous, are associated
by tradition with the name of John and with Ephesus. The
Apocalypse, itself claiming to be written by one named John and
also associated by tradition with Ephesus, is still held by some
modern scholars to be by the same hand as some or all of the
other Johannines: but despite certain contacts in vocabulary and
thought, its style, and, still more, its theological outlook, are
very different. However that may be, it is perhaps a more useful
thing to think in terms not so much of a Johannine *corpus* as of
an Ephesian tradition, and to speculate cautiously about the
courses along which diverse streams of tradition flowed to that
centre. The late T. W. Manson revived, in a modified form,[2]
Sanday's interesting suggestion that there was 'an anticipatory
stage of Johannean teaching, localized somewhere in Syria,
before the apostle reached his final home in Ephesus'. Manson
proposed Antioch as a centre of 'Johannine' traditions *en route*
to Ephesus. Manson did not discuss the relation of the Epistle
to the Ephesians to the Johannine traditions; but it is well
known that, whereas this Epistle (as has been already observed)
does not fit beyond doubt into the typically Pauline mould, it
does present certain affinities with Revelation (e.g., the Church
as the Bride of Christ, and as founded upon the apostles and
prophets). There is not here, as a matter of fact, any necessary

[1] See P. Katz, 'The Johannine Epistles in the Muratorian Canon', *J.T.S.*,
n.s., viii. 2 (Oct. 1957), 273 ff. for an ingenious bid for the inclusion of 2,
3 John in the Muratorian Canon, by suggesting that *duas* (*leg. duae*) *in
catholica habentur* represents an original Greek such as δύο σὺν καθολικῇ, *two
in addition to the Catholic* (*Epistle*). This seems to me to be in principle convincing; but I do not see why the original should not have had πρὸς καθολικήν
—even more natural Greek for *in addition to*, and more easily translated *in*.
[2] See T. W. Manson, 'The Life of Jesus: a survey of the available material,
(5) The Fourth Gospel', *B.J.R.L.* 30 (1946–47), 312 ff., with W. Sanday,
*The Criticism of the Fourth Gospel* (1903), 199.

contradiction to the Pauline phrases about Christ as the one foundation; but may not Ephesians represent the flowing together and fusing of Pauline and other types of thought, and may not Ephesus (possibly with Antioch as a kind of halfway basin or reservoir) be the centre of confluence—especially if much of the Johannine tradition really does go right back to Palestinian sources?[1] Possibly it is worth while to throw into the discussion the fact that Matthew is the only Gospel that speaks of the Church and its (apostolic) foundation, and that there is something to be said for an Antiochene connexion for this Gospel.[2] The letters of Ignatius of Antioch seem to contain nothing that can demonstrate any knowledge of the Fourth Gospel or of Ephesians. But (as H. Chadwick observes) it is not Ignatius' manner to *cite*, but he may allude. In these conjectures, however, we are on a quaking bog of uncertainty. Notions of ecclesiastical authority might seem to provide a more fruitful clue to classification: Matthew, Ephesians, the Fourth Gospel, and the Johannine Epistles are all very vigorously concerned with authority; but again it is impossible to group them together in an undifferentiated way, for, in a sense, the Fourth Gospel is remarkably non-ecclesiastical in its treatment of authority (as indeed throughout). Non-apocalyptic eschatology is, to some extent, common to Ephesians and the Fourth Gospel; but this does not apply to the Johannine Epistles—still less to the Apocalypse; and there is non-apocalyptic eschatology in Rom. viii also.

In short, we know pitifully little about the cross currents of Christian teaching and apologetic at Ephesus or elsewhere that led to the ultimate recognition of those Johannine writings by the whole Church. What we do know is that St John's Gospel was the latest of the four to gain this status and that it was opposed by a group contemptuously known for this reason as the 'Alogi' (the 'logos-less' in relation to the Fourth Gospel

[1] See p. 93, n. 3.
[2] For discussions of Matt's. provenance, see, e.g., T. W. Manson, 'The Life of Jesus: a Survey of the Available Material: (4) the Gospel according to St Matthew', *B.J.R.L.* 29 (1945–46), 392 ff.; G. D. Kilpatrick, *The Origins of the Gospel according to St Matthew* (1946); K. Stendahl, *The School of St Matthew* (1954); P. Nepper-Christensen, *Das Matthäusevangelium: ein judenchristliches Evangelium?* (1958); W. Trilling, *Das wahre Israel* (1959); E. P. Blair, *Jesus in the Gospel of Matthew* (1960).

prologue and therefore 'logos-less' also in the sense 'stupid'); likewise that the Apocalypse was roughly handled by those who were opposed to millenarianism, of which it alone, within the New Testament, is the spokesman.[1] Conversely, it is a familiar fact that certain other writings associated with the name of John never gained wide recognition at all; while writings widely read at one time for edification, such as the Apostolic Fathers, were ultimately excluded. The necessity for decision on authoritative books as against the false or the unauthoritative, was imposed by heresy from within and attack from without. Perhaps a fruitful line of advance may lie (cf. Chapters I and VIII above) in the direction of freshly investigating the purposes of some of the New Testament writings. 2 Pet. and Jude are manifestly attacks on perversions of Christianity, perversions which had arisen, at least in part, through the kind of misappropriation of Pauline doctrines which Paul himself attacks (e.g. in Rom. vi). The Pastoral Epistles are also concerned in part with correcting perversions of Pauline teaching, and it is notoriously possible that James may (though it is far from certain that Paul is presupposed) have something of the sort in view in Chapter ii. The Johannine Epistles, attacking a docetic type of misinterpretation of Christ, may similarly be viewed as a corrective to perversions of the teaching in the Fourth Gospel. And in addition to insidious dangers from within, necessitating a clear recognition of what was sound in Christian writing, there were attacks of opponents from without. In controversy with these, authoritative references were needed; while in times of persecution, it might be of vital importance (as we have seen at Scilli) to define the sacred Christian manuscripts. The story of the fluctuations on the fringe of the canon—on one side the ultimately excluded, on the other the doubtfuls ultimately included (2 Pet. and Jude, 2, 3 John, Hebrews, etc.)—is told in all books of introduction, and need not be repeated here, any more than the final settling down of the present canon, in Athanasius' 39th Paschal letter of A.D. 367 and (?) the Council of Laodicea. The purpose of this chapter has been not to retell the whole story

---

[1] For anti-millenarianism, see Euseb. *H.E.* iii. 28; vii. 25; and (e.g.) I. T. Beckwith, *The Apocalypse of John* (1919), 340 ff. The 'Alogi' opposed the Johannine writings because they seemed to offer a handle to the charismatic anarchy of the Montanists.

but rather to throw into relief—so far as is possible in a realm too remote to focus clearly—some of the motives and principles, theological and disciplinary, behind the long process. All the time, moreover, it is viewed, so far as possible, as a human process. That it is also the tale of a divine overruling of the gropings and mistakes of men is here assumed without further discussion.

## CHAPTER XI

# CONCLUSION

THROUGHOUT this book the general standpoint of 'form criticism' has been adopted, namely, that it is to the circumstances and needs of the worshipping, working, suffering community that one must look if one is to explain the genesis of Christian literature. Probably at no stage within the New Testament period did a writer put pen to paper without the incentive of a pressing need. Seldom was the writing consciously adorned; never was adornment an end in itself. Accordingly different aspects of the community's life have been successively considered, with a view to illustrating how various types of Christian literature grew up in response to these circumstances and needs and can only be adequately understood against this setting.

But if the standpoint of 'form criticism' has been thus adopted, a good many of the assumptions that frequently go with it have been discarded or qualified. A caveat has been entered against too lightly assuming that we have the very words of liturgy in certain passages which are frequently so interpreted. It has been urged that the probabilities favour a more fluid interchange of forms, such that snatches of prayer and hymnody flow in and out of the texture of pastoral exhortation, and liturgical phrases at the close of an Epistle do not necessarily imply that it is being formally linked as a homily to the eucharist. Again, the immense importance and prominence of Old Testament scripture in Christian thinking and reasoning, while it explains and accounts for much in the New Testament, must not, it has been argued, lead to the conclusion that whole sections of Christian narrative were created by the Old Testament. Neither should the essentially theological, apologetic, and edificatory intention of Christian writing lead to the assumption that the early Church took little or no interest in the actual circumstances of the Jesus of history. In particular, it is here maintained that the Gospels, as documents of Christian apologetic (direct or indirect), are very considerably concerned to reconstruct the story of 'how it all began'.

In the chapter on persecution, the view is taken that the greater part of the 'persecution' sections of the New Testament may be explained by postulating primarily Jewish antagonism, without invoking the Roman arm. In the treatment of the edificatory passages, stress is laid upon the relativity of Christian ethics, and the comparative individualism which, of necessity, was imposed upon them by the circumstances of the Christian communities. The last two chapters stress the wide variety of outlook and the often frightening vagueness that must have obtained in the underworld of the congregations scattered over the empire, over against the astonishing uniformity that characterized their leaders and was ultimately reflected in the canon, despite its exceedingly complicated history and seemingly haphazard development. Devotion to the person of Jesus Christ—as was said at the outset—is the clue to this extraordinary phenomenon.

Hundreds of problems remain. Too little is still known about the Jewish background of the life of Jesus and of the primitive Church; the peculiarities of the Christian uses of Scripture still present unsolved riddles; the varying social conditions of the different centres of Christendom are still largely in the shades of obscurity; the story of the canon bristles with unsolved—perhaps insoluble—problems.

But perhaps two conclusions of major importance arising from this study may now be underlined. One is the primacy of the divine initiative; the other is the urgent need today for what might be called the 'ethical translation of the Gospel'.

With regard to the first, a too cursory glance at the chapter headings of this book might lead to the conclusion that the early Church was engaged in an intensely self-regarding struggle—explaining itself, defending itself, edifying itself, unifying itself, authenticating itself. But that would be a quite false impression. It was by deliberate intention that these chapters were prefaced by one on the Church at worship; and it is in fact in a steadily Godward attitude that the Church undertook all its other activities—and still does, whenever it is really being its true self.

Explanation, defence, edification, unification, authentication—none of these is Christian unless undertaken under the compulsion of the Spirit of God and for his glory; and it would be quite contrary to the intentions of this study if the growing self-consciousness of the Church here traced—from the earliest assumption that it was nothing other than 'Israel', to the latest awareness of itself as a *tertium genus* with its own scriptures—were seen as anything but the corollary of a growing understanding of God and his purposes in Jesus Christ.

With regard to the second matter much needs to be said, though it cannot be said here. Perhaps nothing is more urgently needed than a concerted effort to hammer out Christian ethics for the present day. But that requires the 'ethical translation of the Gospel'. It requires joint action by experts in very many different fields, and is quite beyond the competence of a mere New Testament student as such. Indeed, one of the most important lessons of this book is that the guidance of the Spirit of God was granted in the form not of a code of behaviour nor of any written deposit of direction, but of inspired insight. It was granted *ad hoc* to Christians as they met together, confronting the immediate problems with the Gospel behind them, the Holy Spirit among them, and the will to find out the action required of the People of God in the near future. If the pages of the Pauline Epistles are searched, they reveal various lines along which the apostle sought guidance: through direct revelation—in vision or audition; through the words and example of Christ; through the Jewish scriptures read in the light of Christ; through community custom; even through 'natural law'. But it is tolerably clear that the most characteristic Christian way of guidance was in the kind of setting indicated in I Cor. xiv, where the Christians assemble, each with a psalm or a teaching or a revelation or an ecstatic burst of ejaculation: *and the congregation exercises discernment*. That is how Christian . ethical decisions were reached: informed discussion, prophetic insight, ecstatic fire—all in the context of the worshipping, and also discriminating, assembly, met with the good news in Jesus Christ behind them, the Spirit among them, and before them the expectation of being led forward into the will of God. And if there is one lesson of outstanding importance to be gleaned from all this, it is that only along similar lines, translated into terms of our present circumstances, can we hope for an informed Christian ethic for the present day. It will probably be different in different areas of the world: each Christian Church has its peculiar problems and opportunities and its unique conditions. And it will always be based, not on a rigid code of ethics but on the guidance of the Spirit in the light of the unchanging Gospel and of contemporary conditions carefully studied by experts. One of the contributions to this will be hard, scientific, statistical thinking, brought to the Christian group by the Christians who are specialists in various realms of study. Only in the light of this will the guidance of the Spirit be realistically apprehended. Efficient, intelligent historical reconstruction of the past is another necessary contribution: the very writing of the Gospels bears witness to the Christian awareness of the importance of understanding and constantly recalling the origin and movement of the Christian *kerygma*. But only by 'translation' can an applied ethic be hoped for. Unless the Church expects the living voice of the Paraclete in such a context, to lead it forward into all truth, it will look in vain for specific guidance. Christian ethical practice in the past may, and must, be carefully studied. But in the last analysis we shall only know what Christian ethics today should be by letting the Holy Spirit 'translate' the message—by trusting to contemporary guidance. It was only so that the Church progressed and met its problems in those early years.

Many other matters have come up in the course of this enquiry, all of them in some measure important for this always necessary study of Christian beginnings, and some of them, perhaps, unusual. It will be for others to assess the value of the more unusual suggestions offered about some of the standing problems of the period. The estimate of the purpose of the Gospels, the guesses about the character of Matthew and Hebrews, the attitude to the liturgical factor, and the speculations about the relation of Luke the physician to the canon of scripture: these may or may not be well advised. But the problems they represent are ones which the student of the New Testament must constantly wrestle with; and his reading of the New Testament situation will, in its turn, be one of the contributions which it is his ministry to bring to the congregation of

Christian people to which he belongs, as they try, in the light of all the available data, to place themselves under the guidance of the Spirit.

It is hoped that this study, even if indirectly, may be a contribution to the prolegomena to contemporary Christian ethics.

# TRANSLATION GREEK AND ORIGINAL GREEK
# IN MATTHEW

It is worth while asking whether too little attention has not been paid to the word ἡρμήνευσεν in the much-discussed words of Papias quoted by Euseb. *H.E.* iii. 39. 12. Considerable thought has been devoted to the meaning of Ἑβραΐδι διαλέκτῳ (in the light of H. Birkeland and his critics and of others' researches, see p. 186, n. 2); and τὰ λόγια is a phrase round which hundreds of pages have been written.[1] But are not the implications of ἡρμήνευσεν worthy of closer consideration?

Behm, in his article on this word-group in *T.W.N.T.* ii. 659 ff., distinguishes three main senses—(a) *deuten, auslegen, erklären* (explain, interpret); (b) *andeuten, seine Gedanken durch Worte darlegen, ausdrücken* (express); (c) *aus einer fremden Sprache in die bekannte übertragen, dolmetschen, übersetzen* (to translate). All three are Classical—indeed, all three can be exemplified from Plato alone, not to mention other writers; and, although only (a) and (c) are found in the New Testament ((a) only in Lk. xxiv. 27 (διερμ., D ἑρμ.), (c) only in Jn i. 38 (v.l.), 42, ix. 7 (ἑρμ.), 1 Cor. xii. 30, xiv. 5, 13, 27 (διερμ.), Heb. vii. 2 (ἑρμ.), (b) not at all), there seems to be no particular reason why the word in Euseb. should not mean whichever is the most appropriate to its context.

Clearly the second sense ('express') is here inapplicable; but there is at least some option, linguistically speaking, between 'interpret' and 'translate', and it is, I think, just conceivable (in the abstract) that τὰ λόγια might mean a collection of parables and parabolic sayings which were differently *interpreted* by different hearers, just as the sayings in the Gospel of Thomas are being variously interpreted today. In that case Matt. xiii would contain specimens of the process in question. However, I suppose all will agree that the preceding sentence, with its reference to the language of the original, virtually clinches the third sense—translation.

What follows? Surely a much firmer rejection of the theory that τὰ λόγια means Old Testament *testimonia* than is to be obtained from an investigation merely of the meaning of λόγιον. For, had

[1] See T. W. Manson, *B.J.R.L.* 29. 2 (February 1946), 392 ff.; Kittel's *T.W.N.T.* iv. 144 f.

I

Old Testament *testimonia* been intended by τὰ λόγια, in the first place, Ἑβραΐδι διαλέκτῳ is not a completely rational way of expressing 'in their [original] Hebrew' and secondly it is difficult to imagine why it is described as *necessary* for them to be translated by each reader, 'as best he could' (ὡς ἦν δυνατὸς ἕκαστος). It is perfectly true that it is precisely Matthew's *testimonia* that are notoriously not septuagintal; but the fact that Old Testament *testimonia* were individually rendered into Greek still does not justify the phrase ὡς ἦν δυνατὸς ἕκαστος which implies some *necessity* for private translation. There were already well-established Greek versions of the Old Testament available—especially, of course, that of the LXX: why should each reader be compelled to use his own make-shift? The translation clause points, as it seems to me, almost conclusively to τὰ λόγια being some original and hitherto unknown composition. In other words, this clause points strongly to the theory that the writing in question was some such document as we associate with Q, though it certainly does not tie it down to being a collection of nothing but sayings.[1]

If, then, Papias' tradition really does point to variant translations, is there any trace left of these? It has often been observed that a comparison of Matt. and Lk. suggests that, in some cases, they represent different translations of the same sources (see a useful list, based partly on Wellhausen, in C. K. Barrett, 'Q: a Re-examination', *E.T.* liv. 12 (September 1943), 320 ff.). But is it not posssible that, actually within Matt. itself, variant versions of a single source have left their trace? In v. 22, not only may μωρέ be a gloss on ῥακά, but συνέδριον and κρίσις may be alternative translations (see my note in *E.T.* l. 4 (January 1939), 184); xii. 31 f. is possibly a conflation of the Marcan and Lucan versions of a saying, of which the Marcan may be nearest to the original; in xvi. 22, ἵλεως and οὐ μὴ ἔσται are *alternative* renderings of חלילה (see P. Katz, *Kratylos* v (1960), 157 ff.); in xxiii. 8, 10 ῥαββεί and καθηγητής are transliteration and translation respectively; in xxvii. 6 f., both 'treasury', 'ōṣār and 'potter', yōṣēr are represented (cf. Zech. xi. 13, וצר and M.T. respectively).[2]

At any rate, it is clear that the Evangelist was, in many respects, a conservator, conflating, combining, sometimes duplicating. Is it possible to say, further, that the Semitisms in his Gospel are survivals from his sources, while he himself naturally wrote purer Greek?

[1] For warnings against hasty identification of 'Matthew's *logia*' with Q, see B. W. Bacon, *Studies in Matthew* (1930), xii, and J. A. Robinson, *The Study of the Gospels* (1902). For a discrediting of Jerome's 'authentic Hebrew', see P. Nepper-Christensen, *Das Matthäusevangelium* (1958), ch. 2.

[2] See a slightly fuller treatment of this question of the 'anthological' tendency of Matt. in my paper 'St Matthew's Gospel: Some Neglected Features', *T. und U.* (forthcoming).

(i) It is noticeable that at least some passages which are obviously editorial contain fairly clear Semitisms. In the first place, there are the five famous 'link-passages' or 'connecting panels', vii. 28, xi. 1, xiii. 53, xix. 1, xxvi. 1. Here, if anywhere, we may be reasonably confident that we see the hand of the editor himself. And each of these begins with the characteristically Semitic καὶ ἐγένετο ὅτι. . . . Then, again, many a section begins with a vague and strictly illogical use of ἐκεῖνος such as: ἐν ἐκείνῳ τῷ καιρῷ (xi. 25, xii. 1, xiv. 1) or ἐν ἐκείνῃ τῇ ὥρᾳ (xviii. 1) or ἐν τῇ ἡμέρᾳ ἐκείνῃ (xiii. 1)—all of them apparently meaning little more than 'on one occasion' or 'one day'; and I suspect that this, too, is Semitic rather than native Greek; cf. Gen. xxi. 22, Josh. v. 2 (bā‘eth hahî) and Gen. xxxix. 11, 1 Sam. iii. 2 where kᵉhayyôm hazzeh and bayyôm hahû' are interpreted (e.g. by Brown, Driver, and Briggs, Lexicon s.v. יום) as meaning 'on this particular day (when the incident occurred)'. Further, the use of εἷς =τις (which is generally regarded as Semitic) occurs in certain passages where it is simpler to assume that it is Matthew's own introduction than that it came from a source. Thus: εἷς γραμματεύς (viii. 19), ἄρχων εἷς (ix. 18), μία παιδίσκη (xxvi. 69) are instances where the parallel passages are without this idiom; προσήχθη εἷς αὐτῷ ὀφειλέτης (xviii. 24) is in a passage peculiar to Matt., and may or may not have been in his source; only εἷς προσελθὼν αὐτῷ (xix. 16) is paralleled (Mk x. 17). On the other hand, the εἷς ἐκ τοῦ ὄχλου of Mk ix. 17 becomes simply ἄνθρωπος in Matt. xviii. 14, which is a warning against too light an assumption that the construction is systematically introduced by the evangelist. However, enough has perhaps been adduced to suggest that the editor himself did use Semitisms.

(ii) Were these Semitisms, then, spontaneous and natural to this writer, or did he deliberately introduce them? That the latter is the more likely is suggested by two phenomena:

(a) There are passages where we find quite accomplished Greek, free from Semitisms. On the whole, the Aktionsart of the verbs is correct throughout Matt. But the most striking instance of good Greek is, perhaps, xvii. 24-27, the pericope about the coin in the fish's mouth. Here there is a comparatively elaborate use of participles, a wide range of vocabulary, and a liveliness almost like Luke's at his most free and individual (e.g. in the latter chapters of Acts). One may note especially the phrase (xvii. 25) καὶ ἐλθόντα εἰς τὴν οἰκίαν προέφθασεν αὐτὸν ὁ Ἰησοῦς (for this competent handling of participles, cf. ix. 27, xxvi. 71). A reasonably stylish passage of this sort might, of course, come straight from a source and not represent the author's own style; but on the whole the balance of probability, if we allow that Semitic sources lie behind the Gospel tradition at all, is against attributing to a source features which are linguistically the opposite of Semitic. It must be admitted, however, that even here there is (*v.* 26) what Classical Greek would less easily tolerate — an ostensible genitive absolute which turns out to be, after all, not absolute; and throughout this Gospel there are, side by side, correct genitives absolute and this incorrect type (the latter even in so clearly editorial a passage as viii. 1).

(b) Secondly, there is the introduction into otherwise apparently pure Greek of such Semitic phrases as ἰδού. In the story of the magi (ii) almost impeccable Greek is given a slightly Semitic flavour by this means (as also, perhaps, by ἐχάρησαν χαρὰν μεγάλην σφόδρα *v.* 10); and in the narrative of the baptism Matthew seems (iii. 16) to rephrase Mk (i. 10) in such a way as deliberately to introduce this interjection.

On the whole, this adds up to a balance of evidence in favour of the editor's own Semitisms being deliberate and artificial.

(iii) There are, of course, fairly clear signs of the extensive use of sources which already contained Semitic idiom. Very much has been written on the Aramaic behind the Sermon on the Mount and many other passages. Let it merely be remarked here, by way of one illustration, that the use of ἄνθρωπος in apposition with a noun, which is likely to be a Semitism,[1] is, though peculiar to Matt., yet invariably in parables (ἐχθρὸς ἄνθρωπος, xiii. 28, ἄνθρωπος ἔμπορος, xiii. 45 (*v. l.*); ἄνθρωπος οἰκοδεσπότης, xiii. 52, xx. 1, xxi. 33, ἄνθρωπος βασιλεύς, xviii. 23, xxii. 2); and the likelihood, therefore, is that the idiom came by tradition with the parable. This is only one phenomenon out of a wealth of evidence that Matthew simply took over much that already had a Semitic cast.

(iv) Among other features of the language of this Gospel may be mentioned the following miscellaneous items: ὅτι *recitativum* is comparatively rare; τοῦ *c. infin.* of purpose is sparingly used (iii. 13, xi. 1, xiii. 3, xxi. 32); the Marcan εὐθύς is sparingly used, and εὐθέως is much commoner; δεῦτε is frequent, and not only in borrowings from Mk. There are several Latin words: μίλιον, κῆνσος, κουστωδία, perhaps συμβούλιον λαβεῖν (xxvii. 1, 7? =*consilium capere*). There is a wide and rather remarkable vocabulary (in what follows * denotes a passage paralleled in Mk or Lk. or both; † denotes special to Matt.): There is a large number of verbs in -ζω, some of them unusual, e.g.: εὐνουχίζω xix. 12,† ἅπ. λεγ. in N.T.; καταποντίζω, xiv. 30,† xviii. 6,* not elsewhere in N.T.; πυρράζω xvi. 2,† (*si vera l.*), ἅπ. λεγ. in N.T.; σεληνιάζω iv. 24,* xvii. 15,* not elsewhere in N.T. Other noteworthy words include: τὸν δεῖνα xxvi. 18,* ἅπ. λεγ. in N.T.; διασαφεῖν xiii. 36,† xviii. 31,† not elsewhere in N.T.; θαυμάσιον xxi. 15,† ἅπ. λεγ. in N.T.; παλιγγενεσία xix. 28,*

[1] See, e.g., M. Black, *An Aramaic Approach to the Gospels and Acts* ([2]1954) 249 f.

elsewhere in N.T. only Tit. iii. 5; πέλαγος xviii. 6,* in N.T. elsewhere only Acts xxvii. 5; συντέλεια xiii. 39,† 40,† 49,† xxiv. 3,* xxviii. 20,† elsewhere in N.T. only Heb. ix. 26; τὰ ὕδατα *pl.*, viii. 32,* xiv. 28 f.† elsewhere in N.T. only Jn iii. 23 and Rev. *passim*. It speaks strongly for these words belonging to the evangelist's own vocabulary that they are spread over both his peculiar material and passages which have parallels in the other Gospels, which do not, however, use the words in question.

Thus, as a preliminary estimate, one might say that the editor was an educated person commanding sound Greek with a considerable vocabulary; but he derived many Semitisms, and perhaps some Latin, from his sources; and he also had some feeling for Semitic 'atmosphere', occasionally introducing a Semitism on his own account, though less histrionically than Luke. So far as it goes, this conclusion fits well enough with my suggestions about the provenance of the Gospel.

# LUKE AND THE PASTORAL EPISTLES

As for the link between the Pastorals and Lk.-Acts, in addition to the allusions in the Pastorals to persons or situations alluded to in the Acts (for which see the commentaries, and P. N. Harrison, *The Problem of the Pastoral Epistles* (1921), 93 ff.), note the following contacts: 1 Tim. v. 17 τιμή =material reward, cf. Acts xxviii. 10 πολλαῖς τιμαῖς ἐτίμησαν ἡμᾶς. 1 Tim. v. 18 ἄξιος ὁ ἐργάτης τοῦ μισθοῦ αὐτοῦ is the Lucan form (Lk. x. 7, τῆς τροφῆς αὐτοῦ, Matt. x. 10). 1 Tim. vi. 10 φιλαργυρία is a N.T. ἅπαξ λεγ.; Lk. xvi. 14, 2 Tim. iii. 2, both have φιλάργυρος (only here in N.T.). 1 Tim. vi. 17 ὑψηλοφρονεῖν (N.T. ἅπαξ λεγ.), cf. Lk. xvi. 15 τὸ ἐν ἀνθρώποις ὑψηλόν (same context as φιλάργυρος above). 1 Tim. vi. 18 πλουτεῖν ἐν ἔργοις καλοῖς . . . ἀποθησαυρίζοντες ἑαυτοῖς θεμέλιον καλὸν εἰς τὸ μέλλον, ἵνα ἐπιλάβωνται τῆς ὄντως ζωῆς, cf. Lk. xii. 21 οὕτως ὁ θησαυρίζων αὐτῷ καὶ μὴ εἰς θεὸν πλουτῶν and cf. Lk. xvi. 9 (moral from 'Dishonest Bailiff' parable). 2 Tim. ii. 12 εἰ ὑπομένομεν καὶ συμβασιλεύσομεν, cf. Lk. xxii. 28 f. ὑμεῖς δέ ἐστε οἱ διαμεμενηκότες μετ' ἐμοῦ ἐν τοῖς πειρασμοῖς μου· κἀγὼ διατίθεμαι ὑμῖν . . . βασιλείαν . . . 2 Tim. ii. 19 ἔγνω κύριος τοὺς ὄντας αὐτοῦ, καὶ ἀποστήτω ἀπὸ ἀδικίας πᾶς ὁ ὀνομάζων τὸ ὄνομα κυρίου, cf. Lk. xiii. 27 οὐκ οἶδα ὑμᾶς πόθεν ἐστέ· ἀπόστητε ἀπ' ἐμοῦ πάντες ἐργάται ἀδικίας (where Matt. vii. 23 has ἀποχωρεῖτε for ἀπόστητε. But admittedly Matt. also has, vii. 22, the allusion to 'naming the Lord'— κύριε, κύριε, οὐ τῷ σῷ ὀνόματι ἐπροφητεύσαμεν, κ.τ.λ.). 2 Tim. ii. 26 ἐζωγρημένοι, cf. Lk. v. 10 (only other N.T. occurrence of ζωγρεῖν). 2 Tim. iv. 7 τὸν δρόμον τετέλεκα, cf. Acts xiii. 25 ὡς δὲ ἐπλήρου Ἰωάνης τὸν δρόμον; xx. 24 ὡς τελειώσω τὸν δρόμον μου. Indeed, 2 Tim. iv. 1-8 as a whole is reminiscent of the Pauline farewell in Acts xx. 17 ff., and the references to presbyter-episcopi in the Pastorals generally is like Acts xx; but of course it might be said that this is only because both passages are Pauline, not because both are Lucan! Note further that Maurer, in *T.W.N.T.* s.v. συνείδησις, remarks that in the post-Pauline N.T. writings, συνείδησις is almost always qualified by attributes (ἀγαθή, καθαρά, etc.). If this were generally true, it would provide to that extent a less clear connexion between the Acts and the Pastorals in particular; but in fact, while there are only two clear instances in Heb. and two in 1 Pet. (though the implications for one or two other passages point the same way), the others are from precisely our two groups of writings—the Acts (xxiii. 1, xxiv. 16) and the Pastorals (1 Tim. i. 5, 19, iii. 9, 2 Tim. i. 3, ii. 22).

It is interesting that two recent works, not concerned with the present problem, both remark independently on connexions between the Pastorals and Luke: C. K. Barrett, *Luke the Historian in Recent Study* (1961), 62 f.; 'Luke . . . shares the attitude of the Pastorals, though he is prevented by his subject-matter from uttering the explicit: O Timothy, guard the deposit . . .'; J. C. O'Neill, *The Theology of Acts* (1961), 176: 'The author of the Pastoral epistles has emphasized that Paul's defence before the Imperial court in Rome completed the preaching. In principle the Gentile mission was over. Acts assumed the same view of Paul's martyrdom.'

# ΠΙΣΤΟΣ Ο ΛΟΓΟΣ

πιστὸς ὁ λόγος is a phrase common to all three Pastoral Epistles (1 Tim. i. 15, iii. 1, iv. 9, 2 Tim. ii. 11, Tit. iii. 8; cf. the closely similar... ἀντεχόμενον τοῦ κατὰ τὴν διδαχὴν πιστοῦ λόγου in Tit. i. 9) and confined to them, though Rev. xix. 9, xxi. 5, xxii. 6 has the analogous οὗτοι οἱ λόγοι πιστοὶ καὶ ἀληθινοί (εἰσιν).

In 1 Tim. iii. 1 both the connexion and the reading are uncertain. Starting to read at ii. 15 we have... σωθήσεται δὲ διὰ τῆς τεκνογονίας ... πιστὸς [v.l. ἀνθρώπινος D* it Ambst.] ὁ λόγος· εἴ τις ἐπισκοπῆς ὀρέγεται, καλοῦ ἔργου ἐπιθυμεῖ. Is the 'word' in question that which precedes or that which follows? If it is that which follows, then πιστός seems to make nonsense (that volo episcopari is a good wish can scarcely be described as a trustworthy aphorism!), and we are bound to read ἀνθρώπινος—'they say...', or 'it is a human, i.e. common saying...' But may it be that the phrase was intended to refer back to the promise about childbirth, and that it was only a mistaken effort to relate it to what followed that led to the desperate expedient of altering πιστός to ἀνθρώπινος? Hardly; for it would be a very violent and arbitrary alteration; and, besides, ἀνθρώπινος is a v.l. also at 1. Tim. i. 15 (r, Ambst., Aug.), where no such motive could be operative; and the suggestion in W.-H. (notes in loco) that it is there probably transferred from iii. 1 seems unlikely. But even if we are driven to accept ἀνθρώπινος in 1 Tim. i. 15 also, it is in any case there reinforced by a phrase almost equivalent to πιστός, namely πάσης ἀποδοχῆς ἄξιος.

Thus on any showing we have this latter phrase and at least three firm occurrences of πιστὸς ὁ λόγος besides, and the related phrase in Tit. i. 9, all seeming to point to a certain selective consciousness, as though here maxims (they are mostly soteriological) were being designated as 'sound' and worthy of inclusion, as it were, in a canon of Christian aphorisms. Contrast the λόγος of 2 Thess. ii. 2, which is emphatically not accepted.

There seems to be no cogent reason for treating the phrase as a reader's comment (C. H. Turner's Inaugural Lecture The Study of the New Testament, 1833 and 1920, 1920, p. 21): the γάρ in 2 Tim. ii. 11 hardly carries this weight; it seems to imply rather the author's own knowledge that 'some collection of Christian maxims analogous to the' words of Jesus was in process of formation. See W. Lock, I.C.C., on Tit. iii. 8.

## THE PRIORITY OF MARK
### By G. M. Styler

AFTER a century or more of discussion, it has come to be accepted by scholars almost as axiomatic that Mark is the oldest of the three synoptic gospels, and that it was used by Matthew and Luke as a source. This has come to be regarded as 'the one absolutely assured result' of the study of the synoptic problem.

It has also been usually agreed that, besides Mark, Matt. and Lk. shared another source of material, denoted by the symbol 'Q'. Many have explored and accepted the hypothesis that it was a single clearly defined document, which can to a great extent be reconstructed. Others, however, have postulated a number of documents or traditions, known to both Matt. and Lk., sometimes in language closely similar, at other times less so. It may therefore be better to employ the symbol Q to denote the material common to Matt. and Lk. (but absent from Mk) rather than to denote a document, and thus prejudge the question of its unity. For the purpose or re-examining the priority of Mk, the unity of the Q-document or Q-material is irrelevant. But the validity of the Q hypothesis in some form or other is not wholly irrelevant, as will be seen.

The priority of Mk and the hypothesis of Q have been widely accepted in the present century, and are conveniently denoted by the name 'The Two-document Hypothesis', although it should be noted that the documents may well have been many more than two. The classical statement and defence was made by B. H. Streeter,[1] who attempted to reconstruct Q as a unitary document, but restricted it more narrowly than previous scholars. He gave the labels 'M' and 'L' to the material peculiar to Matt. and Lk., or (to be more precise) to the sources from which he took most of their peculiar material to be derived. Here again it may be noted that some scholars have been cautious in accepting the unity of the M or L material, and that since this material appears in only one gospel any reconstruction of its alleged source is even more speculative than the reconstruction of a Q.

It was not necessary to maintain that Mk's version must at every point be older than Matt.'s parallel version, since it was possible to say that anything in Matt. which in fact seemed more original than

---

[1] *The Four Gospels* (1924).

Mk could have been derived from Q. Further, there had been linger-
ing doubts about the existence of Q. But it came as a shock when in
1951 Dom B. C. Butler published his book *The Originality of St
Matthew*, attacking the Q-hypothesis and the priority of Mk at the
same time. In a minutely detailed study he subjected both hypotheses
to a severe criticism, and argued strongly for the priority of Matt.
Mk, he argued, was dependent on Matt.; Lk. was dependent on Mk
for the material which the two had in common, and on Matt. for the
Q-material. Once the Q-hypothesis is abandoned, the priority of
Matt., he claimed, quickly follows[1] from the existence of those
passages in which Matt.'s text seems clearly more original than Mk's,
or in some other way superior to it.

In spite of much close and careful reasoning, and the existence of
at any rate *some* passages which tell in favour of Butler's conclusion,
scholars have not abandoned the usual belief in the priority of Mk.
In this Excursus it will not be possible to examine all Butler's
arguments and instances one by one.[2] But an attempt will be made
to show that the belief in the priority of Mk is in fact securely
grounded, and to make clear the principal arguments on either side,
on which the decision must turn.

First of all, we must admit that Butler has exposed a serious logical
error in many expositions of the priority of Mk. Many of its advocates
have begun by stating certain formal relationships that hold between
the three Synoptic Gospels, viz:

(i) The bulk of Mk is contained in Matt., and much of it in Lk.;
there is very little that is not contained also in one or the other.

(ii) The Marcan material usually occurs in the same order in all
three gospels; where Matt.'s order diverges from Mk's, Lk. supports
Mk's order, and where (but this is very rare) Lk.'s order differs from
Mk's, Mk's order is supported by Matt. In other words, Matt. and
Lk. never agree with one another against Mk in respect of the order
in which material common to all three Gospels is arranged.

(iii) The same relationship holds good for the most part in respect
of wording. Matt. and Lk. are often closely similar in wording in
Q-passages (i.e. where Mk has no close parallel), but in Marcan
passages it is exceptional[3] for Matt. and Lk. to have significant words

[1] Butler agreed with the general assumption that there is no case for
maintaining the priority of Lk.

[2] Nor to consider the various articles that have appeared subsequently.

[3] There are a number of exceptions. Some of these may be coincidental;
others are probably due to corruptions and assimilations in the course of the
transmission of the text. (See Streeter, *op. cit.* 179 ff.) Perhaps there are still
more than can easily be accounted for. But they remain few compared with
the large number of passages when the generalization given in the text
holds true. Butler agrees, and does not attempt to use them to establish
Lk.'s knowledge of Matt.

in common unless Mk has them also; frequently Mk and Matt. will share the same phrasing, while Lk. diverges, or Mk and Lk. will do so, while Matt. diverges.

From these facts it is clear that, as far as material common to all three is concerned, Mk is the *middle term* or *link* between Matt. and Lk.; Matt. and Lk. are not directly related here, but only through Mk.

Now it is obvious that the priority of Mk will satisfactorily *explain* these phenomena. But its advocates have made a serious mistake in arguing (or assuming) that no *other* hypothesis will explain them.[1] Butler is correct in claiming that they are guilty of a fallacy in reasoning. If Matt. were the original, followed by Mk with variations, and if in turn Lk. followed Mk, again with variations, these phenomena could well be the result. Alternatively, (as far as the phenomena go) Lk. might be the earliest of the three, Mk the second, and Matt. the last; Butler agrees that on other grounds that suggestion may be set aside. But he rightly insists that the phenomena are satisfied equally well by the standard view, that Mk is the common source of Matt. and Lk., or by the view which he supports, *sc.* that Matt. is the oldest Gospel, that Mk used Matt., and that Lk. in turn used Mk.

Butler is correct, therefore, in saying that the formal relationships do not by themselves compel one solution to the synoptic problem. The texts of the Gospels must be carefully studied side by side before we can decide on the question of priority. With this we agree. But we part company when he goes on to claim that this comparison points to the priority of Matt. Although the advocates of the priority of Mk have been wrong in claiming to establish it through the statistics etc., yet there are cogent arguments which retain their force. In the present writer's judgment Butler has not succeeded in destroying them, and they outweigh the arguments that Butler has adduced on his side.

Before turning to them, however, let us examine the place of the Q-hypothesis in the enquiry. It is relevant to the priority of Mk to this extent: there are passages, especially in sections of teaching, where Matt.'s version may well be judged more original than Mk's parallel. If the existence of a non-Marcan source is denied, it will be difficult to maintain that in such passages Mk is prior to Matt.; rather, they support the priority of Matt. to Mk. But if Matt. had access to a non-Marcan source, then there is no problem for advocates of Marcan priority. Q is therefore relevant, since it is just what is required—*sc.* a non-Marcan source. The evidence of Lk. therefore

---

[1] A variant theory is that the common source of Matt. and Lk. was not the Mk that we possess but an 'Ur-Markus', an earlier edition of Mk, similar but not identical. The only objection to this theory is that it seems to be unnecessary.

will be relevant to the enquiry if it supports the existence of Q. If, however the Q-hypothesis is rejected, the position of 'Marcan priorists' is weakened; they must still postulate a non-Marcan source for Matt. to have used, but they can no longer point to Q as constituting that source.

Butler's attack on Q, therefore, is an important preliminary to his attack on the priority of Mk. If the former succeeds it increases his chance of succeeding in the latter also. But only slightly. Marcan priorists will be driven on to more uncertain ground; they must now postulate an unknown source, instead of being able to point to one which is partially known. But in this there is no intrinsic improbability.[1] In other words, it is perfectly possible to believe that Lk. obtained his so-called Q-material directly from Matt., and at the same time that Matt. obtained it from an earlier source, possibly known to Mk.[2]

It is agreed that Matt. has not borrowed from Lk. The two possible explanations of the fact that they have some closely similar passages are (a) that Lk. borrowed from Matt. and (b) that both depend on a common source (or sources), i.e. the Q-hypothesis. Any argument against (a) is therefore *ipso facto* an argument in favour of Q. There are three principal ones: first, that in at least some of the parallel passages Lk.'s version seems more original than Matt.'s;[3] secondly, that it is hard to see why, if Lk. has borrowed material from Matt. he has so violently and frequently disturbed Matt's. order; and thirdly, it seems inexplicable why he has consistently ignored[4] Matt. in any passage where he follows Mk, and has made no use of Matt.'s narrative wherever Mk has no parallel account—e.g. of the Nativity stories and Resurrection appearances.

Butler faces these arguments, and dismisses them. He denies that there are any cogent examples of Q-passages in which Lk.'s version is more original than Matt.'s; and he claims that Lk. makes no attempt to put material derived from Matt. into the Marcan context in which Matt. had it. He claims that it would be a tricky task to find out

---

[1] Butler rightly asserts the principle that sources should not be multiplied needlessly. But there is no objection to postulating such a source; and it may be necessitated by other reasons, viz. the arguments for the priority of Mk, if they prove to be sound.

[2] E.g. Dr A. M. Farrer holds (like Butler) that Lk. knew and used Matt. (as well as Mk), but continues to accept the standard view that Matt. used Mk. Cf. his essay 'On Dispensing with Q' in *Studies in the Gospels*, ed. D. E. Nineham (1955), 55-88, and *St Matthew and St Mark* (1954).

[3] Cf., e.g., Lk. vi. 20 ('Blessed are you poor') with Matt. v. 3 ('Blessed are the poor in spirit'). Although it is true that Lk's. version fits his own special interests, it still seems to the present writer that it is nearer to the probable original than Matt.'s 'poor in spirit'. Cf. also Lk. iii. 8 with Matt. iii. 9; Lk.'s μὴ ἄρξησθε may well be nearer to the original than Matt.'s μὴ δόξητε.          [4] Or 'almost entirely ignored'; cf. p. 224, n. 3.

what that context was, since already there are large variations in order in the first half of Matt. and Mk.[1]

But in spite of Butler's arguments, which deserve careful study, the present writer continues to find it hard to believe that Lk. used Matt.

After disposing of Q, Butler turns to the question of the relative priority of Matt. and Mk, and rightly asks that it should be discussed on the basis of a direct comparison of the parallel passages without prejudice. This is a fair challenge, which the 'Marcan priorist' need not evade. Butler himself examines a large number of passages, and claims that here on a straight comparison of Matt. and Mk the preference will nearly always go to Matt.'s version as the more original. The most convincing of his examples are cases[2] where Matt.'s version is a coherent whole, and Mk's seems to be an excerpt, in which knowledge is betrayed of some phrase or fact which Mk does not reproduce. Unless we are allowed to appeal to Q, and say that it is some knowledge of Q[3] (not Matt.) which Mk betrays, Butler's conclusion does indeed seem to be forced on us. Rather less convincing are passages where Mk refers to Jesus' teaching, or to parables (in the plural), and goes on to produce only one example. Certainly Mk here betrays knowledge of more than he reproduces, and certainly Matt. shows more knowledge than Mk; but it is gratuitous to suppose that it must be from Matt. that Mk's knowledge comes.

Less convincing still are passages where Matt.'s version is more smooth than Mk's; rather, they tell the other way. In all his arguments of this type, Butler defeats himself; the better his defence of Matt. the harder it becomes to see why Mk should have altered something smooth into something less smooth. In fact, the relative roughness of Mk is one of the strong arguments on the other side. In textual criticism it is an accepted canon that, other things being equal, the harder reading is to be preferred, since it is more probable that the harder should have been altered to the easier than *vice versa*. Numerous examples can be produced in which, in one way or another, Matt.'s version looks easier than Mk's. They may be grouped under several heads:

(a) Grammatical variants, where Mk is wrong and Matt. correct; e.g. Mk x. 20 ἐφυλαξάμην (wrong), = Matt. xix. 20 ἐφύλαξα (right).

(b) Stylistic variants, where Mk is sprawling, and Matt. tidy;

[1] Dr A. M. Farrer (in *Studies in the Gospel*, 67 ff.) argues that Lk.'s order is typological, and was never intended to reflect the order of Matt. But although his argument is persuasively written, the present writer finds his thesis incredible.

[2] Cf., e.g., the preaching of John the Baptist.

[3] I.e., of Matt.'s source for this passage.

e.g. Mk x. 27 = Matt. xix. 26. Butler argues regularly for the superiority and greater originality of Matt. in such cases, on the ground that his version is closer to an authentic Semitic parallelism and even an original poetic strain in the teaching of Jesus. To the present writer it seems far more probable that Mk represents the earlier version, and that Matt. by careful rewriting has achieved a greater polish.

(c) There are the well-known examples[1] where Mk's version appears lacking in respect for the apostles or even in its estimate of the person of Christ, and where Matt.'s version avoids all such implications. Without attempting to establish any rigid law of development, we must surely say that all such passages tell strongly in favour of the priority of Mk, and that Butler's attempts to evade this inference are unconvincing.

(d) In some passages Mk is suggestive but obscure, and Matt.'s parallel looks like an attempt to leave the reader with an edifying message; but we are left with the suspicion that Matt. has not penetrated to the real sense. Compare, e.g., Mk viii. 14-21 with Matt. xvi. 5-12 where Matt. interprets the 'leaven' against which Jesus warns his disciples as 'the teaching of the Pharisees and Sadducees'.

But the best instance is the difficult passage about the purpose (or effect) of parables.[2] Butler's treatment[3] of this leaves me quite unconvinced. Matt. seems here to be trying hard to extract a tolerable sense from the intolerable statement that Mk appears to be making, sc. that Jesus taught in parables to prevent the outsiders from having a chance of understanding and being converted. He assumes that Mk's 'all things are (done) in parables' means 'I speak in parables'. But recent commentators have suggested a line of interpretation of Mk's text which the present writer finds wholly satisfying; viz. that the same teaching is put before all by Jesus, but whereas some by God's grace penetrate to its inner meaning, for others it remains external, a parable and nothing more;[4] and herein the dark purpose of God, as predicted in Isaiah, is fulfilled. Mk may have partly misunderstood what he recorded; but it seems certain to the present writer that his words are closer to the original, and that Matt.'s version is an unsuccessful attempt to simplify what he found intolerable.

Another example of misunderstanding by Matt. may be claimed

[1] E.g., Mk iv. 38 (cf. Matt. viii. 25); Mk vi. 5-6 (Matt. xiii. 58); Mk x. 17-18 (Matt. xix. 16-17), where Matt.'s question τί με ἐρωτᾷς περὶ τοῦ ἀγαθοῦ, and the appended comment εἷς ἐστιν ὁ ἀγαθός are intelligible as a rewriting of Mk, but most odd otherwise.

[2] Mk iv. 10-12 = Matt. xiii. 10-15.     [3] Op. cit. 90-92.

[4] Or even 'a riddle'; the same word in Hebrew or Aramaic can mean 'parable' or 'riddle'. Cf. J. Jeremias, The Parables of Jesus (Eng. trans. 1954), 12-14.

at Mk ii. 18 ( – Matt. ix. 14). Mk's first sentence ('the disciples of
John and the Pharisees were fasting') sets the scene; then 'they' ask
Jesus why his disciples, unlike those of John and of the Pharisees, do
not fast. The persons who ask are surely *not* the ones who were the
subject of the previous sentence; they are persons unspecified.[1] Matt.'s
sentence is much shorter and neater. But he obviously assumes that
'they' are the disciples of John and the Pharisees.

We have passed on to an argument which to the present writer
puts the priority of Mk beyond serious doubt, *viz.* that there are
passages where Matt. goes astray through misunderstanding, yet
betrays a knowledge of the authentic version—the version which is
given by Mk. The two accounts of the death of the Baptist (Mk vi.
17-29, Matt. xiv. 3-12) contain clear examples of this. Mk states
fully the attitude of Herod to John; he respected him, but was
perplexed; and it was Herodias who was keen to kill him. And the
story that follows explains how in spite of the king's reluctance she
obtained her desire. Matt., whose version is much briefer, states
that Herod wanted to kill John. But this must be an error; the story,
which perfectly fits Mk's setting, does not fit Matt's introduction;
and at xiv. 9 Matt. betrays the fact that he really knows the full
version by slipping in the statement that 'the king'[2] was sorry. It is
surely clear that Matt., in a desire to abbreviate, has oversimplified
his introduction.

Further, both Mk and Matt. relate this story as a 'retrospect' or
'flashback', to explain Herod's remark that Jesus was John risen
from the dead. Mk quite properly finishes the story, and then re-
sumes his main narrative with a jump; Matt., failing to remember
that it was a 'retrospect', makes a smooth transition to the narrative
which follows: John's disciples inform Jesus; and 'when Jesus
heard . . . etc.' (Matt. xiv. 12-13).

Butler rightly asks that the comparison should be made without
prejudice. But, in the course of it, impressions are necessarily received.
One impression which is received of Matt. is that he regularly aims
at giving a smooth version, without any kind of roughness; and also
that he is somewhat pedantic.[3] It is at least in line with this impression

[1] For another clear example of Mk's 'impersonal' plural cf. v. 35. iii. 21
and 32 are other probable examples.
[2] Mk calls Herod 'king'; Matt. correctly calls him 'tetrarch' in xiv. 1,
but lapses into calling him 'king' at xiv. 9. Butler attempts to base an argument for the priority of Matt. on his superior knowledge at this point; and
also on the knowledge he displays from time to time of Jewish and Palestinian
customs. Such arguments are tenuous, and are more than counterbalanced by
Mk's superior knowledge of the story he is relating.
[3] Cf. xxi. 2 ff., where he apparently takes Zech. ix. 9 to mean two
animals. Cf. also xiv. 21, where he speaks of 5,000 men 'apart from women
and children'; surely this is a pedantic gloss on Mk's plain ἄνδρες.

if, as the Marcan priorists maintain, Matt. regularly conflates Mk and his other source. Butler pours scorn on the suggestion, regarding it as cumbrous and pointless; but if Matt. really was pedantic he may not have thought it so.

Of all the arguments for the priority of Mk, the strongest is that based on the freshness and circumstantial character of his narrative.[1] Tradition connects his Gospel with St Peter, and this trait has strengthened the belief that the tradition may be sound. But it should be noticed that the same character is to be found even in narratives of events at which St Peter was not present. Butler concedes this quality to Mk, and explains it by a daring suggestion: he accepts the tradition that St Peter is often Mk's source—hence a vividness and wealth of detail greater than in Matt.—and saves the priority of Matt. by suggesting that St Peter himself[2] had access to a copy of Matt. while speaking.

In effect, this suggestion amounts to the view that Mk had direct access to what was in fact Matt.'s ultimate source; to the authentic version of the story which Matt. has often abbreviated or modified. Clearly it makes dependence on Matt. unnecessary. These are the cases on which the priority of Mk strongly rests, and they counterbalance the rival group of passages, mostly teaching and not narrative, on which Butler relies for his hypothesis. In those, it will be remembered, Marcan priorists are sometimes on the defensive, and appeal to Q.[3]

For those passages,

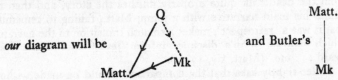

In the narrative passages, the situation is exactly reversed; here the simple view is that Matt. depends on Mk; and it is now Butler who requires a three-term diagram, *viz.*

[1] Including touches that might well come almost directly from an eyewitness, e.g. the cushion in the boat, Mk iv. 38; and the Aramaic words and phrases, of which Mk preserves more than Matt.

[2] Or, presumably, it might have been that Mk, while using Matt. as his written source, called to mind the fuller account he had heard from St Peter. In any case, Matt. is acquainted with the same account as Mk.

[3] Cf. *supra* p. 223; 'Q' need not here mean a source common to Matt. and Lk.; all that is needed is a source used by Matt. which Mk knew, and occasionally used.

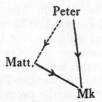

But whereas it seems perfectly credible to the present writer that (i) a non-Marcan source existed, known to both Mk and Matt., and (ii) Matt. conflated it with Mk, Butler's suggestion on the other hand seems to be pure fantasy. Our explanation of *his* favourable cases may be cumbersome; but his explanation of *our* favourable cases is incredible.

In the next place, Mk, if he is using Matt., has used only about 50 per cent of his subject-matter, but has expanded it in the telling.[1] But it is hard to see why he should have omitted so much of value *if* he was using Matt.: not only the Sermon on the Mount and much teaching besides, but also the narratives of the Infancy of Jesus. Mk *does* include teaching; and so it cannot be replied that he was only interested in narrative.[2]

The point may be put like this: given Mk, it is easy to see why Matt. was written; given Matt., it is hard to see why Mk was needed.[3]

If Matt. was using Mk, and incorporating other material, it is easy to understand why he should regularly have abbreviated Mk whenever he could safely do so.[4] In spite of the postulates of the Form Critics,[5] it is likely that Mk's sprawling and circumstantial stories are more original than Matt.'s shorter and more formal ones.

Lastly, an examination of Matt.'s additions tells heavily against his priority. Under this head there are two classes of passage. (i)

---

[1] But has expanded it in a natural way; the extra sentences seldom look like extraneous insertions.

[2] True, he has in any case made his selection from the material available to him. Butler urges this point, and claims that if there is a difficulty here it is almost as great for us as for him. But surely not. It is harder to see why Mk should have omitted these if they were already incorporated in a full-scale document accessible to him.

[3] I.e. by the early Christians. Mk is of course valued most highly by the modern scholar.

[4] The story of Jairus' Daughter is a good example (Mk v. 21-43 = Matt. ix. 18-26). Matt. omits one whole episode in the story. His version is more compact, but as a result it is historically far less credible; according to him, the father tells Jesus that his daughter has just *died*, and begs him to come and restore her to life. In Mk, the girl is *near* to death, and the father appeals to Jesus for help.

[5] The Form Critics postulate that conformity to a regular pattern is an indication that a passage goes back to an earlier date than one which does not conform to the pattern.

First, pieces of teaching included by Matt. but absent from the parallel section of Mk. Butler claims that Matt.'s whole context hangs together; and that if he has really inserted them into a framework provided by Mk he has done so with a felicity that is beyond belief. But, with some exceptions,[1] this judgment will be challenged. Thus, in spite of Butler's claim that the famous *Tu es Petrus* passage has parallels or antitheses with both the preceding and the following verses, few will find him convincing. On the contrary, the passage will still seem to many to be an insertion into Mk's account of Peter's confession of faith[2]—although not, of course, necessarily an invention.

(ii) There are also some narrative additions in Matt. which seem to stem from later apologetic, or even from the stock of legendary accretions which are evident in the apocryphal Gospels. Butler argues strongly that any such judgment is premature and unwarranted; that if the detailed comparison of Matt. and Mk proves Matt. to be older, then that verdict must be accepted, and any suspicion that Matt.'s special narratives are 'late' must be mistaken. But since we hold that the detailed comparison of Matt. and Mk tells in the other direction, in favour of Mk's priority, then the judgment that Matt.'s narratives are late, and sometimes close to the legendary, must be given full weight.

In conclusion it should be said that, although Butler naturally gives most space to the passages which seem to tell in his favour, he does not attempt to conceal the fact that there are strong arguments on the other side. To some extent, however, he weakens their force by admitting them quickly, and attempting to explain them all away in a few words by his suggestion that St Peter had access to a copy of Matt. Until some less incredible explanation is forthcoming, the natural conclusion that Mk is prior to Matt. will continue to hold the field.[3]

[1] *Viz.* the passages where an overlap of Mk and Q is postulated by Marcan priorists.

[2] Mk viii. 27-33, cf. Matt. xvi. 13-23. Cf. also Matt.'s parable of the Labourers in the Vineyard (xx. 1-16), which is placed after πολλοὶ δὲ ἔσονται πρῶτοι ἔσχατοι καὶ ἔσχατοι πρῶτοι, and rounded off with a variant of the same logion. But the real point of the parable is different; in inserting it after this logion, Matt. has accentuated a secondary feature.

[3] For a review of the way in which the priority of Mk came to be accepted, and the dubious arguments often used in its defence, cf. W. R. Farmer, 'A "Skeleton in the Closet" of Gospel Research', *Biblical Research* vi (1961), 3 ff., which the present writer had not seen at the time of writing. But it seems that, however insecure the arguments used in the past, the reasons for accepting the priority of Mk are in fact strong.

# INDEX OF SUBJECTS AND PROPER NAMES

# INDEX OF SUBJECTS AND PROPER NAMES

# INDEX OF SUBJECTS AND PROPER NAMES

# INDEX OF SUBJECTS AND PROPER NAMES

# INDEX OF BIBLICAL AND OTHER REFERENCES

## OLD TESTAMENT

242

## NEW TESTAMENT

# INDEX OF BIBLICAL AND OTHER REFERENCES

## OTHER SOURCES